The Race for Consciousness

John G. Taylor

A Bradford Book
The MIT Press
Cambridge, Massachusetts
London, England

First MIT Press paperback edition, 2001

© 1999 John G. Taylor

This book was set in Sabon by Achorn Graphic Services, Inc.

Printed and bound in the United States of America.

Library of Congress Cataloging-in-Publication Data

Taylor, John Gerald, 1931–
    The race for consciousness / John G. Taylor.
      p.   cm.
    "A Bradford book."
    Includes bibliographical references and index.
    ISBN 0-262-20115-1 (hc : alk. paper), 0-262-70086-7 (pb)
    1. Consciousness.   I. Title.
  BF311.T354   1999
  153—dc21
                                                              98-37294
                                                              CIP

Contents

Preface

This book was written in the excitement of the gathering race to understand consciousness. There is a feeling among scientists that the time is now becoming ripe for the difficult problem of consciousness finally to be solved once and for all. Consciousness has led humans to many weird and wonderful explanations, but the development of new experimental and theoretical tools for probing the brain has produced an atmosphere of unparalleled optimism that the job can now be done properly.

It is as part of this gathering activity that this book was written, and in particular to explain an approach to the problem of mind and brain on which I have been working for the last twenty-five years, originally called the relational mind model. The book describes the complete scene of entries, rider, punters, and racecourses, as well as developing an entry into the race, an upgraded version of my older model, now termed *relational consciousness*.

But consciousness is "hard" in the sense that it is not clear what function it performs, or what explanation it could ever possess. Some claim it must be regarded as an entity independent of the brain. How are we able to prove that a machine (or other animal, for that matter) really does possess consciousness? How can we claim that any model can finally cross the so-called explanatory gap, that of deducing that the activity in the model would necessarily possess consciousness by virtue of its very nature and not by fiat?

These questions have to be considered carefully. Owing to recent developments in tools able to probe the brain in action, it would seem that we are now able to set up experiments that will give us all the possible answers to guide us as far as the objective methods of science can take us. I belong to the group who consider that such knowledge will then allow us to attain a final solution to the problem of how consciousness arises from the activity of the brain.

At the beginning of my formulation of the relational mind approach in the early 1970s, there was much opposition to the deliberate study and modeling of consciousness among those who were most concerned with its experimental analysis—the psychological community. It was therefore difficult to make headway. The atmosphere has, as noted above, changed enormously; there is a wealth of interest in the subject, and consciousness is no longer regarded as a dirty word among serious scientists. At the same time an enormous wealth of data on the brain and mind is coming from new "windows on the mind" achieved by the noninvasive instruments of electroencephalography, positron emission tomography, magnetoencephalography, and magnetic resonance imaging. These are changing our understanding of the way the neural networks of the brain are used in mental processing.

The main thesis I will present is that consciousness is created through the relations between brain states. What is more, this process is a continuing and adaptive one, so that consciousness emerges from past brain activity. It is this emergence of consciousness, through a highly subtle and delicate process, that leads to its complexity. That is explored in the book. I hope that you find in my ideas some grains of truth to help make a little more sense of this exciting but confusing emerging branch of science, and also join with me and my colleagues in our race to scale the "last Everest"—our inner selves.

John G. Taylor
King's College, London/Institute of Medicine, Juelich

Acknowledgments

Many colleagues helped me form my ideas on brain and mind and made me articulate the ideas of relational consciousness that are developed in this book. There are also those whose talks on mind and brain have stimulated me. All of these I would like to thank, most especially Farrukh Alavi, Igor Aleksander, Bernie Baars, Bill Banks, Raju Bapi, Paul Bressloff, Guido Bugmann, Walter Freeman, Chris Frith, David Gaffan, Jean-Phillipe Gaussier, Denise Gorse, Jeffrey Gray, Steve Grossberg, Stuart Hameroff, Simon Hastings, Jim Hopkins, Andy Ioannides, Lutz Jaencke, Bart Krekelberg, Dan Levine, Ben Libet, Tony Marcel, Tom Metzinger, Robin Merris, Luchas Mihalis, Ouri Monchi, Hans Mueller-Gartner, Jim Newman, Gerry Orchard, David Papineau, Roger Penrose, Ras Petersen, Bill Phillips, Karl Pribram, John Shah, Tim Shallice, Neil Taylor, Alessandro Villa, Doug Watt, and Stephen Zrehen. I thank Hans Mueller-Gaertner, Director of the Institute of Medicine, Juelich, for inviting me to work as a guest scientist at the institute for one and a half years to search for consciousness with the new machines, and his colleagues John Shah, Berndt Krause, Andy Ioannides, and Stephen Posse for providing expertise, enthusiasm, and a stimulating environment during my stay there. I also thank my late editor, Harry Stanton (I am sad to say, no longer with us), and his replacement Michael Rutter, for being so supportive, and the reviewers for making such excellent suggestions for its improvement. Finally I thank my wife, Pamela, for her unstinting help in editing the book through several of its drafts.

I

Introduction to Consciousness

1

The Race Begins

Away went Gilpin—who but he?
His fame soon spread around.
He carries weight, he rides a race!
'Tis for a thousand pound!
—Wallace Cowper

The Racing Scene

The race for consciousness has started. Consciousness is the most subtle and complex entity in the universe. With it, humans have duplicated here on Earth the awe-inspiring methods by which stars produce their energy. By creative thinking the forces of nature have been probed from across the vastness of the visible universe to deep inside the atom; a beautiful theme for the construction of the whole has been powerfully constructed: "the Universe in a grain of sand and a twinkling star," to extend the poet William Blake. By artistic imagination humans have created emotionally satisfying alternative universes that allow us to have new and surprising views of this one. These magnificent products have all been achieved by human consciousness.

But what is this elusive thing called consciousness, which is so important in the process of creativity and thinking? Our very experience is based on our being conscious. How does this subtle process, regarding which philosophers and theologians have argued and fought for several millennia, emerge from brain activity in what looks just like "two fistfuls of porridge"? Or is there more to mind than mere matter? To answer these deep questions at the basis of the human condition, science is turning its sights onto the mind; the race is on to be the first ever to discover the scientific nature of consciousness.

We all love winners. We look up to them, even revere them, as well as envy them. In the poem, John Gilpin became famous in peoples' minds because they thought he had entered a race for what was a huge amount of money in those days. While bringing in a tidy sum in prize money, a Grand National winner today will be worth far more (many millions) in stud fees to its owners. But it is not just for the money but also for the sheer guts shown in winning that crowds show such admiration. Red Rum, one of the greatest Grand National winners of all time, had a special place in the hearts of many for his plucky rides over what is acknowledged to be a terrifying course.

Such, then, are the prizes in all types of races—satisfaction, fame, and fortune. But to win, skill and strength must be developed by training over lengthy periods, and strategy must be carefully designed to exploit the weaknesses of opponents. This can be done because races are over well-defined obstacles, and rules are designed to prevent any unfair advantage going to one or other of the competitors.

Scientific races are different. For them, anything goes in trying to win. Scientists race against each other to try to solve some conundrum, but do so without rules about styles, techniques, equipment allowed, or ideas used to help suggest crucial experiments. They can do what they want as long as they produce a solution to the problem that started it and that stands up to the rigorous test: does it work? Any number of scientists may enter the race, but it is usually those who are either most conversant with the particular area or who are best equipped who will win. Two examples of recent scientific races, one of a mathematical nature, the other experimental, clearly demonstrate this difference.

Fermat's last theorem had been unproved for over 200 years. It is very simple to state: lots of pairs of numbers have squares that, when added, give the square of a number, for example, $3^2 + 4^2 = 5^2$; are there any pairs that when cubed and added give the cube of a number? The French mathematician realized that this was a simple but interesting problem and claimed to be able to show that no such pairs of numbers can exist: this is Fermat's last theorem. However, his proof never surfaced; he died without ever writing it down. Since then many have labored mightily to prove the theorem; a prize was awarded several times for supposed solutions that were all later shown to be wrong. Numerous mathematicians (and others with little technical training) still entered the race to prove Fermat's last theorem, in the process giving an enormous advance in understanding general aspects of number theory (the relevant branch of mathematics).

In 1995 British mathematician Andrew Wiles, working in Princeton, finally produced a proof (his first effort was not quite right, but the latest version has now been accepted). Wiles struggled with this problem with dedication and secrecy over several years. To throw his colleagues off the scent he published a trickle of papers in mathematics journals on an altogether different problem. His dedication, cunning, and enormous technical expertise in all the branches of number theory together allowed him to produce a proof of the theorem before anyone else, and so win one of the most important mathematical races of all time.

A completely different race was run to find the elusive and subtle W and Z mesons, particles that justified the beautiful theoretical unification of electromagnetism and radioactivity suggested in the 1960s by Salam, Weinberg, and Glashow. The photon is the "glue" that binds charged particles together, carrying the force of electromagnetism between them; it was suggested that analogous glue would carry the force of radioactivity. It was even predicted how massive these glue particles should be, in addition to some of their other properties. Italian physicist Carlo Rubbia persuaded the powers that be to have a machine built, the big electron-proton collider particle accelerator at the particle physics laboratory CERN in Geneva. This particle smasher would generate enough energy in particle beams as they clashed that they could produce, out of the debris, a few of these glue particles—the W and Z mesons. This was done, and when the experimental results were analyzed they showed clear traces of the exotic short-lived particles. Rubbia and the designer of the machine were awarded the Nobel prize for their work.

These are two scientific races in which the winning posts were crystal clear, as were the winners when they reached them. The race was won by those with appropriate technical equipment, whether it was expertise in number theory or access to a very large particle accelerator.

The race for consciousness seems to be different. Is it a race at all? What can be scientific about it? Where is the winning post? Is there only one? If the race exists, can it be run by amateurs, or is it only the professional scientist who is expected to win, as in the two examples above?

The Consciousness Scene

The interest in consciousness is exploding. Many are involved across the whole spectrum of intellectual life, from philosophers to quantum physicists. All are having their say and claiming things about consciousness from their own viewpoint. All well and good, and they have every right to have opinions about things that cannot be proved. That is what opinions are for, to make up for lack of real knowledge on which all have to agree if possible. The recent spate of books on consciousness only confirm such a feature—philosophers and quantum physicists and others joining the battle to air their opinions on the subject.

Yet the subject of consciousness is now moving out of the arena of opinion against opinion into that in which the problems are being clarified. Scientific tools and expertise are becoming available to provide competitors with the best sorts of support to enable them to win. Noninvasive instruments—so called because they can be used without cutting open the skull and sticking electrodes in the brain—are allowing enormous strides to be made in appreciating the magnificence of the brain as the most subtle and powerful natural system ever looked at scientifically. These tools are exposing the mysteries of the brain and giving new direction to the search for how consciousness is supported.

These enormous advances are such that opinion is being replaced by science. Opinions are now seen as either irrelevant or helpful only as a ground-clearing exercise before the true scientific race can begin. However, the core problem of consciousness as a subtle inner experience remains. Many still ask, "How can science ever get to the 'inside' of my experience?" Science considers the outside only, in an objective manner. How can it ever probe the subjective inner world we each inhabit? What is more, how can it construct a clear winning post, that of giving a truly scientific explanation of consciousness, if it cannot get inside this subjective world, which must remain terra incognita to its methods and approach?

Are we not back to the opinions of all those who, we claimed earlier, were not part of the scientific race for consciousness? Are their opinions not just as valid as those of researchers who are exploring this prohibited inner world? Indeed it could be claimed that no progress has really been made by importing more science into a scientifically intractable problem.

The Scientific Approach to Consciousness

More clarity is being brought to the consciousness arena than these pessimistic remarks would grant. A clearer vision is arising not only from results flooding in from noninvasive instruments and new understanding of the brain thereby obtained, but also from ideas of a more theoretical nature.

The brain is composed of myriad living nerve cells (the "atoms" of the brain, the nerve cell being the smallest living unit). The manner in which these nerve cells combine to enable the brain to support the mind is being tackled by workers in the discipline of neural networks. This was initiated over fifty years ago in a remarkable paper by American scientists Warren McCulloch and Walter Pitts (1946). They showed that a network constructed of the simplest possible kind of such cells influencing each other was powerful enough to perform any logical computation that we ourselves could do. This amazing result was a big fillip to the development of the digital computer and ushered in the age of the computer.

That was only the beginning. Additional neural networks were designed by keeping closer to the way the living nerve cells work in the brain. This led to numerous artificial neural networks that were developed to solve difficult problems, such as tracking unexpected changes in buying and selling shares on the Stock Exchange so as to catch insider trading, or so as to make better investment of bonds or shares by predicting how their prices would change in the near future. Many artificial neural systems are now in operation in a wide range of industries and across commerce.

All these developments have gone hand in hand with similar increases in theoretical understanding of how the neural networks of the brain perform. From the retina (an approachable part of the brain) to the frontal lobes (the thinking center), artificial neural network models are being built that attempt to capture ever more closely the patterns of activity and response possessed by people or animals (e.g., monkeys, cats, and rats). This work is proceeding at an ever greater rate now that noninvasive machines are pouring out their results; attempts are even being made to construct very simple models of the whole human brain. Such is the present avenue of neural networks—more properly called computational neuroscience—that is adding a deep theoretical underpinning to the neuroscientific approach to the brain and mind.

It is this experimental and theoretical underpinning that I claim is beginning to make a difference in the investigation of consciousness. It brings a broad theoretical framework inside which testable models of behavior can be constructed and refined by further experiment. The analogy to the two races—Wiles's proof of Fermat's last theorem and Rubbia's discovery of W and Z particles—is that Wiles used the latest tools of number theory (some of which he helped to construct) and would not have been successful without them. In the search for W and Z particles Rubbia had the accelerator designed solely on the basis of the unification of radioactivity and electromagnetism, a theory of highest scientific subtlety based on the latest and fullest knowledge of the intricacies of particle physics.

The race to discover the W and Z particles represents just a minute part of scientific knowledge; the vast remainder is an impressive monument to the creativity and dedication of scientists increasingly to master the material world. From the time of Sir Francis Bacon's eloquent *Novum Organum* published over 370 years ago, the scientific method has probed the mysteries of matter using his guidance: ever more precise experiments to test present understanding lead to its continued improvement.

What a head start the science of matter has had over that of mind! The beautiful ideas of Sir Isaac Newton in the seventeenth century began the race toward the center of the atom; this was speeded up by the genius of Albert Einstein at the beginning of this century, and since the late 1920s knowledge has moved ahead even faster, until we are now inside the inside the inside of the atom, so to speak.

Despite some of the ancient Greeks coming close to modern ideas of the brain as the controlling organ of mind, the dead hand of the past restricted knowledge of the mind vastly more than that of matter. Only in the last century did the science of mind begin to emerge from antique traditions and appeals to ancient authority.

Finally, toward the latter part of the last century the brain was convincingly shown to be divisible into parts specialized for different functions. For example, in 1861 Parisian surgeon Paul Broca revealed that patients with certain speech disorders usually had damage to a particular area of the cortex. Since then our understanding of brain and mind gathered speed, and is now neck and neck with research into unthinking matter. At a recent neuroscience conference in New Orleans in October 1997, 23,000 brain scientists attended; the subject has come of age.

The time has come for the race to understand consciousness to proceed with the most appropriate scientific tools available—noninvasive instruments, neuroscience of the brain (neuroanatomy and neurophysiology), and the theory of computational neuroscience. Those who do not avail themselves of these tools will be heading down the track in the wrong direction, away from the winning post. They will still keep galloping as fast as ever, and some spectators may cheer them on. But the spectators themselves will be rallying around the wrong post.

But where is the winning post? Isn't that one of the main problems in the first place? No one knows where the elusive winning post is or even if it exists. If we have no scientific definition of consciousness, all the scientific tools and theories in the world will never help us reach a winning post.

Science proceeds by reducing a problem to looking at its parts; in general, the parts are much easier to solve than the whole. Then partial solutions are combined eventually. This is sometimes called the method of divide and conquer. It is the way to proceed with consciousness, and inch by painful inch move toward a definition of it. Consciousness is not a monolithic whole, as seen by the way that bits of it become "chipped off" when a person has an injury to part of the brain from a stroke or accident. Parts of its structure and neural support are easier to understand than others. The manner in which the whole of conscious experience arises can be tackled in terms of the decomposed parts; that is indeed the manner in which science is approaching the brain.

In that case, won't there be several winning posts? Even the notion of a race for consciousness may have to disappear, since it may be seen as part of a more general and broad approach to the total problem of brain and mind. However, that is not the case. One very difficult and basic problem exists whose scientific solution would correspond to winning the race: the crucial ingredient in the neural activity of the brain that sparks consciousness into life. It is this so-called hard problem—to discover that added value that guarantees the presence of consciousness—that is the final winning post we seek. Once that feature has been discovered, we are there!

Yet such optimism still does not seem to carry us past the problem of the "innerness" of consciousness. How can science solve that? My answer: by producing a neurally based model that not only satisfies all scientific criteria by agreeing with all of the observable effects, but also one that leads to features that indicate that such a system constructed according to the model would have the sort of inner experience that we do ourselves, as shown by introspection. Such an aspect could never, however, be proved scientifically. It has to be accepted that science cannot enter into the inner life. However, it must be shown by analyzing its features, that such a model would be expected to have an inner life. That is indeed a tall order, but it is what I try to outline in this book. Even if the proposal set out here only points us to the right track we will be making progress.

These are features that we cannot explore further in detail without beginning the real work: exploring the complexity of consciousness, describing noninvasive instruments and neural network tools being used to understand what is going on in the brain, and beginning to construct a model of the brain that would grant inner experience. So we need to begin to look at the tools being applied in the race for consciousness as well as some of the entries themselves.

The Road Map

This book is about the nature of consciousness and the race to be the first to understand it scientifically. It was written to be read sequentially, since we require carful preparation before we are ready to jump the ever harder jumps in the great race for consciousness. The race put up complex hurdles over the past millennia and there is no reason why it will not continue to do so; that is why it must be approached with care and patience.

Let me describe in more detail what is before us. First, in the next chapter I begin with a brief tour of the mind and lay out the general nature of the racecourse, so to speak. In the process we will see some of the complexities in the structure of the conscious mind: it is not a monolithic entity at all but can be decomposed into simpler components. It has, however, a unity that will have to be constructed as part of the overall model combining those parts. Some problems we face in understanding the conscious mind are explored in the next chapter, and further clarification is attempted as to the nature of the race.

In the second part we will travel in chapter 4 to view the tools being developed—noninvasive instruments, elements of neuroscience, and the theoretical framework of computational neuroscience. Chapter 5 evaluates some of the earlier entries and savors how they have helped give the beginning of a sense of direction to the race. It is important to remember that science is a constructive exercise, one scientist building on the work of previous ones. Some like Einstein, suddenly emerge with their heads high above the others and see how to create new images and models that are then worked on by many others. But even Einstein had to stand on the shoulders of his predecessors to get his vision; earlier work is of great relevance, to be appreciated and used in further development. To complete the second part of the book, a proposed composite model—relational consciousness—is suggested as combining important features of earlier ideas and helpful in guiding us into the center of the conscious mind. The model states simply that the content of consciousness arises from memories that are relevant to present input. In this way the past is used to interpret the present, a process of learning and being guided by earlier events that appears to possess good survival value. The way this idea relates to some of the earlier ones is then explored. In this chapter the main ground rules for the race are laid.

The real work begins in the third part. Various features of the neural underpinning of various components of consciousness are explored: to achieve its unity, to explain its use in reducing ambiguity, to understand its relation to memory, to determine how the active component involving higher cognitive processes could be constructed, and how the self can emerge. The five chapters of part III form the framework from which we hope to launch our entry into the race.

Part IV is where we face the greatest difficulty: how any dross matter can conceivably possess the amazing phenomenon of being able to think! We start by setting out principles that encode the relational approach to consciousness and discuss evidence for their support. Possible sites in the brain where consciousness first emerges are considered from the point of view of results flooding in from new sources. The final chapter of part IV gives a glimpse across the gap between matter and consciousness by positing the existence of a special form of neural activity—"bubbles"—supported by particular areas in the cortex. These are analyzed and shown to possess some of the important characteristics we ascribe to the raw feels of our own experience.

The final part mops up things that have not been touched on thus far: varieties of conscious experience and how they can be explained using relational ideas, answers to the most critical philosophers, and a final chapter indicating the relevance of it all to society and our future. This leads to tasks for the third millennium: the creation and direction of conscious machines.

2

The Nature of the Conscious Mind

I balanced all, brought all to mind.
—William Butler Yeats

How does the mind work to produce the experiences written about by poets such as Yeats? We do not know. No machine has yet been constructed that can be said to think in the way that you and I are doing at this moment. Some claim that there never can be such a machine, because the human mind is able to do things, such as be creative in the arts or prove new mathematical theorems, that no machine ever could. Even more remote, they argue, is the possibility of an emotional machine, able to appreciate such things as beautiful paintings or musical compositions; machines, they insist, will never be able to feel like you or I do. Others suppose that mind is separate from the body and may even have an independent and direct action on other people's minds. The recent surge of interest in the paranormal as shown, for example, by the enormous popularity of the television program "The X-Files" gives some indication of how widespread is such a view. That is not surprising since, even if they do not believe them, many people implicitly subscribe to one or other of the world's religions, which are based mainly on the idea of a separate mind or soul. For example, according to a recent newspaper poll in the United Kingdom, 59 percent of respondents stated they believed in extrasensory perception (precognition, telepathy, or clairvoyance). And it is said that one-fourth of Americans believe in angels!

We are faced, then, with an enormous range of positions on the nature of mind and a correspondingly large range of lifestyles supported by those views. Such a wide range of beliefs about the mind cannot all be right. What is the nature of this mental apparatus we all use so effortlessly, yet of which we have little or no comprehension? Is it possible to probe its nature more closely and bring some consistency out of disagreement? How do we really get to grips with the mind, particularly with its conscious part?

Parallel with this controversy, a race is developing among scientists to discover exactly the neural mechanisms underlying the mind, and especially conscious experience. New tools are being developed to resolve the difficult issues involved. It is hoped that this understanding will finally solve the problem of consciousness. As Francis Crick, codiscoverer of the structure of DNA and Nobel prize winner, wrote (1996), "Consciousness is now largely a scientific problem. It is not impossible that, with a little luck, we may glimpse the outline of the solution before the end of the century."

It is my purpose to describe some of the aspects of this exciting race. The promising new tools, both experimental and theoretical, for probing the brain and mind will be explained and the results they are providing explored. An entry into the race will be developed using guidance and support from the latest scientific knowledge presently available. We will abstract from this entry the basic principles of the conscious mind and consider the explanation of human consciousness and the reality of a machine version of it.

The Nature of Mind

Much controversy has raged regarding the definition of mind. Among the many definitions is that of Chamber's Dictionary: "that which thinks, knows, feels and wills." I think this suits our purpose well, fitting our own experience: I take the mind to consist of the four factors of thinking, knowing, feeling, and willing. A minimum of one of these, if not all four, must be present for mental activity to be claimed to occur. Yet one feature is essential if you are to continue to read: namely, that you be conscious. Without awareness of what you are reading, it would not be possible to consider that you are reading at all; you would just be staring vacantly at the pages of this book. However, you would still be aware of your surroundings and you would be able to report on them if you were asked. So consciousness, which I take mainly to be identifiable with awareness, is necessary to be able to state what it is you are experiencing at any one time. Such a report need not be spoken out loud but can be used as an internal "story" of what is happening to you; this running record is of value in planning future actions and being ready for rapid reaction to a threat. The report may actually not be necessary owing to the need to respond to pressing events. You can lose yourself in your present activity so that you do not even notice you are in a conscious state.

The mind therefore has at least two levels of activity, *conscious* and *unconscious*. I have just introduced consciousness; the unconscious was made popular by Sigmund Freud. Understanding of the manner in which unconscious mental activity can affect responses is increasing. There is also peripheral processing of inputs to our brains, such as by our retinas or by the subcortical relay parts of the thalamus (at the top of the brain stem), of whose specific form we are now indubitably unconscious and will always remain so.

The term unconscious covers a broad range of mental activity. I dissociate those brain activities that never directly enter awareness, owing to their primitive level in the processing hierarchy, from those of which we are presently unaware but that may have been repressed at an earlier time and still influence our actions. The term *nonconscious* will be used specifically for the former brain activity and *unconscious* for the latter, in case of ambiguity.

Why not equate mind with consciousness alone, so that we could avoid nonconscious or unconscious components; it would make things so much simpler? But that is not how we usually speak about them: mind includes both nonconscious and unconscious mental states since they both affect consciousness. States of mind are taken to be those based on all forms of brain activity.

Thus the mind has three levels: nonconscious, unconscious, and conscious, with the last two comprising knowledge, emotion, and drive and, in addition, the conscious level supporting thought. Creativity, for example, involves a nonconscious processing stage, occurring after the conscious hard work of setting up a data base together with prior conscious manipulations in attempting to solve a problem. In general we can regard the nonconscious stage as coding knowledge of the environment so as to help make sense of one's surroundings. Evidence shows that at least some of these early processors in the brain are learned, very likely at critical early phases in development. For example, a kitten brought up in surroundings in which it can see only vertical lines is unable to detect the presence of horizontal ones when it grows up.

We have therefore some structure in the mind, with its nonconscious, unconscious, and conscious components. But when we turn to analyze more closely the details of that structure we realize the full magnitude of the problem facing us.

Processing occurring peripherally at a nonconscious level, such as by the eyes or ears, is increasingly probed by neuroscientists. The detailed manner in which nerve cells combine their activity to handle incoming information is now understood well enough to allow simplified hardware versions of, for example, the retina and ear (Mead and Mahowald 1988) to be constructed. Some of the principles involved are also becoming clearer (Taylor 1990).[1] Aspects of low-level processing are therefore beginning to be understood, although considerable further investigation is required to explain all of the principles and related details.

But we must accept that the important advances being made in understanding such peripheral processing in the brain are sadly absent in other nonconscious processes, such as those involved in creativity or emotions, mental disease, or drug addiction. Important parts of the cognitive disturbances involved in mental disorders such as schizophrenia are thought to arise from defects in nonconscious levels of activity in frontal and midbrain regions. The neural regions are highly complex and only beginning to reveal the secrets of their modes of action.

Similar lack of understanding is glaringly present for the unconscious and conscious levels of the mind. As noted earlier, even their material nature is debated. As has been said, "What is mind? No matter. What is matter? Never mind." Since unconscious mental activity is closely related to consciousness, and consciousness is introspectively experienced by each of us, it is easier for us to attempt to look into consciousness before worrying about unconscious levels of processing. But we cannot leave out the nonconscious level since it is a crucial component of creativity and other important aspects of thinking. Even more important, it is used in the emergence of consciousness itself out of nonconsciously processed activity; nonconscious activity is the gateway to consciousness, so we cannot neglect it. Yet consciousness is where the greatest difficulty lies in trying to understand the mind.

The Problem of Consciousness

What is consciousness? It has proved notoriously difficult to define. It has even been stated: "The term is impossible to define except in terms that are unintelligible without a grasp of what consciousness means." Not much help for us there! More pithily, American philosopher Thomas Nagel (1974) stated "without consciousness the mind-body problem would be much less interesting; with consciousness it seems hopeless." Daniel Dennett (1987) wrote, still unhelpfully, consciousness "is the most obvious and most mysterious feature of our minds." More recently he changed his mind and claimed to explain it (Dennett 1991) but in the process tended to reduce it to a less difficult problem by downgrading it. The following glossary definition appears to be a little more positive: "the totality of one's thoughts and feelings; awareness of one's existence, sensations and circumstances" (Dennett 1987). This indicates the complexity of consciousness: it involves both thinking and emotional elements and self-awareness, as well as the more elemental sensations of so-called phenomenal consciousness. The first of these, involving thinking and self, consists of abilities possessed only by more advanced animals in the evolutionary tree: humans, orangutans, and chimpanzees perhaps alone in the animal kingdom. On the other hand the lower level of experience, the raw feels of sensations such as the redness you sense when you look at a red rose, are most likely shared by a much larger number of animals. This shows that, at least initially, we should investigate the nature of consciousness not only in our own species but also in lower animals. That we will do shortly, and we will find a remarkable range of levels of ability that reflects different levels of conscious experience. This only underlines my claim that consciousness is a collection of a set of components that we have to try to disentangle.

In spite of some valiant attempts, it is perhaps not appropriate at this stage to present a hard and fast definition of consciousness; this is the position taken by Francis Crick and Christof Koch (1990), who wrote,

We feel it is better to avoid a precise definition of consciousness because of the dangers of premature definition. Until we understand the problem much better, any attempt at a formal definition is likely to be either misleading or overly restrictive, or both (Crick and Koch 1990).

That may not please you, and you can well ask, "How can you investigate a topic or a subject if you cannot describe what it is you are looking for?" More especially, how can I claim that there is a race to understand consciousness if I do not know what the winning post looks like, or even that it exists at all, a question raised in the first chapter?

The answer is that we all know roughly what consciousness is, but our knowledge is not precise enough to give a definition that might satisfy a jurist; the fine print, even the not-so-fine print, is missing. Part of the purpose of this chapter is to try to fill in some of that not-so-fine print in a nonrigorous manner. Various features of consciousness will be explored so as to have a better appreciation of the nature of the beast. We will then be much more prepared for the discussion of models of the mind to which we turn in chapter 4, and the more complete model developed later in the book. I will give a preliminary definition of consciousness at the end of this chapter and relate it to the main thesis of the book, although it will not be until somewhat later that I can be specific. Only then will we define the winning post with any precision. My purpose through the next sections of this chapter is to present evidence that will guide us toward such a preliminary definition. We know that consciousness is made up of different parts, and any definition must be flexible enough to encompass that complexity.

The Controlling Brain

Fossil records over the last seven hundred million years give evidence of a gradual evolution of complexity in living forms and more recently of increased brain power and the resulting intelligence in coping with the task of staying alive. An enormous range of intelligence evolved during those millenia, and that is especially true of humans. As details are increasingly filled in of the missing link between us and our earlier relatives from bone relics and the manner in which the genetic heritage changed becomes clearer, our emergence from animal ancestors becomes more apparent.

The differentiation of humans from other living beings occurred in a relatively continuous manner. At no point can we detect any sudden jump in evolution, as we would expect if consciousness was suddenly fused with brain. Such a fusion should produce a decided advantage for its possessor; that does not seem to have happened. This is strong support for the thesis that consciousness, as an important concomitant of intelligence, has to be looked for in terms of brain activity alone; it evolved along with the brain.

This thesis has an enormous amount of evidence for its support. Consider the case (Whitworth 1997) of a man who, because of brain damage in a car crash, cannot prevent himself from pestering any woman he meets. He cannot hold down a job owing to this proclivity; his marriage has broken up because of it; yet he is powerless to prevent himself behaving in this highly asocial manner. He is in the grip of his rerouted brain circuitry.

Even more tragic are the gradual disintegrations of personality and mind from Alzheimer's disease. This is the most common degenerative neurological disease in many countries, and it has been estimated that between 5 and 10 percent of the population over sixty-five years of age suffer from the condition. It is not even uncommon for people between the ages of fifty and sixty-five to have it. The disease can begin insidiously after a long and productive life. A typical case is described as follows (Zomeren and Brouwer 1994):

Our patient, TB, was a 66-year-old retired businessman who had led an active social life. In World War II he had flown a fighter plane as a Dutch volunteer in the US Air Force. After the war he had a successful career in publishing. He came to the Department of Neurology outpatient clinic because of forgetfulness that had been noted by his wife and had developed over the past few years. A neurological examination revealed no convincing signs, but the neurologist noted that the patient was disoriented in time. It also struck the neurologist that TB underwent the examination passively, leaving the talking to his wife (Zomeren and Brouwer 1994, chap. 4).

TB was examined thoroughly and showed no motor difficulties. However,

Memory functions were clearly affected, as the patient scored beneath the normal range for his group on verbal and nonverbal tasks of learning, recall and recognition. In an interview with his wife, she stressed that forgetfulness was the first sign that started her worrying. Later she noticed that her husband was often disoriented in time and sometimes in place. For example in the car he might stop at intersections, not knowing whether to turn left or right. He stopped playing bridge, with the comment that his play demanded too much thinking.

TB was diagnosed as having Alzheimer's disease, not only having problems of loss of memory but also of attention.

There appeared to be a striking discrepancy between performance elicited by well-known or obvious environmental stimuli and performance requiring active mental control. TB's visual reaction times were within the normal range on a basic reaction task, but he was completely unable to handle two more complex conditions. When distracted by irrelevant additional lights, and when a dual task demanded divided attention between visual and auditory stimuli he became confused and made so many errors that the testing had to be discontinued.

More rapid changes of behavior, sometimes reversible, are also the product of the damaged brain. Consider the following case reported by his physicians (Mark and Ervine 1970):

Donald L was a short, muscular, 43-year-old man, who, when we first saw him in the hospital, was restrained by heavy fish netting. Even so, his behaviour was impressively threatening. He snarled, showed his teeth, and lashed out with either arm or leg as soon as any attendant approached him. His wife and daughter were too frightened to give a detailed history. All they could say was that for no apparent reason he had taken a butcher's knife and tried his best to kill them. They had called the police, who had observed Donald's garbled and inappropriate speech and promptly brought him to the hospital. Further questioning of his family elicited the information that Donald had undergone a genuine change in his personality over the previous 6 months, and that during this time he had also complained of severe headaches and blurred vision (Mark and Ervine 1970).

Careful examination of the man showed he had a tumor underneath the right frontal lobe that was pressing on his limbic system. With removal of the tumor, his symptoms completely disappeared, he regained his equable disposition, and went back to work.

Aggressive behavior has also been shown by patients with similar tumors affecting the limbic system, associated with assaulting, suicidal, depressive, fearful, or seclusive symptoms. These and many other cases where the emotions are out of control are aptly described by Henry Fielding: "Oh this poor brain. Ten thousand shapes of fury are whirling there, and reason is no more." This all supports the importance of the brain in determining the emotional response to life, and makes the study of the brain as basis of emotions of great relevance; it is why so much attention in the life sciences is now being focused on it.

Such cases underline the complete but subtle dependence of the conscious mind on suitable brain mechanisms. Any suggestion that consciousness has an independent existence from the brain has first of all to deal with the patients described: TB and his disintegration with Alzheimer's disease, Donald L's running berserk under the influence of a brain tumor, and the sober citizen turned compulsive womanizer after he damaged his brain in a car crash. These and an enormous number of similar cases completely justify the strong thesis: consciousness depends solely on brain activity.

Strong evidence also exists for brain-based consciousness from the study of animal behavior. This can add to our understanding of the detailed nature of consciousness, and in particular some of its component parts.

Animal Consciousness

Do animals have consciousness? If so, what form does it take, and how can it help in our search for a better understanding of human consciousness? These questions are increasingly being explored by animal ethologists and animal psychologists. The answers have great relevance to those of us who are concerned about animal suffering, such as that caused by inhumane methods of transporting livestock from one country to another and their slaughter.

Our search for animal consciousness is clearly prejudiced by our understanding of consciousness itself, which is something we will clarify by turning to animals. In spite of the apparent impasse we can look for conscious behavior of animals in terms of levels of intelligence they display, of their keeping a goal "in mind" and trying to achieve it, of being able to report on their experiences, and so on. We immediately meet the obvious problem that animals cannot normally or easily describe their experiences by means of language. In addition, we can usually only observe their behavior in the wild or under controlled conditions. Thus it is difficult for us not to ascribe a level of consciousness to some animals, but it is still controversial exactly what those levels are. Let me give some examples to show the difficulty.

Numerous attempts have been made to teach animals to communicate directly with human trainers. Chimpanzees were taught human speech; for example, one named Viki learned to say the words *papa, mama, cup,* and *up,* although the words were enunciated poorly. From such studies it became apparent that apes do not possess the vocal apparatus necessary to reproduce human speech sounds efficiently.

Although apes cannot speak, they do communicate with each other. Chimpanzees have a repertoire of about thirteen sounds that they use to maintain contact in the undergrowth, and allow other members of their group to know their position, emotional state, and likely behavior. Yet it is uncertain whether or not they can use language in a creative way, as we humans can. Are they able to produce "sentences" by stringing together their different sounds? Even more important, can they go on "talking" by creating any number of sentences? We just do not know.

Other species use calls to give information to members of their troupe about the presence of predators. Vervet monkeys, for example, have different alarm calls for when they sight a python, a leopard, or a martial eagle. Young monkeys learn which ones to use with which sighting by observation, without direct teaching from their mothers. In the wild, mothers have shown inability to recognize or correct any ignorance displayed by their offspring. As noted by animal psychologists (Seyfarth and Charney, 1992), "Such reliance on observational learning is widespread among animals and can, in our view, ultimately be traced to the adult's failure to recognise that their offspring's knowledge is different from their own."

The high-level ability to attribute knowledge to others—to possess what some have called a theory of mind—arises in animals other than humans. Anecdotes tell of chimpanzees deceiving others in several different contexts and by a large variety of gestures, postures, and facial expressions. This occurs especially when an animal wishes to lead members of its troupe away from food that it has hidden in the forest. Anthropologist Jane Goodall once watched an adolescent male chimp, Figan, deceive others to protect a hidden cache of food. As a group of chimpanzees assembled in the feeding area, Figan suddenly stood up and strode into the woods in a manner that caused the others to follow him. Shortly thereafter Figan abandoned his companions and circled back to eat his hidden bananas. This and similar anecdotes indicate the possibility of a theory of mind in such apes.

Evidence of this sort agrees with the superior powers of self-recognition of chimpanzees compared with other apes and other animals. When chimps were allowed to become used to playing with a mirror, and under anesthesia had colored dye painted on their faces, they would acknowledge the presence of the dye by touching the affected part after observing it in the mirror. Such activity of self-realization did not occur if the chimps had not previously become used to handling a mirror. Nor did gorillas or other apes (other than orangutans) display a similar sense of self by means of the mirror test.

The chimpanzee is closest to ourselves in its ability to use symbols in communication. In particular it can use gestures in the sense of "knowing that" instead of merely "knowing how." Some animals know how to make a gesture to obtain a reward, but do not at the same time realize that such a gesture will actually produce the reward. In humans, "how" knowledge is associated with skills and in general is connected to nonconscious states. Playing a stroke in golf or riding a bicycle can be performed in a purely automatic manner in which there is little or no conscious content (and it is usually more effective). Experiments with chimpanzees Lana and Sarah using symbols for communication instead of spoken words, revealed that the apes could learn the meaning of the symbols. Lana was able to name correctly either a banana or a piece of candy, presented to her on a tray, by typing the name on a keyboard. Sarah was also able to learn the concept of "name of" for various objects she ate or played with. Evidence of this sort is suggestive, although not compelling, that chimpanzees have more than skill memory and are truly conscious of their responses.

An important aspect of behavior is whether it is guided by some representation of a goal. Such behavior would be beyond haphazard performance or be under the control of habits. It would correspond to having some guiding goal in mind. But the main problem in attempting to detect conscious mind in goal-directed behavior patterns of animals is whether the goal is held consciously or unconsciously.

Some behavior patterns appear to have a great deal of evident goal-directedness. The sandpiper, for example, attempts to draw off an intruder from its nest by leaving it and acting as if injured, such as trailing an apparently broken wing. Experiments indicate that in the process the bird can distinguish between enemies intent on a close approach to its nest and those not so inclined. Again, evidence is equivocal as to the extent of conscious content of the experience.

One indicator of higher-level brain processing that can be expected to have some conscious content is use of tools. Numbers of animals are known to use a tool as an extension of their body to attain an immediate goal. Crows take whelks up into the air and drop them on a rock to break them open. Song thrushes hold snails in their beak and smash them against a rock, and ravens and vultures drop bones to crack them open and feed on the marrow. An elephant or horse will pick up a stick with which to scratch itself. Such behavior appears to be intelligent and, as such, gives us an indication of the animals' conscious brain states.

More creativity was observed in a population of macaques on the Japanese island of Koshima. One particular animal, Imo, invented the technique of washing sand-covered sweet potatoes in a stream, a habit that spread over ten years to most of the monkeys on the island. Imo later removed sand from grain scattered on the beach by throwing the grains into the sea; the sand sank, whereas the grains floated and could be scooped out and eaten. Even if Imo had made her discoveries by chance, she was aware of the value of the results and used them. That again seems like consciousness at work.

Animals are also able to express emotions strongly, although the level at which they experience pain is presently unclear. However, the amount of force they use in attempting to extricate themselves from unpleasant situations indicates that they do indeed suffer. It is difficult to understand such response patterns without accepting a conscious experience driving the behavior.

Finally, it is possible to train animals to report on their own experiences. A rat can learn to press an appropriate lever to indicate that it "knows what it is doing." Experimenters waited until a rat in a cage made one of four responses of face washing, rearing on its hind legs, walking, or remaining stationary. To obtain food, the rat had to press one of four levers that the experimenters labeled for each activity. The rats were able to learn the correct response and gain the food reward. Monkeys are expected to be able to achieve similar responses.

In all, evidence gives no clear indication that such and such an animal is conscious but that slightly more primitive ones are not. At no point in evolution can we suspect that animal consciousness suddenly arose; we should expect that from the clearly complex nature of consciousness. It supports our thesis that consciousness emerged gradually as animals evolved. Moreover, it is totally created by activity of the brain. Various combinations of the components of consciousness were selected differently by our ancestors for the extra survival value they offered. But we cannot expect the full panoply of human consciousness to be present in animals lower than ourselves, and the attempt by some to do so is misguided. Animals appear to possess some parts of the complex of human consciousness, and studying them could well allow teasing out the more primitive parts.

This leads us to conclude that consciousness is composed of separate parts, with various combinations created by particular animal brains. At the highest level the sense of self is possessed only by ourselves, chimpanzees, and orangutans. Lower down the scale are the additional possession of empathy for others of one's own kind and of the ability to consider the minds of others (as by the cheating chimpanzee). There is also dissociation of the ability to hold a goal in mind, and of being able to value the results of chance experience. Finally, the lowest level of consciousness, that of phenomenal experience, apparently is possessed by a large range of animals who demonstrate the ability to report their state of mind by acting on it. These animals have no sense of self. They cannot suddenly flip in and out of realizing that "they" are having a particular conscious experience, as I can as I write these words. Yet they have awareness of their experience, as their commentary on it shows. This phenomenal level of experience therefore can be dissociated from awareness of self.

In summary, results of animal studies support the thesis that consciousness is made up of several components: of self, of others, of intentions to act, of emotions, and last but decidedly not least, of phenomenal experience. We may be reading some of our own experience into that of animals, but this knowledge helps us clarify our understanding even if it reflects ourselves more than the animals. We may be in danger of committing the same fallacy when we look at the development of babies, but the changes we observe in them are also relevant to our search for understanding our consciousness.

The Development of Consciousness

As studies of animals indicate, levels of mind and of consciousness range from lower animals to the great apes and humans, with the last two possessing self-recognition. A continuum of levels of consciousness is also displayed in the fetus and infant. Can we observe discrete steps in the emergence of consciousness as the infant develops, and if so, can we use them to help us understand consciousness better?

A fetus acquires an increasingly coordinated set of responses as it grows. Movements begin at about eight or so weeks after conception and develop into a wide range of movement patterns by about twenty weeks. The fetus also begins to give clear sensory responses. Sound, initially in the low-frequency range and later at higher frequencies, produces a change of heart rate at about twenty-eight weeks and also brings about movement patterns.

It is known that the fetus learns. The fetuses of twenty-three women were classically conditioned by pairing a 12-second burst of music with a period when the mothers relaxed. Before birth, fetuses moved sooner when presented with the sound (Feijoo 1975, 1981). After birth, presentation of the music reduced crying, increased eye opening, and reduced the number of rapid movements (Feijoo 1975, 1981).

That the fetus can learn indicates its ability to perceive stimuli. Studies show that the memory for prenatal events is present immediately after birth, but exactly how long this lasts is not known. It is difficult from the evidence presented above to deduce exactly when and if the fetus may be said to be conscious. There may even be a continuum of consciousness, as the fetus acquires memories and enlarges its repertoire of responses. Once born, such development increases apace, but again, it has not been possible to focus on a specific time of which one might say, "The infant has become conscious NOW." The mind appears to emerged gradually from a complex process of growing and learning.

The seamless sensitivity of response of the infant to its surroundings indicates it is gradually developing its powers of phenomenal experience. At the same time developmental watersheds indicate that factors such as self-awareness are relative latecomers to the structure of consciousness. Experiments point to several possible indicators for the development of self-awareness in the infant. An investigation (McFarland 1993) into the age of onset of empathy determined when an infant would go to the aid of another in distress (McFarland 1993). Above a certain age an infant shows emotional concern and compassion, whereas a younger infant either remains indifferent or responds by seeking comfort for itself. Between sixteen and twenty-four months of age a change occurred from noncomforting to comforting other distressed infants. This transition was closely related to the changeover from nonrecognition to recognition of themselves in the mirror. It is as if self-realization develops at the same time as realization of others, yet the two faculties, need not be present simultaneously. This is seen from the fact that compassion for others of a group is known to occur in numerous animals besides humans, as mentioned earlier; such animals have empathy for each other but do not simultaneously have self-awareness. Yet again we see the mind having several faculties that are independent of each other and that are possessed by animals lower than ourselves in reduced degrees.

What we learn from the developing infant about consciousness reinforces our lesson from animals: to understand consciousness we must look at its different parts, the reduce and conquer technique used in science.

Adult Consciousness

Studies in animals and fetuses and infants indicate that consciousness is a combination of many parts. Adults in full possession of their faculties will therefore have a complex experience under the heading of consciousness. That is one of the reasons why it is not possible to give a simple or short definition of the experience without enormous simplification and loss of clarity. It would be better to use the term *states of consciousness* than the single word *consciousness* to describe this complexity wherever possible. However, to keep to normal usage, I will use the latter for the whole range of conscious experiences, although we must keep in mind that the more complex interpretation is necessary. When specific forms of consciousness are considered I will be precise and speak of phenomenal consciousness, self-awareness, or emotional consciousness, as appropriate.

A different approach to the range of possible states of consciousness is given by Bernard Baars (1988) in his excellent discussion.[2] Baars lists conscious states on a continuum going from those possessing "clarity" to those that are more nearly unconscious.

Clearly conscious phenomena

↓Attended percepts

Clear mental images

Deliberate inner speech

Material deliberately retrieved from memory

Fleeting mental images

Peripheral or background perceptual events

Abstract but accessible concepts

Active but unrehearsed items in immediate memory

Fuzzy, difficult-to-determine events

Presuppositions of conscious percepts

Fully habituated stimuli

Subliminal events that prime later conscious processes

"Blind sight" in occipital brain damage

Contextual information, set

Automatic skill components

Unretrieved material in long-term memory

Perceptual context

↑Abstract rules, as in syntax

Clearly unconscious events

Baars uses "unconscious" as involving either nonconscious or unconscious mental activity, according to the discussion in the first section. His list indicates an important new division of consciousness in terms of memory representations stored in various parts of the brain and used to support various conscious states. One of the most important of these distinctions is between memory used consciously and that which is not. Such a distinction was made by a number of philosophers early in this century. Henri Bergson distinguished, in 1911, between habit, "a set of intelligently constructed mechanisms" that enables people to adapt themselves to their environment, and true memory, coextensive with consciousness, "truly moving in the past" and capable of marking and retaining the dates and orders of happenings. Bertrand Russell (1921) strongly endorsed Bergson's distinction, claiming that despite the difficulty "in distinguishing the two forms of memory in practice, there can be no doubt that both forms exist."

These ideas led to the differentiation between what is called *declarative* and *nondeclarative memory*. Declarative memory contains material of which one can be conscious, such as the meanings of these words you are reading. Nondeclarative memory contains only representations, such as skills, of which we have no such awareness. Consciousness is therefore supported explicitly by declarative memory and possibly by further input from nondeclarative memory.

Declarative memory was recently further divided into two separate systems (Tulving 1972). One is semantic memory, which involves material used in a conscious manner but for which we have no memory of when it was first experienced and learned. This contains what is usually called general knowledge, such as the name of the capital of the United States (Washington, DC) or Churchill's first name (Winston). That is to be set against memories that contain the percipient, the "I." These are called episodic memories and involve autobiographic memories: what you ate for breakfast or did on your last vacation.

Consciousness involves not only declarative memories but also percepts that arise from preprocessing in peripheral systems, such as the eye, ear, and early parts of the posterior cortex. When you experience the percepts of the words you are reading on this page, they have been created in your brain by considerable processing in different parts of your visual and auditory cortices. The neural connections needed to achieve such percepts were created by suitable learning after you were born and also by genetic guidance. Both of these are parts of what can be termed *perceptual memory systems.* You use them to filter and analyze sensory inputs to produce the percepts you experience.

Structure in Consciousness

These divisions of memory are important as they allow us to divide consciousness into those states in which only perceptual and semantic memories are predominant, compared with those in which episodic memory has become the major aspect. These are two quite different states of mind. The perceptual sort occurs when you passively experience your surroundings, such as when you savor delicious food or drink or look at a beautiful sunset; you need have no sense of self. At the other extreme is the case of more reflective consciousness in which you are moved by personal memories or are aware of yourself as the experiencer. An autobiographic component may be present when you experience a percept, such as recalling an event, where it occurred, and when. However, that happens only infrequently at a conscious level during the day; it would get in the way of effective processing if it occurred too often.

A third, active form of consciousness is present in thinking hard about a problem. This requires the inhibition of perceptual input, which could prove too distracting for thought processes to work effectively. It also requires prevention of autobiographical recall, unless this is undertaken to use experience in solving similar problems. This mode of thought contains active processing, with various brain activities transformed internally to achieve a solution to a problem. Active consciousness is supported mainly by the frontal part of the brain, so such activity is especially difficult for those with damage to that area.

Finally, most states of consciousness have an emotional component, even to the extreme of emotion completely taking over awareness. The phrase "blind rage" aptly summarizes a state of mind in which emotion fills the whole of consciousness. However, we will not postulate an independent emotional component or element of conscious experience, since emotion is always a coloration of what we experience in the other parts of consciousness; emotion tinges phenomenal, active, or self experience.

From our discussion we can divide consciousness as passive (or perceptual), active, and self consciousness. These are the parts out of which our waking experience is composed. To understand them better, let us look at where roughly in the brain they are based. This will strengthen the relation between brain and consciousness. In fact I have already presented several instances—damage to frontal lobes causing loss of planning or social response, loss of cortex in Alzheimer's disease causing loss of attentional capabilities, loss of primary sensory regions leading to blindness or loss of hearing—that are part of the enormous range of evidence for such localization of consciousness in brain sites. Based on effects of brain damage, the three components of consciousness are sited as follows:

1. Passive or phenomenal: mainly posterior sites, after initial activity has been processed in the primary input regions of visual, auditory, or somatosensory cortex.
2. Active: mainly in the frontal lobes, which are more extensive in humans than in any other living animal.
3. Self: also mainly in the frontal lobes, but with relevant episodic memories based in posterior regions.

To be complete (although I discuss these further sorts of consciousness in more detail in the final part of the book), I should mention emotional components of experience (which can get out of control, as in the case of Donald L): they appear to arise mainly in the frontal lobes, although lower down in the brain. However, that emotional consciousness has a separate site is unclear, since emotions are so strongly determined by nonconscious and unconscious mental states. In addition, conscious experience during dreaming appears to be mainly posteriorly sited; in slow-wave sleep, whatever conscious experience occurs has strong frontal components. According to present thinking, consciousness has at least three separate components, with possibly two or three more in sleep and emotional states. These three components depend on episodic and semantic memory systems.

Further Structure in Consciousness?

The components of consciousness are related to the memory structures, enabling content to be given to consciousness. Philosophers and psychologists have identified additional divisions that can give us more insight into the subtlety of consciousness. They separate consciousness into three more parts (Searle 1991, 1994).

Phenomenal

This involves raw feels, or, in the term used by philosophers, *qualia*. These are regarded by some as the most primitive elements of conscious experience, and as such form the ultimate basis of consciousness. You will have a raw feel of "red" when you look, say, at a red patch of color on the wall, or at an exquisite rose, or the taste of a full-bodied red wine. Qualia are supposed to have various highly debatable characteristics, such as being intrinsic, and so with no relationship to other objects. They are also claimed to be ineffable; they cannot be described to someone else. They are also supposed to have the character of transparency, so that they can be looked through, presenting no resistance to their experience. A fourth important characteristic is atomicity, that is, they cannot be decomposed into anything smaller or more primitive.

Such properties are supported at an informal level by introspection of our conscious experience at the phenomenal level of raw feels. But the notion has been battered by certain philosophers who claim that qualia do not exist as primitives anywhere in the brain. In spite of such criticisms, an undeniable "phenomenal feel" to our consciousness possesses these characteristics, and it would be difficult to argue it away by fiat. We all have phenomenal experience that has some of these characteristics. We must try to determine how a neural model of consciousness accounts for the nature of experience encapsulated in these properties, even if qualia themselves do not actually exist as primitives.

We identify phenomenal consciousness in the sense of qualia with the passive or perceptual consciousness introduced earlier; the memory structures used to create qualia must involve perceptual memories. Our first glimmers of consciousness must be from already filtered inputs to give them some level of coherence. How far back down the processing path in the brain toward the input raw feels actually arise is one of the interesting but unresolved questions in brain research. It is that question, and the associated one of added value, that leads to the initial raw feel emerging from nonconscious neural activity that is at the heart of the consciousness race.

Intentional

A second important structure in consciousness is intentionality, a medieval concept that arose philosophically from Aristotle. Its etymological root is the Latin verb *intendo,* meaning "to aim at" or "to point toward." Intentionality was resurrected by Franz Brentano, a contemporary of William James, who distinguished between mental acts and mental contents; my belief that the earth is round has intentional content [the earth is round]. There is meaningful intentional content in desires, hopes, expectations, memories, loves, and hates; in fact, in all mental acts. Brentano's thesis is that intentionality is a necessary component of a mental phenomenon.

A basic problem of mental states is how to explain their intentionality, their "aboutness," the meaning or sense to be attached to their content. This problem has been realized for some time by those attempting to construct a purely physical framework for the mind, as is being done here (the physicalist or materialist program). The problem raised by the meaning of the content of thought was noted clearly by Armstrong (1968):

. . . any theory of mind must be able to give some account or analysis of the intentionality of mental states or else it must accept it as an ultimate irreducible feature of the mental. . . . No Materialist can claim that intentionality is a unique, unanalyzable property of mental processes and still be consistent with materialism. A Materialist is forced to attempt an analysis of intentionality.

This aspect was discussed extensively by philosophers such as John Searle (1983), who regarded it as the content or meaning of conscious experience. Earlier in this chapter we met a practical form of intentionality when we discussed animal minds in terms of goal seeking. It is used here in an extended sense to indicate the more complete sense of significance that an object of conscious experience will possess as part of that experience. Intentionality at this level is therefore mainly concerned with the semantic content of the representations of objects entering conscious experience. This involves the passive component of consciousness since, as I argue later, it is composed mainly of semantic activations in addition to the input that is causing the conscious experience. However, active contributions are also associated with actions, since meaning has an active aspect. An approach to semantics as virtual actions is developed in part III in which this active component is given due weight. Intentionality as reaching out to objects is thus based on parts of both passive and active consciousness. Such a formulation is consistent with the ideas of existentialist philosophers, especially Merleau-Ponty, as emphasized by Freeman (1995).

Introspective

Introspective means awareness arising from looking into one's own experience. Through introspection we become aware of the content of our conscious experience. Given this ability, it is possible to study this content in more detail by a process of self-reference. This ability appears at about sixteen to twenty-four months of age in the human, as shown in studies we noted earlier. This character of consciousness is most prevalent when autobiographic consciousness, that of self, is predominant.

I stated earlier that consciousness is complex; we have recognized so far at least three divisions or parts to it: passive, active and self, with possible additional components arising from emotions, during dreaming and during slow-wave sleep all waiting in the wings. Now we have brought in the notions of raw feels or phenomenal experience (which we identified with the passive component), intentionality, and introspection. We will identify intentionality later as a part of active consciousness, and introspection can be clearly seen as part of the self component, so we have not increased the overall complexity of consciousness. Even so, all of the components separated out for more complete discussion—passive, active, and self—are themselves complex. This we know from our own experience: in our active state we can think or plan or attend to what is around us, each of these states itself being different from the others. We can flip from one to the other with no apparent difficulty. Yet how can we reconcile such complexity with our experience of being only one person throughout these different consciousnesses?

The Unity of Consciousness

Each of us is sure that we experience the world in a unified manner despite splits in our consciousness. "I" claim to be an undivided whole and to know all that is going on in my mind. That is the traditional view, termed the *thesis of the unity of mind*. It was this indivisibility of the mind, especially of its conscious component, that led French philosopher Rene Descartes to his hypothesis of the duality of brain and mind: the brain can be separated into parts but the mind cannot. He solved this paradox by requiring the mind to be incorporeal, with quite different properties from the divisible brain. In particular the soul, the essence of the mind is, he claimed, indivisible and indestructible, so providing a basis for the continuation of personality both during life and after death.

Such a simplified picture of the mind as an indivisible whole is not consistent with the fact of separate mental faculties—imagination, will, understanding, and so on—nor with splits of consciousness discussed so far in this chapter.

Nor is the claim that the mind is a unity consistent with a number of facts about the manner in which the brain controls experience. We considered some effects of brain lesions on behavior; they can cause loss of specific faculties either at a high cognitive or a low sensory level. Frontal injuries cause a person to lose the ability to plan and to hold objects in mind over a period of time: the ability to make decisions is reduced and leads to difficulties in occupation and personal life. On the other hand, brain injury in the posterior part of the cortex causes loss of sensation in a given modality. Oliver Sacks (1996) recounted vividly the painter who lost the ability to see in color due to a brain injury when he hit his head during a car accident. From then on he could see only black and white. Before the accident he responded to and used his experience of colors brilliantly in his painting; afterward he had to try to compensate for this loss of color experience. So again, there is no simple unified mind but a collection of experiences bound together in a way that is immensely vulnerable to brain damage.

Another form of brain damage underlines the fragility of the sense of unity of consciousness. Patients with excessive epilepsy that is uncontrollable by drugs have had their brains split into two parts by cutting the fibrous band, the corpus callosum, that joins the cerebral hemispheres. In normal people the corpus callosum carries information about activity on one side of the brain to the other, allowing the activities to be related by literally pooling the different knowledge each side possesses. Unity of experience is thereby created. The knowledge possessed by each hemisphere is known to be different: the left side for logical and linguistic knowledge, the right for artistic and emotional knowledge and global analysis of inputs. These differences are combined to make a single personal experience in the normal brain by information flowing in both directions across the fibers of the corpus callosum. If the hemispheres are separated by severing the corpus callosum, unification is lost. One half will have the majority of the language skills, although the other side may still have a modicum of language and respond to questions. But in some people, a difference of experience and motivation can produce strong conflict between the responses of the two halves.

One such woman who was operated on to control epilepsy had a severe case of conflict. She was unable to name sensations in her left side since they were transmitted to her right hemisphere, although both hemispheres could organize speech. She was aware of being touched on her left hand, which she indicated by nodding her head. Yet her hands would fight with each other over responses to certain questions, and conflict also showed in alternating rapidly and vigorously in her replies, "Yes!," "No!," "That's not right!" She had two definite personalities inside her head, each controlled by a separate hemisphere.

Even more common are the gradual disintegrations of personality and the mind due to Alzheimer's disease. How can the brain, in spite of its fragility, produce in a healthy human being the apparently unified experience that is "I"? It seems like a miracle. Yet my examples show that we have to start from the brain itself, and in particular its detailed structure, to obtain an answer. There is no easy way; it will be a hard slog to gain even a glimmer of understanding, but it will be worth it if we can also in some small way help to understand how the destruction of the brain can produce the ravages of Alzheimer's and other mental diseases. So besides having to understand different components of consciousness we have recognized so far, the "dividing" part of the divide and conquer strategy, we also have to recombine the parts of consciousness to produce its experienced unity. Only then will we have truly conquered the brain.

A Tentative Definition of Consciousness

We are now in a position to compose the tentative definition of consciousness promised earlier. What is clear so far is that consciousness involves memory structures or representations of the past of episodic, autobiographic, semantic, preprocessing, and emotional character. These structures are used to give conscious content to the input in a manner that endows that experience with meaning related to the past. Thus consciousness arises from the intermingling of recorded past experiences with incoming present activity; as such the process is dynamic. In using the past, the system so endowed (in ourselves or other animals) is given extra efficiency by providing the input with the significance acquired during earlier encounters with it. If there is no past memory and the input is completely novel, special strategies are available to deal with it. One is that an animal will freeze, remaining stationary while watching the novel object carefully. It will then approach the object cautiously. In this way it will gradually develop memory structures that will be effective in dealing with what was initially a new and threatening object.

By using the past to fill in the present, the content of consciousness—the experience itself—is given by the filling-in material; that is, by the memories activated being used to help in further processing. This leads us to the relational aspect of consciousness: it arises by means of the activation of suitably related past memories giving meaning to present input in terms of suitably similar past encounters (either of an episodic or a semantic nature or at the level of preprocessing). Even though the memories being used in this manner need not be declarative themselves, as in the case of perceptual processing at the early stages of cortex, they still give content to consciousness.

Such a relational approach can be applied to all of the components of consciousness we have recognized so far. Each of them has conscious content that arises from activation of suitably relevant memories. Thus for phenomenal consciousness there is a range of semantic and episodic memories associated with a given input that in total are the sources of the experience; the more active component of consciousness will also have similar memories to call on as well as those involved in actions. Self-awareness has its own set of memories associated with the self, as does emotional memory. The other two components draw on relevant memory structures for their content. The nature of these memories is more problematic since they are little studied, but would in any case involve different combinations of the memory structures.

From these arguments I propose a relational definition of consciousness:

Consciousness arises solely from the process by which content is given to inputs based on past experience of a variety of forms. It has a relational structure in that only the most appropriate memories are activated and involved in further processing. It involves temporal duration so as to give time to allow the relational structure to fill out the input. This thereby gives the neural activity the full character of inner experience.

We will build further on this definition throughout the book to make it more precise.

Summary and Conclusions

In this chapter I considered various features of mind and consciousness to appreciate better the race for consciousness: the components of mind (conscious, nonconscious, unconscious), the evolution of consciousness over eons, its presence in animals, its development in fetus and infant, its structure in normal awake activity, and its reduction in brain-damaged people.

The main conclusion I reached is that consciousness is a complex of a number of different components. One basic subdivision is between an active, mainly anteriorly based form, and a mainly posteriorly based and more passive perceptual one. This subdivision is seen also in the manner in which posterior and anterior brain damage lead to different effects on conscious experience. I expanded the division to include a self component based on further analysis of the informal inner feel of conscious experience. Waiting in the wings is a further variety of forms of conscious experience: emotional, in dreaming or in slow-wave sleep, as well as a whole host of forms in altered states (under drugs, hypnosis, or fasting).

Further structure was introduced in terms of phenomenal, intentional, and introspective components of consciousness. They were seen to depend on the components introduced earlier, in particular the passive, active, and self parts. Finally, there was the important feature of the unity of consciousness, which has to be explained as part of the total conscious experience.

The analysis so far allowed me to propose a preliminary, relationally based definition of consciousness. This bolstered the component division of consciousness by relating the different components to relevant memory structures. We are making progress in reducing the complexity of consciousness to simpler components. But we still face difficult problems about consciousness. To analyze them better, in the next chapter we consider other important aspects of the structure of consciousness that have been developed by philosphers and psychologists.

3

The Racecourse of Consciousness

Sole judge of truth, in endless error hurled: The glory, jest and riddle of the world.
—Alexander Pope

Growing children present anew the miracle of being able to behave as if controlled by a mind similar to one's own. They appear to have the ability to feel strong emotions or to create works of art or, when older, science. It is through the responses of those around them, guiding and enlarging their own developing sense of enjoyment as well as through their own creative acts, that people emerge from childhood as mature individuals who can take their place effectively in society.

The complexity of this process leads many to suppose that the mind will never be comprehended or duplicated. Attempts to understand it have been continuing, especially over the last 2,000 years, against a background of disbelief by the majority that real progress can ever be made in this area. People tended, therefore, to accept the simplest solution by embracing wholeheartedly the views and beliefs of parents, teachers, and peers. That has the advantage that societies have a built-in stability and inertia arising from such traditionalism, so engage in less civil strife. This situation is changing, and consciousness is being explored extensively.

In this chapter I discuss some of the main problems that arise when trying to explain consciousness scientifically, and the pressures to choose one solution over another. I outline some criteria as to how to handle these pressures and suggest tentative solutions to guide further development. Finally, I come to the truly hard problem of the mind, which I relate to the divisions of consciousness described in the previous chapter.

Who is involved in the race? Traditionally the domain of theologians and philosophers, the mind is being probed ever more precisely by psychologists and brain scientists. The latter category covers a broad church of neural networkers, neuropsychologists, neuropharmacologists, neurophysiologists, and computer scientists. It more recently acquired physicists, mathematicians, and engineers among its numbers. Using the methods of these disciplines, considerable progress has been made in understanding some of the complexities of the mind and brain. Conscious and unconscious brain activities are being analyzed more deeply and some of the subtleties of the physical concomitants of these different states of mind are beginning to be unraveled. It is clear from what was said in the previous chapter that the conscious state is not a simple monolithic one but has a detailed structure as well as the possibility of occurring in a variety of guises. All of the various forms of consciousness have preceding unconscious and nonconscious neural activity creating them. To obtain a complete understanding of this neural activity we have to understand most, if not all, of the complexity of the brain.

The problem of explaining consciousness in terms of unraveling the complex action of the brain requires a high degree of interdisciplinarity, since research can proceed at many levels. All approaches are important, but each is involved in a different manner. We can recognize the following researchers as especially relevant to the quest:

1. Philosophers, to analyze the logical nature of the problem of brain and mind and of possible solutions

2. Psychologists, to look at inner report and how it is affected by various stimuli or tasks

3. Neuropsychologists, to investigate neural concomitants of psychological responses

4. Neuroanatomists and physiologists, to look at the structure and function of nervous tissue in the brain

5. Neural network researchers, to develop theories of the neural networks of the brain

6. Engineers and computer scientists, to help build apparatus to probe the brain and analyze data

7. Physicists, to develop better tools and theories

8. Mathematicians, to use mathematical analysis to help understand the implications of theories of the brain

We can develop a clearer understanding about the problem of mind by seeing that there is a crucial gap between approaches 1 and 2 and the rest. This is the deep divide between psychology and the neurosciences: the former considers and experiments with mental states, the latter probes the brain and its constituent neurons. The two disciplines investigate mental and material aspects of the brain, respectively.

However, psychology has not always acknowledged that its domain is the mind. During some periods in this century it denied the efficacy and even the existence of mind and mental states as relevant to the analysis of behavior. Behaviorism denied the existence of consciousness or kept its investigation at a very low level. American psychologist Mandler tried in 1975 to redress that when he wrote in his article, entitled "Consciousness: Respectable, useful and probably necessary" (Mandler 1975), that "Another statement, however imperfect, may be useful to undo the harm that consciousness suffered during fifty years (approximately 1910 to 1960) in the oubliettes of behaviourism." Biologists also neglected and suppressed the study of the mind. Walter Freeman (1995) put it aptly: "For centuries the concept of psychology has been regularly re-introduced into biology at intervals of fifty years or so, suggesting that alternating generations have felt compelled to expel it after those preceding had rediscovered it."

Psychology and biology are again evaluating consciousness and the nature of the mind: conferences are held on the subject of consciousness (Hameroff 1996), new journals are devoted to it, and grants are awarded for research into it. In addition, several interdisciplinary groups are attempting to develop brain models that possess the elements of cognition (Taylor 1995a).

At the same time pressures from the fields of medicine and mental health are increasing to gain a better understanding of the mind in order to ameliorate the lot of those with mental ill health. Mental diseases stem from a variety of causes, such as chemical imbalance in the brain, brain pathology, brain damage, aging, and trauma. All of these disorders are best treated by a deeper understanding of the manner in which brain and mind interrelate. Thus it is important to model the mind as thoroughly as possible. The approach of building partial models of mental features and observing how they can explain deficits such as dyslexia and schizophrenia is actively pursued in the neural network community (Plaut and Shallice 1993; Cohen and Servan-Schreiber 1992; Monchi and Taylor 1995).

In addition, industry is increasing pressure to develop systems better able to handle complex tasks in an intelligent manner. That is especially true for the Internet, where the information overload is large and where increasingly intelligent agents are necessary to extract requisite information from a large number of sources. It is also difficult to communicate rapidly and easily with computers. There is as yet no computer to which its owner can say, "Do this," and the machine complies. Think how easy it would make using a computer, instead of the decidedly alienating software we all have in our word processors. To solve these tasks requires understanding semantics, even up to the level of natural language. The process of building a mechanical brain with close to our own cognitive powers will provide a solution to some of the problems facing the information industry (Taylor 1995c).

With the improved interdisciplinary work occurring in the study of brain and mind, I believe that the whole broad range of investigation is stable enough to prevent a swing away from the subject by biologists or psychologists. The problem of consciousness, I suggest, is a subject of scientific research in its own right, and is not to be taken up or put down as fads and fashions change.

The Rules of the Race

I have already warned that many proposed solutions to the mind-body problem are lying around to trap the unwary. They are associated with one or other set of possible models of the world and the nature of its contents. Acceptance of a particular solution usually corresponds to acquiring, at the same time, the concomitant worldview with all its implications. The manner in which these lead to antagonistic responses to others with different worldviews has been commented on.

Many proposed solutions to the mind-brain problem are seductive to those outside the main relevant disciplines (namely, psychology and the brain sciences listed above). For example, physicists are naturally attracted to the idea that consciousness arises from some sort of coherent quantum state of the brain. But it is clear that these biases are dangerous in the search for truth. We must face the real facts and attempt to build models on them, not allowing our ideas to drift off into the clouds and away from reality.

The real facts about consciousness are that brain activity and conscious experience are completely intertwined. This infinitely close relationship forces us to accept that it is the mechanism of the brain, as a connected set of neural ensembles, that is the root cause of conscious experience. We reached this conclusion in the previous chapter, but it is worth emphasizing it once again since it is the starting point for my approach. We should compare this natural starting point with the much more removed one of quantum mechanics or quantum gravity. Such features of the material world as these latter theories are required to explain seem remote from the arena of neural networks of the brain. Quantum effects become important only for very small objects or those at enormities of temperature or pressure, as in the case of neutron stars or superconductors; however, their proponents seem to think they are relevant to consciousness. I consider these claims in chapter 5 to see if they provide a runner worth betting on in the race for consciousness.

One way we can respond to these quantal approaches is to develop an effective model of the mind through the neural ensembles in the brain, which should be closely related to experience and can be tested ever more closely by experiment. It is then to be compared with a similarly effective model based on coherent quantum states (if one is ever produced).

The neural model of mind and consciousness to be pursued in this book as an entry in the race is based on ideas developed at the end of the previous chapter and subscribed to by the majority of brain researchers:

The general relational thesis: consciousness necessarily emerges from the relational activity of suitably connected neural networks.

This thesis contains various words whose meaning is not yet properly defined. "Relational" and "suitably" have to be made precise. What are the relations? How are the neural networks "suitably" connected in order that consciousness can emerge? The answers to these questions will take up considerable portions of the book.

A much more difficult feature of the thesis to be proved involves solving what has come to be accepted as the hardest problem of all in consciousness research, explaining why neural activity of any form must necessarily lead to the creation of conscious experience. Such a problem arises for any approach to consciousness, not just that through neural networks, but we must face it and attempt to find a solution. We will consider this most crucial hard problem in more detail later in this chapter; it is indeed so hard that some think it will always be impossible to solve.

To help us on our way I will develop some criteria to be used in developing justifications of the above theses; I will use them to guide the style of our approach to understanding the brain.

Criterion 1

Any model of consciousness should be developed with as much guidance (hints or clues) as possible from relevant data from the fields of at least psychology, neurophysiology, and neuroanatomy. These fields contribute as follows.

1. Psychology, in which there is both behavioral response and subjective report. The latter corresponds to the use of the subject's conscious experience, a feature that has been used over a considerable period by psychologists, although they were wary about admitting it too loudly in the past.

2. Neurophysiology, in which concomitant brain activity is investigated at several levels, as by noninvasive methods: electroencephalography (EEG) and magnetoencephalography (MEG), which measure electric and magnetic fields of the brain, and positron emission tomography (PET) and magnetic resonance imaging (MRI), which measure blood flow and oxygen take-up in the brain, all of which have increasing accuracy. For the first time, experimental results from these instruments are giving us a chance to bridge the gap between these disparate domains.

A level down is multiunit recording, where the averaged activities of hundreds of neurons are measured by implanted electrodes. This is mainly carried out in animals, although it is also used in patients undergoing treatment for certain diseases, such as implanting electrodes directly in the brain to detect the source of epileptic activity.

At the lowest level is measurement of the single unit or nerve cell. Results at this level in animals performing a broad range of learning tasks provide much insight. However, it is carried out on humans only in exceptional circumstances, so that concomitant psychological experiences are unknown and can only be inferred.

3. Neuroanatomy, in which the connections between the different neural modules active in various psychological experiences are determined. This allows better comprehension of the possible causal sequences that may be involved in the flow of activity between modules as mental experience occurs, allowing decomposition of that experience into its subcomponents.

Criterion 2

The models must be tested to (possible) destruction. This accords with the falsifiability principle of Sir Karl Popper, who posited that the only good scientific theory is a dead one and the next theory is in the process of being created from the skeleton and the recalcitrant death-dealing data. Such an approach led to the success of modern science, with a trail of discarded theories about the material world increasing as better theories are created to deal more effectively with the increasing range of data. Newtonian mechanics was destroyed by phenomena at the atomic level and replaced by quantum mechanics, or by phenomena at high speeds and replaced by special relativity. And so it goes.

Ideas and theories about consciousness must be tested in terms of the data mentioned above. The first criterion indicates how data that are already available are to be used; the second states that more data must actively be searched for in order to put any model through as large a battery of critical tests as possible. A theory can claim to be successful only if it has been put through its paces and survived.

Criterion 3

A global viewpoint should be kept for as long as possible.

This is a restatement, that to start with we must experiment and model at a global level how the brain and mind interact and how, in particular, the brain is able to support the activities that produce consciousness. Too much time spent determining the manner in which a single neuron responds to various sorts of input leads us away from a solution to our main task. It is very likely true that "the human brain is the most complicated object on earth," as aptly stated by Harvard neurobiologist Gerald

Fishbach. However, it would not be very efficient for us to attack the problem of modeling how consciousness emerges from brain activity by modeling the brain in its minutest detail at the outset; we would soon lose the forest for the trees.

Having given a set of criteria to help us advance effectively on the problem of consciousness—the rules of the race, so to speak—I turn next to what is rightly regarded as the most difficult problem regarding understanding consciousness.

The Hard Problem

The divisions of consciousness we have met so far have not crossed the divide between mind and matter, the really hard problem: how can consciousness arise from the activity of nonconscious nerve cells? The apparent separation between body and mind was heightened in 1974 when Thomas Nagel pointed out, in a paper descriptively entitled "What is it like to be a bat?" (Nagel 1974), that it is impossible for science ever to penetrate the subjective character of a mental experience. "The fact that an organism has a conscious experience *at all* means, basically, that there is something it is like to *be* that organism. . . . Fundamentally an organism has conscious mental states if and only if there is something that it is like to *be* that organism—something it is like *for* the organism." Furthermore Nagel stated, ". . . every subjective phenomenon is essentially connected with a single point of view, and it seems inevitable that an objective physical theory will abandon that point of view."

This subjectivity of the nature of mental experience was developed further by other philosophers and in particular by David Chalmers (1996a,b) in a clear account of why the hard problem is just that: hard. He points out that one can divide the whole set of problems raised by the brain and mind into two classes, easy and hard. The first class is composed of problems about consciousness that have a possible explanation in terms of computational or neural mechanisms. These easy phenomena of consciousness consist of

• The ability to categorize and respond to inputs
• Integration of information across different modalities

- Reportability of mental states
- Ability to access one's own mental states
- Attentional control mechanisms
- Behavior control
- Possession of a wake-sleep cycle

Although these are all involved with consciousness, explaining them does not get to the root of the matter. As Chalmers succinctly states:

The really hard problem of consciousness is the problem of *experience*. When we think and perceive, there is a whir of information processing, but there is also a subjective aspect. As Nagel put it, there is *something it is like* to be a conscious organism. This subjective aspect is experience.

It does not seem possible, claims Chalmers, to uncover a functional explanation of subjective experience since no ability or function that it performs would guide us to a mechanism that would then explain it. It seems possible to suggest mechanisms, at least in principle, for all of the easy problems listed above, even though their detailed explication will no doubt take many years, if not centuries, to work out. A similar situation does not occur for phenomenal experience. It has no function, it is claimed, so no mechanism can be called upon to explain it. This is the nub of the hard problem. For without a function for consciousness we have no clue as to a mechanism for it. Scientific modeling cannot even begin in this case; it has nothing to get its teeth into.

This separation of the domain into easy and hard problems by means of their functional grounding, or lack of it, is important and puts Nagel's concerns into a fuller perspective. It makes the real difficulty facing any neural approach to consciousness clear, and is related to the existence of an *explanatory gap* (Levine 1983): what are sufficient conditions for consciousness to emerge? What is it in the firing of neurons that leads to consciousness? Why cannot information processing go on in the dark, so to speak? Can we not all be zombies, without the spark of consciousness to lift our experience beyond that of the stones or the earth on which we tread?

As part of the cult of voodoo practiced in Haiti and in the New Orleans area of the United States, zombies are occasionally created (Littlewood 1997). They are humans who have been drugged so as to be completely paralyzed (by poison from the monkfish, e.g.), assumed by their loved ones to be dead and so buried by them, and some hours later dug up by voodoo priests. The experience so disturbs the personality of the poisoned person that it turns the victim into a zombie, someone with complete docility and no mind of his or her own. But are they real zombies with no consciousness? Very unlikely; these people are not totally devoid of consciousness, but act as if in a hypnotized state. Yet philosophers of Chalmers' persuasion claim that true zombies—persons who behave like you or I but have no conscious experience at all chugging away inside them—are "logically" possible to contemplate. Consciousness cannot therefore have a function; a person could exist in a nonconscious state yet appear to be exactly like you or me.

To repeat, the difficulty Chalmers raises is that there is no clear corresponding function that consciousness performs and whose modeling would explain it. Thus he states, "But if someone says 'I can see that you have explained how information is discriminated, integrated and reported, but you have not explained how it is experienced' they are not making a conceptual mistake. This is a nontrivial question."

Chalmers does admit that it might be possible, in the course of explaining any supposed function of consciousness, for a key insight to be discovered that allows an explanation of experience. However, it is not the case, he claims, that this explanation of function would automatically produce such an explanation of experience.

The basic difficulty of the hard problem, then, is that it appears to be conceptually coherent to assume that the processes of the brain could continue without experience accompanying them at all; true zombies are possible. In other words, consciousness is not entailed by the activity of the brain. If this claim is true, it completely destroys the relational consciousness model we will build throughout the book, as well as annihilating other models of consciousness based solely on the brain that claim to solve the hard problem.

We have now come face to face with the real difficulty that presently has no accepted solution: how to construct inner experience from the activity of the material of the brain. Chalmers, who underlined the nature of this problem as outlined above, decided that it was impossible to solve it directly using reductive methods that break down the phenomenon into more basic physical processes. As he said about consciousness: "When it comes to problems over and above the explanation of structures and functions, these methods are impotent." Instead, he took a more dualistic approach in which conscious experience is a fundamental ingredient, but with an informational basis. However, this separate component has to be integrated in a delicate and subtle manner with awareness and the functional easy processes. This integration is one of the unsolved problems of the dualistic approach, and is also counter to my strongly supported claim that it is solely in the brain that we must search for consciousness.

But I make an even stronger claim: analysis of the brain must lead us *inevitably* to discover the function of consciousness after the experiments and their modeling are completed at a sufficiently detailed level. As far as I can see, no no-go theorem states that inner experience can never be constructed from the activity of a suitable system of connected neural tissue. Nor that we will never be able to discover the function of consciousness by careful enough scientific analysis (involving experimentation and modeling). If we follow the scientific path properly and look ever more closely at the brain, there is nothing to stop us from reaching an answer to the hard problem about consciousness, including the possible answer that consciousness indeed has no actual function, but is merely an epiphenomenon.

To see the strength of this possibility, consider a well-endowed laboratory attempting to create artificial consciousness. Furthermore, assume that the funding available to pursue this method has no limit (an assumption certain to be false everywhere on Earth). Then increasingly large numbers of brain cells would be assembled into different modules and connected together into ever larger groups until something resembling a human brain was created (together with external sensors for certain of the modules). Given that the system was also provided with effectors so it could move itself around, and suitable nutrients to continue growing connections between its assemblies, what principle could prevent it from ultimately developing inner experience?

It would not develop into a zombie, at least as far as the billions of similar experiments successfully carried out on developing humans from birth are concerned; no zombie has ever been reported as having been born or grown up. On those grounds alone the chances of zombiehood of the artificially created brain is vanishingly small.

Are we missing any known principle that really does prevent the purely neural assembly, laboriously constructed over many years by the assiduous efforts of the laboratory staff, from having inner experience? Not that anyone has ever discovered or thought of.

The main claim that Chalmers makes, other than various similar arguments to the one that zombies are logically possible, is that, "For consciousness to be entailed by a set of physical facts, one would need some kind of analysis of the notion of consciousness—the kind of analysis whose satisfaction physical facts could imply—and there is no such analysis to be had." But that is where scientific analysis must enter; it is clearly essential to investigate how the brain has been so sculpted as *necessarily* to lead to the experience of consciousness. There would appear to be no reason why a more careful analysis of the stuff of the brain, along with the notion of consciousness itself, will not ultimately yield up its secrets, in spite of the pessimism of philosophers like Chalmers. It will not be an easy task, but *we have no reason to expect it to fail*. Only pessimism engendered by the subtlety of the brain will cause us to give up.

Such pessimism often occurs in the face of a difficult scientific problem. One clever researcher despaired of ever understanding the specificity of a particular enzyme involved in a certain biochemical process. A few years of making no progress led him to give up his research and retire to a monastery to contemplate the unknowable in more general terms. A few years later a detailed solution to the problem was arrived at by another group in terms of the geometric structure of the molecules involved. A scientific question will always have an answer; nil desperandum!

The problem raised by Chalmers about lack of functionality for inner experience has not been met by the above argument. The function of consciousness is very difficult to solve. I will not attempt to try for a solution immediately, but delay discussing the problem until later when sufficient understanding will allow for a reasonable attempt at a solution.

So how do we proceed? It is appropriate to consider at this juncture how best to analyze the stuff of the brain, and consciousness itself, to uncover the possible mechanism of conscious experience. I have already cursorily described the levels on which evidence about brain activity is being collected. We must consider this in more detail, since only by a more careful analysis of that evidence can understanding necessary to solve the hard problem emerge. At the same time we must determine the manner in which the content of inner experience is more closely related to the working of the brain. Ultimately, we will have to return to the qualia or raw feels to appreciate what sort of neural architectures would be able to produce the sorts of experience to which qualia correspond. So we will attempt to bridge the explanatory gap by working from both ends—neural and experiential. This will involve building ever more sophisticated neural models until we recognize the emergence of qualia-like properties of activity. We have to accept that at the same time we must develop models of some of the easy problems since we may not be able to solve the hard problem on its own. This is typical of the brain, in which there is so much interconnection that it is not easy to divorce the function of one part from that of another, or the manner in which one function is carried out as opposed to another.

How Many Consciousnesses?

That mind and consciousness are complex I have clearly demonstrated. There are several sorts of consciousnesses: passive, active, self, emotional, during dreaming, during slow-wave sleep. But then it would seem as if we are dealing with not one race for consciousness but several. Moreover different species may have different forms of consciousness. And what about the possibility of machine consciousness? So which of these consciousnesses are we trying to understand?

To answer, let us define three broad types of consciousness: human, animal (nonhuman), and machine. The first is decidedly the hardest to understand owing to the complexity of the brain and of human behavior. However, it has the clear advantage that people can tell of their inner experiences, sometimes in dramatic and graphic form. The second certainly exists, but nonhuman animals provide only a limited form of report. The third, machine consciousness, does not as yet exist so is the most difficult with which to experiment. The added problem is that any machine that claims to be conscious requires very careful analysis to ensure that its claim had not been programmed in by its creator. The trivial

Table 3.1
Pros and cons of investigating the three categories of consciousness

Type of consciousness	Pro	Con
Human	There exists inner report	Few experiments with intercranial electrodes
Animal	Can perform many experiments on animal brains	No inner report
Machine	Can build directly (if know relevant principles)	No data at all No report at all

solution of a tape recorder repeating the phrase "I am conscious, I am conscious" over and over again shows the danger to be guarded against. The final criterion to prevent this happening does not seem trivial.

The pros and cons of investigation of the three categories of consciousness are given in table 3.1; they all have their attractions. To decide which ones to analyze in detail, let us consider how easy it would be to justify at any point the claim by scientists that they have fully and completely explained consciousness.

I gave a tentative definition of human consciousness at the end of the previous chapter; it was relational and only hinted at the possible emergence of inner experience as the result of suitable dynamics of neural modules over a long enough time span. But it was exactly this question that we noted earlier as the hard problem: why does the neural activity of the brain produce inner experience at all? In comparison with it, other problems of human and animal consciousness are, in principle, trivial.

If we regard the hard problem as the ultimate goal or winning post, it does not seem helpful to attempt to solve it through machine consciousness. Machines can be created to solve a considerable range of pattern recognition and control tasks and be better than humans in the process. But none has been made intelligent at anywhere approaching the human level. Moreover, problems arise as to the criterion to apply to machine consciousness, as noted above. Finally, machines give no clues as to how truly human consciousness might be explained; the hard problem again.

Animal consciousness is also problematic, although not quite at the same level as machine consciousness. A great deal of controversy still surrounds it. No very strong hints as to how consciousness might emerge in animals have yet emerged.

On the other hand, humans decidedly have consciousness and they can describe the inner experience involved; they should therefore be the prime target for analysis. It will be there that we expect a winner of the race for consciousness first to become apparent.

We still have to decide how we can judge that a particular model of the brain will incorporate phenomenal experience. Two sorts of data must be taken into account: emergent and introspective. The first requires observation of brain circuits that are involved at the interface between the final stage of nonconscious processing and that where consciousness occurs. We have various forms of data on this:

• The effects of subliminal (nonconscious) material on later conscious processing
• The manner in which the emergence of percepts depends on the stimulus
• The detailed spatial and temporal courses of brain activity as related to the emergence of a percept

I will consider these and related phenomena in part II; they will form crucial scientific support for the model I propose as an entry for the race.

Data from introspection give us a description of the properties of raw feels. These have no relational character at all and comprise, among others, features mentioned earlier:

• Intrinsicality
• Ineffability
• Transparency
• Privacy
• Infinitely distant

It behooves any neural model to show how such decidedly nonrelational characteristics could ever arise from purely neural activity; we will consider that in particular in chapter 11. It is especially important for us to do so from the relational approach to consciousness introduced at the end of the last chapter and to be developed further in chapter 6.

Introspective properties, such as those listed above, have some powers of experimental validation. If a model cannot, in principle, possess them, it cannot be a starter in the race for consciousness. But it is difficult to use properties gained by introspection as the final test for a supposed scientific model of consciousness, since no objectivity is associated with them. Only hand-waving descriptions of features, such as those listed above, are available to guide us in building models of the emergence of consciousness, but these are not scientifically precise. In the end we must return to objective, external, experimental data with which to make a final assessment.

I propose that what is required of any model of consciousness is that it must be based on the way the brain works, as well as be able to stand up to the increasing onslaught of new data from new tools applied to the brain and mind, which we will meet in the next chapter. How could you explain the creation of a television picture without looking in detail at the television set and the transmitter? It would be useless to give a theoretical analysis in terms of your pet interest, say economic theories as to the nature of exchange rates or how seashells grow in nature. Let us apply the facts of the case, in this instance, those of the brain. I will go even farther; if a model is successful in correlating and explaining the way the brain explains behavior, it must lead to an understanding of the creation of consciousness in all its complexity. Our careful analysis of the objective nature of brain states and behavioral response will, I claim, therefore lead to a solution to the hard problem. However, we are some distance from a model of the mind being able to stand up to the onslaught of the wealth of available data.

Summary

The participants who are entering the debate on consciousness were described, leading to realization of the interdisciplinary nature of the task. I suggested criteria for approaching the problems of consciousness that emphasize the experimental nature that the whole program should take. I described further structure for consciousness: the division into phenomenal, intentional, and introspective components. This naturally led to division of the problems into easy ones with a computational and neuro-cognitive solution and the hard one of the inner or subjective character of experience. This hard problem was explaining why any neural activity, of whatever form, could generate inner experience of the nature that we possess owing to the activities of our brains. I regard a solution to this hard problem as the winning post in the race for consciousness.

I rejected the claim that the hard problem was not solvable by the method of reduction to underlying basic physical processes, and instead proposed a program to discover in detail the mechanisms that created inner experience out of brain states and their dynamics. This led to a further analysis of the nature of the race for consciousness. Of the three tasks on human, animal, and machine consciousness, respectively, only the first two were considered able to provide sufficient clues to proceed. I suggested that human consciousness is the richer of the two, and so the appropriate one to tackle first. I then developed criteria to specify how to judge when success has been attained. This involved the modern program of brain research.

In the next chapter I consider the specific tools necessary to carry out this program—new experimental tools to measure the human brain in action, and theoretical tools of neural networks required to model the results of those experiments. Scientists entering into the race for human consciousness hope that these tools will lead them to the winning post.

II

Looking at Consciousness

4

New Windows on the Mind

The proper study of mankind is man.
—Alexander Pope

What happens in the brain during various mental states? We must answer that question to develop a detailed scientific theory of consciousness based on the neural structure of the brain, and in particular begin to tackle both the easy and hard problems raised in the previous chapter. Do specialized regions of the brain support vision and olfaction? What of thinking and reasoning? When an animal searches for food? Even more relevant, what parts of the brain "light up" when one becomes conscious of an object in the environment? Do these areas differ between animals and humans?

The answers to these questions provide the grist to our mill of theorizing. But before they can be answered we must consider the level at which we should seek the answers. Are single nerve cells, the atoms of the brain, most appropriate, or are aggregates of such cells more critically involved? If the latter, how large are the aggregates used in various tasks? If the former, are there so-called grandmother cells that respond only to one's own grandmother and nothing else? How are such representations, either as single cells or aggregates of cells, set up and used?

All of these questions are at the heart of the continuing activity of brain research. Not only are aggregates of neurons and single nerve cells themselves at the center of the investigation, but so also are chemicals involved in transmitting activity from each nerve cell to others in the brain or to muscles. Information about such neurochemical effects is proving crucial in understanding mental diseases such as schizophrenia and autism, as well as giving important clues to causes of Alzheimer's and Parkinson's diseases or Huntington's chorea that cause cognitive and movement deficits.

The general result of these investigations is that a clear model is emerging of the manner in which brain activity supports various mental states. In the main, a network of brain regions is active in a given mental state or while a given task is being solved. Each of the regions, or modules, performs a specific function as part of helping the whole network to be effective. Thus both tracing the network and discerning the manner in which each module achieves its own activity has to be pursued. The former corresponds to assessing more global activity among modules, the latter to understanding how separate nerve cells contribute to the function of each module. We must therefore work on a variety of levels.

We have already noted that the brain is composed of separate areas or modules, that each area is itself composed of many single nerve cells, and that each nerve cell is a complicated electrochemical machine. Such complexity causes some to despair that we will ever be able to comprehend the brain fully. Yet it should be anticipated and even expected when we consider the subtlety and breadth of Shakespeare's creations, or the scientific powers of Einstein. To begin to comprehend the brain, an overall view of its structure is necessary.

The Structure of the Brain

As shown in the lower part of figure 4.1, the brain is composed of a brain stem and midbrain regions, with two overhanging cerebral hemispheres that completely hide the brain stem, as shown in the upper portion. The bodies of nerve cells appear gray to the naked eye; these nerve cells are connected by long nerve fiber outgrowths that appear white. The cerebral hemispheres are pink-gray on the outside, having a cortex of cell bodies

Figure 4.1
The important areas and nuclei of the human brain. (*Top*) Lobes of the cortex, including areas devoted to sensing the body surface and to controlling voluntary muscles. (*Bottom*) A view of the midline of the right hemisphere. (Reprinted with permission from Bloom, Lazerson, and Hofstadter 1985)

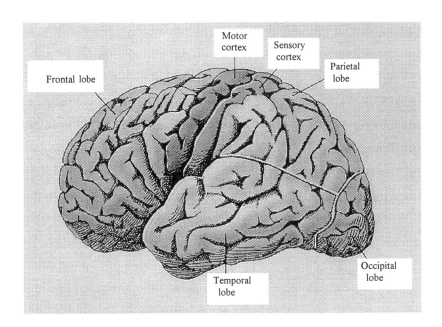

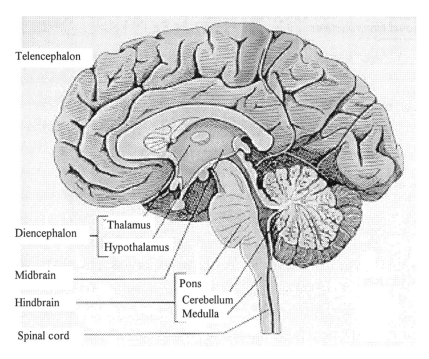

to a thickness of about 2 millimeters, with an enormous bundle of white nerve fibers passing to and fro between different cortical areas or between these areas and various of the subcortical processing centers. The main nuclei inside the cortex—the subcortical nuclei—are the thalamus, composed of numerous subnuclei, some of which relay input to the cortex, others involve output relays for motor response, and others still interact intimately with the frontal cortex or globally with the cortex to give it tone and whose loss can cause coma; the hypothalamus for passing signals describing and controlling the state of the body; the basal ganglia for motor control; and the septohippocampal and amygdala systems for fact and value memory. The last form what is called the limbic systems (from *limbus,* meaning "border," "edge," or "rind," a term introduced by Pierre Broca to denote the physiologically primitive cortex forming a border around the brain stem). It is basic to emotional activity and long-term memory.

The cortex is divided into four areas or lobes[1] as shown in figure 4.2: *occipital* (at the back), where entering visual input is analyzed; *temporal* (at the sides and bottom toward the back, called *ventral* regions), where higher-order visual processing of object images and auditory signals occurs; *parietal* (at the top and upper sides toward the back, the *dorsal* region), where analysis of visual and proprioceptive signals occurs; and the *frontal* lobes, where motor control and higher order cognitive and executive functions, especially thinking and planning, are sited. Numerous other functions are carried out by the lobes and subcortical nuclei, but these are the main features.

The general manner in which visual input is processed is beginning to be understood. Processing in the retina leads to less redundant activity by means of detecting and responding more to moving edges and ignoring regions of constant intensity. Retinal output is then further analyzed at successive cortical levels as it progresses forward from the occipital lobe toward the temporal lobe (along the pathway building object representations) or toward the parietal lobe (for spatial representations), as evident in figure 4.3. The former of these paths is termed the "what" channel for object recognition, the latter the "where" (or "how to") coding, where objects are and how that knowledge might be used to guide actions toward them. Further processing is done by the hypothalamus and

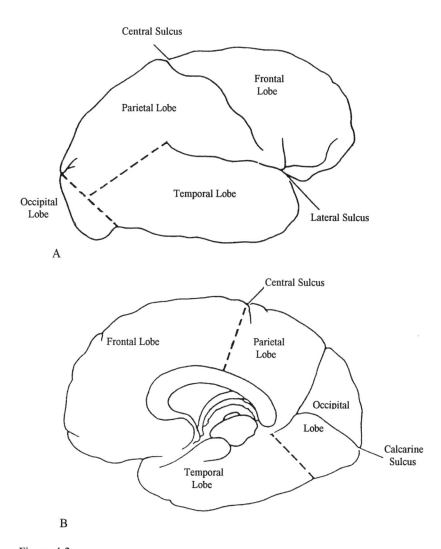

Figure 4.2
(A) Side (lateral) view of the right cerebral hemisphere showing temporal, parietal, occipital, and frontal lobes, and their dividing lines.
(B) Medial view of the right cerebral hemisphere showing lobes. Dashed lines indicate approximate positions of boundaries between the lobes, although no sulci are there.

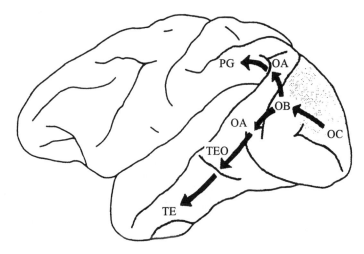

Figure 4.3
Lateral view of the left hemisphere of a rhesus monkey. The shaded area defines cortical visual tissue in the occipital, temporal, and parietal lobes. Arrows schematize two cortical pathways, each beginning in primary visual cortex (area OC), diverging within prestriate cortex (areas OB and OA), and coursing either ventrally into the inferior temporal cortex (areas TEO or TE) or dorsally into the inferior parietal cortex (area PG). Both cortical visual pathways are crucial for higher visual function, the ventral pathway for object vision and the dorsal pathway for spatial vision. (Reprinted with permission from Ungerlieder and Mishkin 1982)

amygdala to add "value" to the input representation, and temporary buffering takes place in the hippocampus.

Automatic (nonconscious) motor responses are carried out by motor parts of the frontal lobe, basal ganglia, and cerebellum, a magnificently characterized neural structure at the back of the brain working as an additional motor control brain. When predicted responses prove ineffective, conscious processing in other (nonmotor portions) of the frontal lobe occur to help determine the most appropriate course of action. However, as in other parts of the brain, the division into what activity is truly conscious and what is not has yet to be discovered.

Figure 4.4 gives a more realistic picture of complexity of the cortex, displaying corrugation and folding of the cortical surface into valleys called *sulci,* the hills between them being termed *gyri.* It is through this considerable folding that the total area of the human cortex is increased very effectively, separating us from lower mammals, such as the dolphin, which have smoother cortices with less area.

Certain sulci are important in that they separate areas of cortex involved in different functions. An example is the central sulcus, which divides the cortex into the posterior somatosensory and visual areas in the parietal and occipital lobes behind it from the frontal cortex in front of it involving motor and higher cognitive processes. There is also the general division of the frontal cortex into the motor part, just in front of the central sulcus, from the prefrontal regions involving the superior and inferior frontal sulci. The prefrontal area is also divided into the dorsolateral (at the top and side of the upper surface near the superior frontal gyrus), involved in thinking about spatial problems, and the lower area in the inferior frontal gyrus involved in thinking about objects. The frontal lobes are divided into two separate areas on the outer and inner sides; they are involved in action and cognition and in evaluation, respectively.

Each of us has a little motor "homunculus" in our motor and touch cortices. Figure 4.5 shows which regions of the cortex are active when a movement of a particular part of the body is made; note the enormous amplification of the face compared with the body, indicating the importance of these regions in our daily actions. In addition, representations of the external visual scene arriving at the retina exist in the occipital cortex in a one-to-one form, giving a topographic map of what one looks at in the initial stage of cortical processing. Several of these topographic maps are repeated in later processing regions of the visual cortex as the information flows along the paths shown in figure 4.3; similar maps of the external inputs occur in touch and hearing. These maps are created partly by coding in the genes, but an important involvement of activity-dependent learning is also involved.

At the same time it is possible to separate areas of the cortex by means of differences in their cellular composition; one of the simplest is that of the primary visual cortex, which has a striated appearance, causing it to be called striate cortex. Thus whereas it is often said that the brain is homogeneous, like "two fistfuls of porridge," that is a gross oversimplification, and as Mesulam (1985) rightly states, "The neurons that make up the human brain display marked regional variations in architecture, connectivity and transmitter neurochemistry." This more detailed cellular

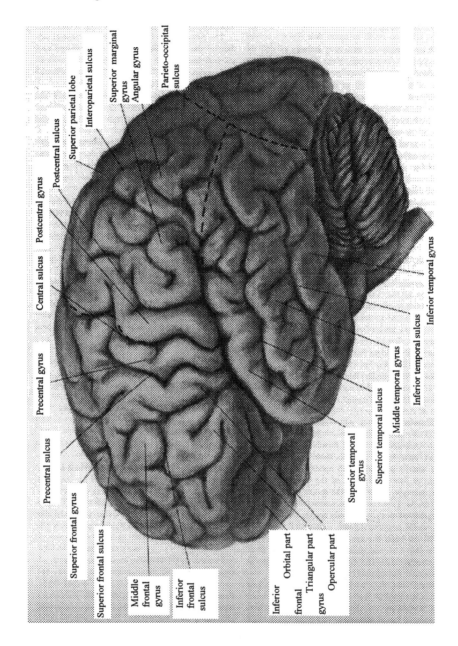

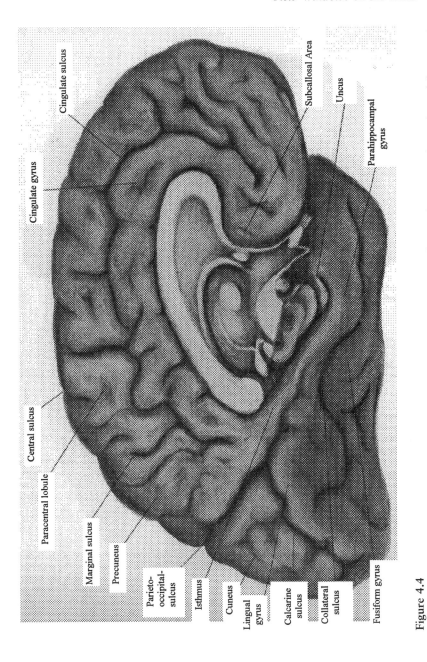

Figure 4.4

(A) Lateral surface of the brain, indicating the detailed nature of the set of gyri (plateaus on the surface of the cortex) and sulci (valley between the gyri).

(B) Medial surface of cerebral hemispheres indicating the main gyri and sulci.

(Reprinted with permission from Heimer 1983)

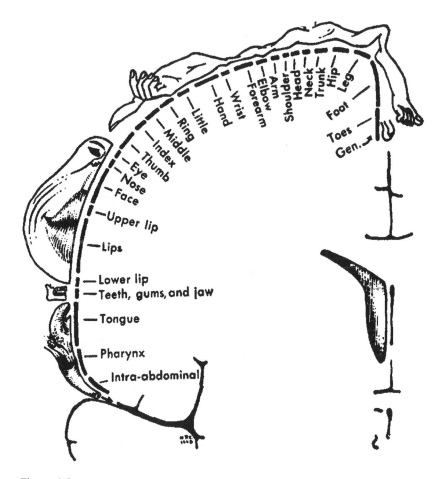

Figure 4.5
The homunculus, indicating the areas of cortex active when the appropriate part of the homunculus is touched. (Reprinted with permission from Heimer 1983)

analysis, which requires careful microscopic and chemical analysis of a number of human brains, allows the brain to be divided up into disticnt regions or modules. Such labeling is completely distinct from the subdivisions of the skull, which went under the name of phrenology and was popular in the nineteenth century. This "science" is now in total disrepute, in spite of the important basic idea of its founder, Joseph Gall, of locating function in the brain. Of the various systems subdividing the

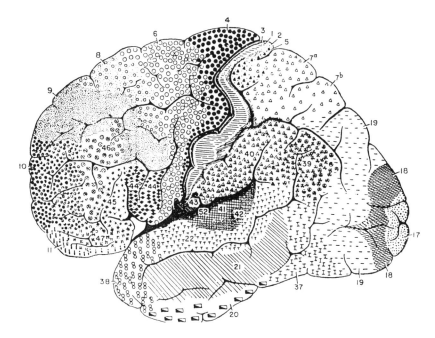

Figure 4.6
Brodmann's (1908) psychoarchitectural map of the human brain. Numbered areas represent subtle but real differences in the neuronal distribution and organization of the cortex. (From Crosby, Humphrey, and Lauer 1962)

brain, the most widely used is that of Brodmann (figure 4.6). It gives the lowest numbers to areas first encountered when steadily slicing away horizontal sections starting at the top. Thus the striate cortex at the back of the brain is Brodmann's area 17, the motor cortex at the top is area 4, and somatosensory areas are 1, 2, and 3. Hearing enters the cortex at areas 41 and 42 in what is called the sylvian fissure, the large sulcus running down diagonally and dividing the frontal cortex from the temporal one at the side of the brain.

This thumbnail sketch stating modes of action of various parts of the brain is an enormous simplification. It is a brief summary of the vast amount of knowledge of functions performed by brain regions that has been gained as a result of painstaking research into the effects of brain injury and surgery in humans and of similar analyses in animals. In animal studies, the activities of sets of cells are monitored in the brain when a cat, rat, or monkey performs a task such as discriminating a remembered object among newly presented ones (a reward of food being given for a correct choice).

One result of such experiments is that meaningful activity, at least that relevant to successful responses, is coded in a whole population of nerve cells. Suppose a monkey is required to put out its arm in a particular direction. It uses the averaged activity of 30 to 100 cells in a suitable part of the motor cortex to code that this action is about to be performed and what direction it should take (figure 4.7). This population coding, persisting over a suitable length of time, gives a signal highly correlated with a successful response even for a highly complex task such as choosing one of two objects over a delay of a second or so. Such activity, persisting over several seconds, has been called "active working memory" (Fuster 1993), and corresponds to the animal holding in mind the signal to which it will later respond (Desimone 1995).

Neural activity is localized in specific regions and not distributed about the brain in a homogeneous manner, as is seen from the fact that damage to small regions can cause specific deficits. After a stroke, some patients lose the ability to remember words of, say, only man-made objects, or lose the power to hold words in posteriorly sited "buffer working" or short-term memory for the normal 1 to 2 seconds (Baddeley 1996).

We should be in no doubt that the activity of nerve cells is closely correlated with processing information in the brain and that mental expe-

Figure 4.7
Population studies of motor cortex discharge in the primary motor cortex of monkeys. (a) The apparatus. The monkey had to hold the manipulandum in the center of the working area. Light-emitting diodes (LEDs) were placed at eight different positions on a concentric circle of about 20 cm diameter. When the LED was illuminated, the monkey had to move toward the light. (b) Trajectories that the animal made in thirty different movements to each target. (c) The discharge of a typical motor cortex neuron in the shoulder region of the cortex is plotted as rasters for each different direction of movement. The rasters are aligned on the onset of movement (M): five repetitions of each movement are shown. The time of the "go" signal is indicated by the bar labeled "T." Movements to the left are associated with an increase in firing of this cell; movements to the right are associated with a decrease in firing. (Reprinted with permission from Georgopoulos et al 1983)

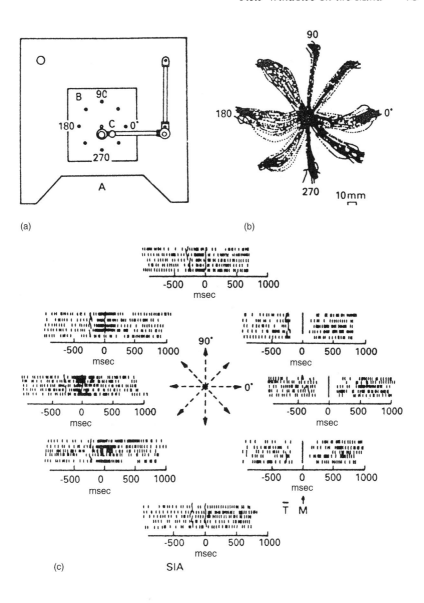

(a)

(b)

(c)   SIA

riences are thereby created. To pursue this further, I will describe in detail the single nerve cell before I turn to networks made of them and how to simplify their description.

The Atoms of the Brain

The nerve cell is called excitable because it can be excited by activity arriving at it from its colleagues, and it responds in kind with a pulse of excitation that it sends to suitably chosen neighbors to which its nerve fibers connect. The excitation is a pulse of electricity; the nerve cells are little batteries, each generating its potential difference from the energy obtained by burning a portion of the food we consume. It is through the passage of a wave of electrical potential—the nerve impulse—down its nerve fiber outgrowth (axon) that nerve cells communicate with each other that they are excited by what they have just received and wish to pass the news on. It is as if the brain was composed of millions of gossips, all spreading the news that each has just received to others. Yet these are specialized gossips; those in the occipital lobe are involved with visual inputs, in the temporal lobe with hearing or special aspects of visual inputs, and so on. Some cells even gossip about all sorts of things—they are called multimodal—and are ready to pass on anything they hear. It is through this gossiping with each other that the brain becomes conscious; it is not all idle chatter!

The brain is composed of an awesome number of such gossiping cells—roughly one hundred thousand million (10^{11}, a 1 followed by 11 zeroes), each receiving input from about 1,000 to 10,000 other such cells, and even up to 100,000 arriving on each of the major output cells, the Purkinje cells, in the cerebellum.

As I stated earlier, the single nerve cell is a complicated electrochemical machine in its own right (Levitan and Kaczmarck 1997), as a picture of a typical one shows in figure 4.8. It sends pulses of electricity to others, and each cell responds with its own output pulse if more than a certain threshold, number of nerve impulses, has recently arrived from other cells. Thus nerve cells signal continually to each other about their own internal level of activity caused by nerve impulses of others. In this way the total activity of the nerve cells in a network can modify

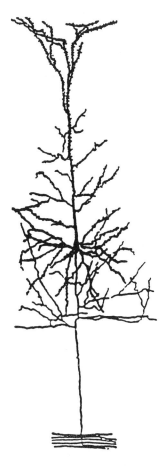

Figure 4.8
A pyramidal cell from the cortex of mammal. The outgrowths covered in spines are dendrites; the smooth outgrowths from the cell body is the axon, which branches profusely in the white matter at the base of the cortex.

inputs from outside or can control motor responses by their outputs to muscles.

Not all cells are the same. At least several dozen different types of nerve cells are recognizable in the brain, with names that usually characterize their appearance when seen under the microscope: pyramidal cells, basket cells, chandelier cells, and so on. There are also beautifully elaborate cells from the cerebellum (the motor brain). These different cell types perform different functions owing to their different structures, although much of this has still to be clarified.

One clear feature is the presence of two sorts of cells. One has an excitatory effect on the others to which it is connected, making them respond more strongly (more likely to gossip among themselves) and is called an excitatory cell; they form the majority of cells in the cerebral cortex. The other class are the inhibitory cells, with a corresponding inhibitory or reducing effect on cells to which they send signals, diminishing the response of these other cells so they are less likely to gossip with their neighbors. In general a cell is either excitatory or inhibitory in its effects on all other cells (either excitatory or inhibitory ones) to which it sends a signal under normal operating conditions.

Cells send their signal down their axon by means of a pulse of electrical activity; this is the nerve impulse mentioned earlier. But when the nerve impulse arrives at the end of the axon and has to get across the gap, the synaptic cleft, that exists between it and the cells to which it is sending information, there is a changeover from an electrical to a chemical mode of signaling. The nerve impulse, when it arrives at the end of the axon, causes the release of a chemical neurotransmitter. This release is also a complex process, as is the life story of the transmitter as it makes its way across the synaptic cleft to affect the nerve membrane of the next cell that is listening in to the gossip. Some of the details of this chemical transmission are shown in figure 4.9.

The changeover from electrical to chemical transmission of information at the synapse brings into consideration the whole world of biochemistry, with not only the dynamics of release of primary transmitters but

Figure 4.9
The main principles of action of a nerve cell. (1) A nerve cell is composed of outgrowths called dendrites (covered in spines), a cell body, and a single smooth outgrowth, down which the cell sends its nerve impulse signals; (2) nerve impulses arrive at the dendrites of a cell from the axons of other cells; (3) the nerve impulse is emitted by a cell if the net activity it is receiving from its neighbors is above a certain value (its threshold); (4) the interior of a nerve cell is held at a negative electrical potential; a nerve impulse is sent down the axon as a wave of sudden positivity of this potential and as sudden (in 1 msec) return to negativity of the axon interior).

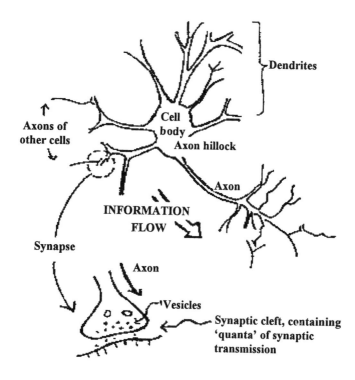

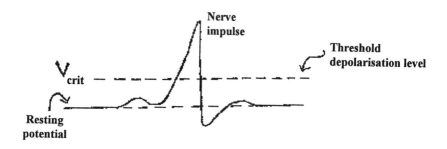

also the effect of secondary transmitters, which can affect the efficiency of the signal being transmitted in the first place. For example, dopamine is crucially involved in modulating signal transmission in the frontal lobes without being directly involved in actual signal transmission. It is concerned with how rewards are represented in the brain, and as such is important in understanding how drugs such as heroin, opium, and amphetamines have their action. Its essential involvement in conditions such as Parkinson's disease is also becoming clear.

Neural Networks

We can picture the brain in action as consisting of a multitude of connected nerve cells or a neural network. Each nerve cell responds when it receives a large enough signal from other cells or from outside sources and then sends a signal—a nerve impulse—down its axon to its companion cells. The strengths of the signals (heights of nerve impulses) are all the same, usually being chosen to have the value of 1. However, the amount by which each cell affects the ones to which it is connected is altered by connection strengths or weights. These change the effect of the nerve impulse arriving at a given synapse on a given cell from another cell by increasing or decreasing the amount the next cell receives proportionally to the connection weight. This mechanism allows the neural network to be flexible in its response to inputs, and even to learn to change the manner in which it responds to an input by altering the connection weights by a suitable learning rule.

In general, the total activity arriving at a given cell at any time is the sum of the input nerve impulses from other cells, each weighted by its appropriate connection weight. If the weight is positive the cell will be excited to fire, if the weight is negative it will be less likely to fire. In this way a cell with only excitatory connection weights on its synaptic endings will always cause the cells to which it is connected to be more likely to respond, and so is excitatory; one with only negative connection weights is an inhibitory cell.

The manner in which the activity of the neurons develops in the neural network depends on the way they are connected. If the activity flows through the cortex from one area to the next in a feed-forward fashion, the response of neurons will die away if there is no input. This is the manner in which activity develops in early sensory regions of cortex, such as in vision, audition, and touch. A typical feedforward net is shown in figure 4.10, where activity starts on the left, feeding in to what is termed the input layer. The cells in this layer, once they have assessed how much input each is receiving from the inputs on the left, respond if the input is above the threshold for their emitting a nerve impulse, and remain silent if it is not. This activity then moves to the hidden layer, which repeats the process; this layer is so called because the neurons in it are not directly visible to either inputs or outputs. Finally, output layer neurons assess the strengths of their inputs and respond according to the activity arriving at them and their own thresholds for responding.

As an alternative neural architecture, neurons in a particular region may feed activity mainly back to other neurons in the same region, so there is considerable recurrence. In that case activity initiated by an input does not die away but settles down into a steady level. The final activity in general depends on the initial neural activity set up by the input, so different final activities may be used to classify different inputs; these have been used considerably to solve problems of classifying inputs. Nets of this kind are called attractor nets since their final states can be regarded as attracting initial activity to become similar to their own (Hopfield 1982; Grossberg 1976). A typical form of an attractor network is also shown in figure 4.10.

I mentioned the concept of connection weights in the neural network. They determine how strongly a given neuron affects one to which it is sending a nerve impulse, and they may be modified by a succession of inputs and cell responses. A possible rule for such modification, or learning law, to change the weights was suggested in the late 1940s by Canadian psychologist Donald Hebb (1949): "When an axon of a cell A is near enough to excite a cell B and repeatedly and persistently takes part in firing it, some growth process or metabolic changes take place in one or both cells such that A's efficiency as one of the cells firing B, is increased." In other words, if activity is fed from one cell to another that is also active, the synapse joining the two should be strengthened and they should be more likely to fire together in the future.

(a) Feed-forward net

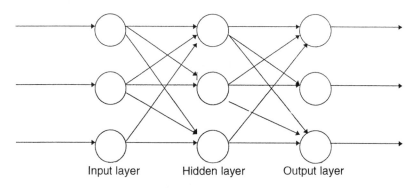

Input layer   Hidden layer   Output layer

(b) Recurrent net

Figure 4.10
(a) A feedforward neural network, in which external neural activity arrives at the input layer on the right, moves through the net to the hidden layer, and then moves on to the output layer at the right; these cells then signal the total response of the net to the external world. (b) A recurrent net, in which every cell feeds back its activity to all the other nerve cells in the net; the activity finally reaches a steady state, in which any further recirculation of activity will not change the activity. This state of the net is called an attractor since activity similar enough to it in the net will ultimately become that of the steady state.

This learning rule was proposed as the basis of learning associations between inputs at the level of nerve cells. It results in a permanent change in the connection between sets of cells, leading to the formation of an assembly of such cells that would thereafter tend to fire together for the inputs they previously experienced. For example, a dog salivates at the sight of food. If it hears a whistle each time it sees the food it will ultimately salivate when it hears the whistle. The creation of such an association between hearing the whistle and salivating can be understood at a nerve cell level by Hebb's law as follows: the strength of the connection of the neural system inputting the sound of the whistle onto the salivary response neurons is strengthened (by Hebb's law) by simultaneous activity of the neural system inputting the view of the food producing the salivary response. After a number of joint exposures to the food and the whistle, only the whistle need be sounded to produce salivation, since the connection strengths of the inputs from the whistle to the salivary neurons has become so strong. A very simple one-neuron implementation of this is shown in figure 4.11.

We can include a reinforcement factor arising from the environment in the learning law to guide an animal or other system controlled by a neural net to maximize the reward it might receive. Such adaptation is termed reinforcement learning. We mentioned earlier the reward signal might be carried by a diffuse signal through the brain by the chemical modulator dopamine. In the case of the salivating dog the reward signal from the sight of food would flow as dopamine to the synapse carrying the sound of the whistle to the response nerve cell, and cause its connection weight to be increased. If that increase is large enough, through suitable learning, the nerve cell will ultimately be activated solely by the sound of the whistle.

A great deal of interest has been aroused by systems composed of the simplified neurons described—simple decision units—with the effects of one cell on others given by connection weights, plus learning laws similar to Hebb's or the reinforcement law to change those weights. Systems of simplified neurons are called artificial neural networks. They are capable of solving problems of pattern recognition, industrial control, time series prediction, and difficulties arising in increasing numbers of other areas. (In fact, they are able to mimic any real system as closely as necessary,

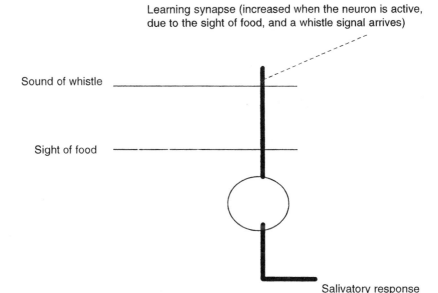

Learning synapse (increased when the neuron is active, due to the sight of food, and a whistle signal arrives)

Sound of whistle

Sight of food

Salivatory response

Figure 4.11
A simple model of the development of conditional learning in an animal. Neural signals indicating the sound of the whistle and the sight of the food converge on the neuron, which generates a salivary response; by suitable adaptation through the response of the neuron (due to the signal about the food) there is an increase of the effect of the sound of the whistle (by increase of its connection strength onto the neuron) so that in the end the sound of the whistle alone will cause it to bring about salivation in the animal.

the universal approximation theorem.) Any problem area in which the rules for a solution are difficult to discern, data are noisy, rapid processing is needed, or any combination of these features, is suitable for tackling by neural network techniques. When combined with further processing methods—fuzzy set theory, genetic algorithms, and statistical methods—a powerful tool kit of adaptive information processing methods becomes available.

As expertise in neural networks has grown, so has the theoretical underpinning. In comparison with early and misplaced euphoria in the 1950s and 1960s regarding universal applicability of neural networks, together with some excessive enthusiasm in the 1980s, our understanding of neural networks is broader and assessment of what they might do is more realistic. If evidence that neurons are the basic atoms of the brain supporting the mind is not misleading, ultimately a neural network model of the mind should be achievable. But the important question remains as to the levels at which such modeling must be attempted.

Neurons used in artificial neural networks are pale shadows of living neurons of the brain. Some of the complexity of the latter was described in the previous section, where we noted that the activities of aggregates of at least thirty or so such neurons were required to code activity relevant to response and information processing. If so, do we have to include all of the enormously complex details of living neurons to understand the principles of brain processing leading to mind? In answer, I suggest that the simplified neurons of artificial neural networks should be sufficient, although not allowing such a complex repertoire of responses as that achieved by their living counterparts. We should be able to discover the principles of consciousness with these simplified models.

Numerous questions can be asked about a given neural network:

1. How many patterns can it store?
2. What is the dynamics of the learning process (involving such questions as lack of learning a task or its being learned suboptimally)?
3. How long will it take for any one pattern to be retrieved?
4. What is the optimal architecture to select for the network to solve whatever task it is being set (classification, storage, motor control, prediction, etc.)?

Thus one could choose among feed-forward and recurrent (and feedback) networks or have a mixture of recurrence with feed-forward character as well. This might be appropriate to describe most cortical regions, with their observed feed-forward and feedback connections between areas.

A particularly useful approach to a class of neural networks similar to those in the brain is to consider them as forming a continuous sheet. This was investigated initially in the 1960s and 1970s and led to some intriguing results about the manner in which activity can persist without input, owing to suitable excitatory feedback. If this recurrence also has longer-range inhibition, these autonomous bubbles of activity can be localized spatially. The bubbles were investigated intensively in the one-dimensional situation, and were relevant in helping understand the learning, along the lines suggested by Donald Hebb, of the regular ordering of inputs to the cortex—so-called topographic maps.

In summary, a neural network is a system of input-output nodes whose strengths of connections can be trained so that the network produces an effective response to a set of inputs. That response may be to classify the inputs into a well-defined set of categories (e.g., speech or visual pattern recognition), to attempt to learn the pattern that may be presented next in a time series (e.g., financial forecasting, say of the dollar to pound exchange rate), or to give a response of a specific form for a given input (e.g., needed in a control problem).

Fields of the Brain

The nerve cells of the brain are electrically excitable. They respond to enough incoming electrical excitation by firing a nerve impulse (pulse of electrical change) down their axon to stimulate their colleagues either nearby or at distant locations in the brain. All of this activity produces minute but observable electrical field effects outside the brain. The beautiful theory of James Clerk Maxwell in 1864, unifying electricity and magnetism, allows us to predict a concomitant magnetic field activity around the skull. In spite of the smallness of these electrical and magnetic fields, they were measured during the past few decades with increasing accuracy and are providing remarkable insights into the details of neural networks as various sorts of task are carried out. Both sleeping and awake states have been probed.

The existence of spontaneous, continuous electrical activity of the brain was first noted in 1875 when Caton recorded from electrodes laid directly on the exposed brains of dogs. A few years later German psychiatrist Hans Berger showed that electrical activity could be recorded directly from the intact brain by pasting electrodes firmly to the scalp and amplifying the resulting signals. This was the origin of electroencephalography (EEG). In 1929 Berger published records that showed differences in EEG patterns of different conscious states of his son Klaus. The frequencies at which brain waves mainly oscillate is related to the state of awareness of the human subject, with slow waves in deep sleep, desynchronized fast

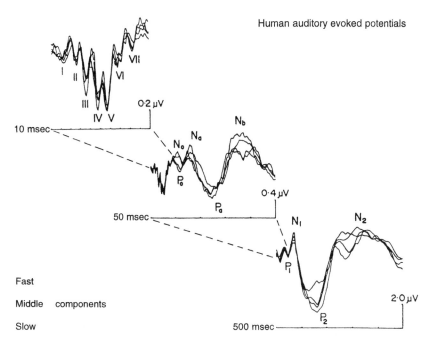

Human auditory evoked potentials

Figure 4.12
The shortest latency (from the brain stem, top), middle-latency (from the midbrain, middle), and long-latency (from the cortex, bottom) deflections of the auditory event-related potential (recorded between the vertex and the right mastoid) to a click stimulus presented to the right ear at a rate of one per second. Relative negativity at the vertex is represented as an upward deflection. Each tracing represents an average of 1,024 individual responses. (Reprinted with permission from Picton 1980)

waves in an alert, awake state, and low-frequency alpha waves in an awake, relaxed state.

The development of EEG to analyze localization of brain activity has proceeded slowly, in spite of the remarkably good temporal resolution of the measurements. Figure 4.12 shows that signals as short as a millisecond or so can be detected; there is, however, an uncontrollable flow of electrical currents in the conducting fluid filling the brain during extensive neural firing. Such conduction currents make it difficult to find the source of the electrical signals arising from underlying nerve cell activities. This delayed discovering the exact source of such activity until powerful computer techniques became available to analyze localized signal averaging and frequency, and provide better methods for solving the inverse problem of extracting underlying nerve cell activity from conduction currents compounded together in the total EEG signal. It also is important to time the onset of the task carefully to allow signals from many similar trials to be averaged together; such averaging smooths away noisy components in the signal, revealing the information-bearing part.

Results on the averaged signal indicate the ability of EEG to give signals of the brain processing at both automatic and conscious levels (Naatenan 1992). At the same time we have to accept that localization of brain activity by EEG is still difficult, especially of subcortical activity. This problem is solved by measuring the magnetic field of the brain, to which we now turn.

Powerful amplifiers of electrical currents and of electrically shielded rooms allowed the development of EEG analysis to reach its current level of sophistication. In a similar manner, the discovery of superconductivity and its deployment in the superconducting quantum interference device (SQUID) allowed detection of very low magnetic fields arising from nerve cell activity around the head (Hamalainen, Hari, Knuutila, and Lounasma 1993). This is called magnetoencephalography (MEG). Neuromagnetic signals, magnetic fields arising from brain activity, are typically only one part in one hundred million (10^8) or so of the earth's magnetic field, so that cancellation of external magnetic "noise" is essential to capture such low-level signals. This can be achieved by designing the coil used to pick up the magnetic signal, such as having two coils close together but wound in opposition so as to cancel out effects from distant magnetic fields.

The first detection of magnetic fields from the heart was achieved in 1963, and the magnetic counterpart of the alpha wave of the brain reported five years later (Cohen 1968). Much advance has been made in recording the magnetic field of the brain since then, especially in the use of many detectors simultaneously, and in the development of more powerful techniques to solve the inverse problem of unscrambling from the data where the sources of the magnetic field were actually positioned.

A helmet formed of many detectors into which the subject's skull fits without touching is shown in figure 4.13. The subject is presented with a visual stimulus, resulting in detailed time courses of measurements from

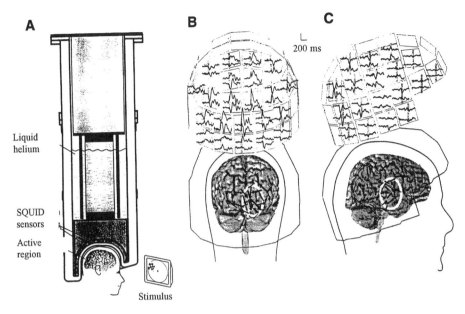

Figure 4.13

Measurement using magnetoencephalography. (A) The magnetic field surrounding the head is measured by a 122-channel SQUID magnetometer in a magnetically shielded room; the SQUIDs are kept superconducting at a temperature of 4K by suitable low temperature technology (B top) Magnetic field signals from the occipital sensors; the strongest sensors are over the occipital cortex. (Bottom) The best fit of the current pattern on the cortex which fits the observed signals. The white oval shows the strongest activation at 90 msec after a stimulus. (C top) Magnetic field signals from the right temporal channels (bottom) best fit to the observed fields at 210 msec after stimulus onset. The oval shows the activity in cortex. (Reprinted with permission from Nastanen et al, 1994)

the sensors, shown on the right of the figure. As can be clearly seen, sensitivity to the temporal changes is as great as could be obtained by EEG measurements. Moreover there is concurrent spatial sensitivity, so it is possible to follow the change of the position of greatest activity as time develops. As seen in parts B and C, the region of maximum activation moves from the visual cortex (at 90 msec after stimulus input) toward the speech area (210 msec). Another process, magnetic resonance imaging (MRI), which is considered in the next section, allows a detailed map of brain structure to be superimposed on the magnetic field map, giving a beautiful account of the localization of processed input as it travels through the brain.

The other important development in MEG, besides its increased sensitivity, is its more powerful methods to determine where in the brain the activity resides that causes the resulting magnetic field. Increasingly sophisticated solutions to this inverse problem have been presented, starting with the equivalent-current dipole. This assumes a localized single-current dipole (a flow of current over a short distance) as a good approximation to the source of the magnetic field in the brain. This can be extended to a distribution of a finite number of such current dipoles, whose position may be optimized to give least discrepancy between the resulting magnetic field distribution they would produce and that actually are measured by the sensors.

The most sophisticated technique to solve the inverse problem is presently magnetic field tomography (Ionnides 1994). This uses the lead field of each sensor (the magnetic field produced at the sensor by a current at a given and known point in the head). Lead fields may be obtained by experiments using currents in model heads composed of similar conducting material to the real head. These fields allow for effective computation of the current distribution throughout a real head, especially when the a priori distribution of neural tissue is measured by MRI. Magnetic field tomography has led to the production of remarkable videos of neural activity flowing through different regions in the brain as various tasks are performed.

Mapping such activity flow in real time is being actively pursued, and over the next few years will undoubtedly result in greater precision as to time and place of brain activity while performing tasks. In particular, subcortical activity is able to be observed with reasonable spatial accuracy. The time course of such activity is shown in figure 4.14. The different levels of cortical activity observed by magnetic field tomography in normal people, patients with mild Alzheimer's disease, and those with more severe disease indicate the exciting use of this method as a diagnostic tool.

In summary, great strides have been made in MEG measurements of brain activity since its initiation in 1968. Much still has to be done, especially in obtaining greater spatial accuracy than the present few

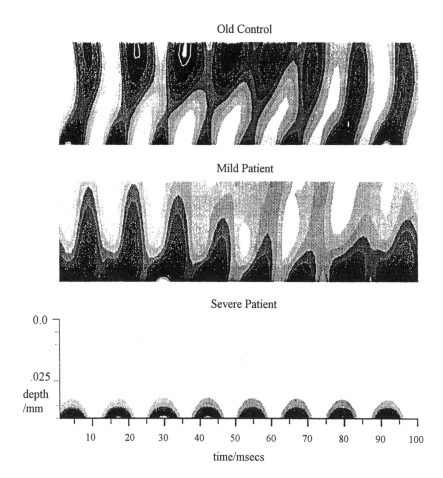

Figure 4.14
Comparison of magnetic field levels of activity from three subjects: an older person (old control), a person with mild Alzheimer's disease, and one with severe disease. The activity is shown as it varies across the depth of the brain (shown vertically) with time along the horizontal axis. Differences among the three people indicate those expected to be met by the person with severe disease, as well as the possibilities of using the technique as a diagnostic. (Reprinted with permission from Ioannides 1995)

millimeters or so by magnetic field tomography. The ability of MEG to observe both deep and surface components of brain activity over a very short time makes it appear to be one of the most important windows on the mind for the next century; it will add immeasurably to our present knowledge as to how the brain works. In particular it will be a crucial tool for testing models of consciousness.

Blood Flow in the Brain

Nerve cells need energy for their activity; energy comes from burning fuel, and this requires oxygen, which is brought to cells by blood. So an important clue to nerve cell activity is increased blood flow. Two techniques are available to measure blood flow: positron emission tomography (PET) and functional magnetic resonance imaging (fMRI). Each allows for remarkably accurate spatial detection of brain activity to within a few millimeters or less, but has far poorer temporal sensitivity than EEG or MEG. Nevertheless, PET and fMRI have led to important breakthroughs in understanding localization of brain activity. Thus the distinguished neuropsychologist M. Posner wrote (1993):

It is a popularly held belief in psychology that the cognitive functions of the brain are widely distributed among different brain areas. Even though the organisation of the nervous system suggests that the sensory and motor functions are localized to special brain regions, the failure of phrenology and difficulties in locating memory traces for higher functions have led to a strong reaction against the notion of localization of cognitive processes. Nevertheless imaging studies reveal a startling degree of region-specific activity. The PET studies show clearly that such visual functions as processing colour, motion or even the visual form of words occur in particular prestriate areas

(where prestriate denotes regions in front of or anterior to the primary visual area). Let us consider PET and fMRI in turn.

The PET uses radioactive decay of material injected into a person's blood to locate regions of high blood flow; the decay products are the clean signal of the increased blood required by nerve cells. It is possible in this way to measure accurately and rapidly changes in local blood flow. Studies with PET have been conducted during a variety of psychological tasks. Thus during sustained visual attention (Pardo et al. 1991), listening to words (Peterson et al. 1991), naming the color of a color word when

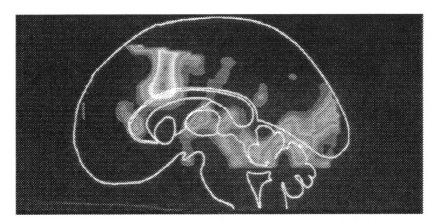

Figure 4.15
The anterior cingulate is strongly activated during trials of the Stroop effect in which color and name are incompatible. The strength of activity in PET images made by subtracting scans taken during the compatible condition from scans taken during the incompatible condition. (From Posner and Raichle 1994)

the word is presented in a different color (Stroop test) (Pardo et al. 1990), willed actions (Frith et al.), and mental imagery (Posner et al.), PET measurements have led to ever more detailed maps of active regions of brain (Posner and Raichle 1994). An example is the demonstration (figure 4.15) of frontal activation during performance of the Stroop task, in which a subject has to read the word of a color that is printed in a different color.

This advance has led to the comment by one of the main practitioners: The PET and other brain imaging techniques hold considerable potential for making crucial contributions to, and advancing the understanding of, the functional organisation of the human brain. Each technique, with its unique assets and the more direct control over structures and processes it can study, provides information inaccessible through more classical approaches, but none has predominance and none is self-sufficient.

These remarks are also true of fMRI, which I alluded to as allowing for remarkably accurate noninvasive three-dimensional maps of the brain. It requires the application of a strong magnetic field. Atomic nuclei have their energies slightly shifted, some increased and some decreased, by the interaction of their magnetic moments with this magnetic field. They then emit a signal under the influence of a suitable applied radio frequency

Table 4.1
Comparison of noninvasive instruments

Method	MEG	EEG	PET	fMRI
Time resolution	1 msec	1 msec	1 min	5 sec 1 slice 10 min echoplanar
Spatial resolution	5 cm	1 cm	5 mm	5 mm
Limitations				
Intrinsic	None	None	Restricted by blood dynamics	
Truly noninvasive	Yes	Yes	Injection	Yes
Whole brain transparancy	Yes	No	Yes	Yes
Nature of sources	Best parallel to brain surface	Surface only	Blood flow only	Blood flow only
Time averaging needed	Single epoch possible	Yes	Averaging by blood flow	Averaging by blood flow

field. These signals contain information about the density of nuclei contributing to the signal, and so give an image of the object, for example, involved in oxygen flowing in the brain to feed nerve cell activity (producing the so-called blood oxygen-level dependent or BOLD signal).

The fMRI technique has been used at a number of centers to detect brain regions active in performing tasks, similar to PET, EEG, and MEG. With strong enough external fields (several million times that of Earth) applied to a subject's brain, cortical regions jointly involved in speech generation and memory tasks have been detected that are consistent with those discovered by other methods. The various features of these techniques are summarized and compared in table 4.1.

Conclusions we reach on brain imaging are as follows:

1. EEG and MEG have comparable temporal resolution of down to 1 msec and spatial resolution of several millimeters (although only surface analysis is possible with EEG), whereas PET and fMRI have similar

spatial resolution of a millimeter or so but much poorer temporal resolution (on the order of seconds).

2. Localized brain regions are sequentially activated during task solution.

3. Different brain regions may combine in different groupings for different tasks.

4. Complex tasks can be decomposed thereby into subtasks carried out by separate brain regions.

5. Averaged activity is apparently all that is necessary, with activity from aggregates of tens of thousands of neurons being measured.

Let us move on to consider important information being gained by analyzing the loss of abilities sustained due to brain damage. Allied to noninvasive instruments, highly important results are being obtained about the manner in which different parts of the brain are involved in the different components of consciousness mentioned in the previous chapters.

Lesions and Defects

Loss of different regions of the brain leads to different deficits in mental faculties. Destruction of areas devoted to input—vision, olfaction, touch, audition, taste—causes loss of conscious experience of these inputs. We would expect that to occur, since without input stages, no information is being carried to higher regions for further elaboration. Damage to more remote regions leads to considerably modified forms of conscious experience and even to dissociation of knowledge from awareness. For example, the phenomenon of "blindsight" (Perennin and Jeannerud 1975; Poeppel et al. 1973; Wieskrantz et al. 1974) occurs in people who have lost a portion of their visual cortex and seem to be blind in a certain portion of their field of view; they cannot discern the position or even presence of a spot of light in that region. Yet if they are asked to guess as to the position of the image they will be successful well above chance, in spite of the fact that they may insist they are only guessing and even feel embarrassed about their response. Blindsight is well documented and is strong evidence for knowledge without visual awareness.

Another example of unconscious information processing arises in face recognition: patients (Tranel and Damasio 1988) who could not consciously recognize familiar faces gave a clear change of skin resistance that was significantly greater for familiar faces than for those of people they had never met. A similar dissociation occurs for semantic knowledge: patients with semantic access dyslexia had no explicit knowledge of what a stimulus was, but could make certain correct decisions requiring knowledge of its meaning (Warrington and Shallice).

Loss of awareness of stimuli that is processed up to quite high nonconscious levels also occurs in people who have suffered a stroke leading to "neglect." These patients typically do not react to or search for stimuli coming from the opposite side to the region of brain damage (Mesulam 1981). They do, however, possess residual knowledge of input from the opposite region of space to their lesion, but are just not aware of it. A famous example of this (Marshall and Halligan 1988) is a woman with severe visual neglect who explicitly denied any difference between the drawing of an intact house and that of a burning house, when the features relevant to the discrimination were on the neglected side. Nevertheless when forced to choose the house in which she would prefer to live, she consistently preferred the intact one, showing implicit knowledge of information she was unable to report.

There are many similar examples of the manner in which dissociation of awareness from knowledge occurs after brain damage. This also agrees with studies using noninvasive instruments in healthy subjects to determine the brain regions involved in certain types of tasks, as mentioned earlier in this chapter. These results are bringing about a revolution in research, the most important result being that the brain processes information in a modular manner, with numbers of areas of cortex involved in any particular task. Moreover, the modules involved in certain tasks are those that have been destroyed or damaged, with resulting loss of one or more faculties.

The Processing Brain

The results of studies in damaged and intact human brains give a general description of the manner in which tasks are distributed around the cortex (Mesulam 1985): processing is from primary cortex (input regions for sound, vision, touch, or smell, and output region for motor acts) to modules that elaborate the information in a patrticular sense. This unimodal associative cortex is placed around the primary cortical receiving areas, or motor cortex. In addition, limbic cortex is associated with values, drives, and emotions, and elaborates the emotional connotation of various cortical inputs. Finally, inputs arrive at the heteromodal cortex, in which elaborated inputs from various modalities are fused together. The deficits and results of noninvasive imaging help us to understand the manner in which parts of these different levels combine to achieve task solutions. There is also important feedback from higher to lower areas so as to control and "fill out" the input patterns for more efficient processing.

The overall plan appears to be that of a flow from input to motor output (as well as in the opposite direction) through the sequence

input → primary cortex → associative cortex → heteromodal cortex → motor cortex → motor output (in a given modality) (also one modality to a number of modalities).

A typical flow pattern is seen in figure 4.16 when a subject performs the task of first looking at a face and then of looking at a pair of faces (one identical to that seen earlier, the other a new one) 21 seconds later and chooses one of these as identical to the one seen first. The flow of activity is remarkable, involving a number of areas in both the posterior cortex and in the frontal lobe. There is activity in the temporal lobe (area 37), known from other studies to be active when a person looks at faces, as well as the hippocampal regions used to encode and retrieve memory of the face over that period. A remarkable loop of activity also circulates around the brain from the temporal lobe to the hippocampus and so on. The functions performed by the different regions in this loop, and more generally those active in the other parts of the brain, are presently under close study. This is also being done for other tasks, so that ultimately the overall nature of processing will be understood at the level of separate brain areas.

Questions that we are led to by this flow diagram are, at what stage does consciousness enter, and how does it do so? We will attempt to answer them in due course. The data presented so far in this chapter do not give any clear hint as to the answers; no experiment described has

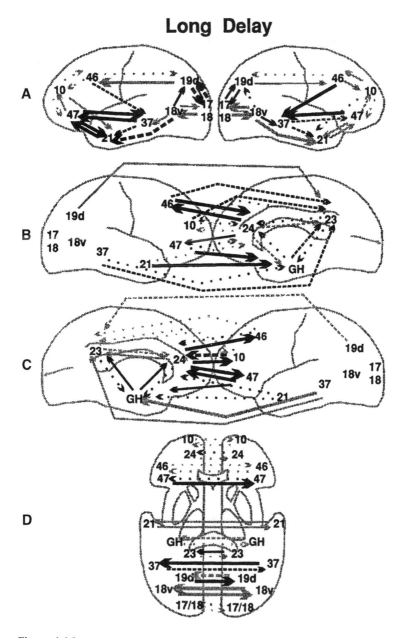

Figure 4.16
Strengths of neural connections between centers of cortical activity involved in face matching over 21 seconds. The thicker lines between regions correspond to stronger interconnections; the dotted lines correspond to inhibitory connections. (Reprinted with permission from McIntosh et al, 1996)

indicated conclusively the existence of any region of which it might be said, consciousness emerges here. No noninvasive instrument has discovered a region in the brain that with certainty is dedicated only to the emergence of consciousness. If its site of emergence is unknown (although hints are being discovered), so is its mode of action. Such ignorance is not surprising in view of the facts, indicated earlier, that consciousness has many components and is not a monolithic entity. Many regions are dedicated to vision, at least twenty, and at least seven are involved in hearing, so the nature of their contribution to consciousness is expected to be difficult to unravel. However, that unraveling has begun in earnest and is described later.

In spite of this complexity, we can be sure that the activity of nerve cells is the basis of information processing and that mental experiences are thereby created. The activity is localized in specific regions and not distributed in a homogeneous manner. That such localization occurs is made even clearer by the fact that brain damage to small regions can cause specific deficits.

Tools such as the noninvasive apparatus and theoretical neural network models give us hope that the complexity of brain processing can be tackled in a progressive manner. They also indicate that it is appropriate to attempt to discern the principles underlying consciousness by looking in great detail at brain processing. Consciousness is created solely by brain activity, so we should be able to uncover these principles.

Summary

In this chapter I described the structure and activities of the brain, from its global modules and cortical lobes down to living nerve cells. I outlined the approach of neural networks to this complexity and extended that to the powerful new windows on the brain that look at its global activity by measuring associated electrical and magnetic fields and related blood flow while a subject is involved in solving tasks. I then described the implications of these measurements and simple attempts to model them, concluding with an outline of the nature of deficits in behavior and experience after brain damage.

All aspects of this chapter involved activity only at the mechanical (more specifically electrochemical) level. The inclusion of task-specific modules would be a step toward the hoped-for inclusion of some level of cognition. However, it is correct to say that as seen from the position we have arrived at in this chapter, the problems of consciousness and mind seem remote. We have yet to build the bridge between mechanical and psychological variables. We analyze what models of that bridge are available in the next chapter. It is the best features of these, together with some of my own, that I try to preserve in our examination of the conscious mind.

5

Past Models of Consciousness

The summer's flower is to the summer sweet.
—William Shakespeare

Considerable numbers of neural models have been developed in an attempt to explain the mind, especially models trying to give a basis for the key feature of consciousness. That such attempts are being made is itself encouraging for the possibility of ultimately obtaining a neural solution to the problem. Each model can be regarded as making further progress resolving the enigma of our nature. It is a putative entry in the race for consciousness. In spite of the fact that none of the approaches has so far succeeded, it is still important to consider them and attempt to build on them further.

In this exercise we will divide the models into two classes, as suggested by Chalmers (1996) and discussed in chapter 2. First are models that tackle the easy problems of mind and consciousness, such as the manner in which visual processing occurs or how motor actions are guided by visual inputs. These are problems that a mechanical model of the type discussed in the previous chapter is designed to solve. Not that the epithet "easy" should be regarded as denigratory, since most of these problems are still difficult and many as yet have no agreed solution. One approach we can take to the easy problems is to construct detailed neural network models that simulate the behavioral responses observed in animals or humans.[1]

The second approach is to tackle the easy problems from the information-processing point of view. This analyzes the psychological machinery of mind rather than neural activity and is based on a "boxes" approach, where each box corresponds to a supposed information-transformation system. The boxes involve preprocessing in separate modalities, data fusion, short- or long-term memory systems, scheduling systems, and control systems for output response. The underlying implementation of such modules is not regarded as important in this class of models; it is the function they perform that is crucial. The main data helping to guide their construction arise from psychology determining, for example, whether short- or long-term memory systems are dissociable or if attention is early or late in the processing hierarchy from input to output. Such models are of great value in understanding a more global level of information processing and are important in seeing what sort of global information processing more detailed neural network models should be carrying out. They are thus to be seen logically before the more detailed models, so we will treat them first.

Hard problems associated with the mind and consciousness are concerned with the nature and origin of qualia, or raw feels, and the source of self-awareness. These are undoubtedly difficult, since they pose questions that lie at the very core of mind and consciousness: the inner, subjective character of the mind and its remarkable fluidity and seamlessness. Presently, very few models try to solve them and certainly none gives much of a hint as to the form a solution might take.

From what I have just said, we can divide models of the mind into three classes according to the nature of the problem and the relevance of the underlying machinery, as follows:

Easy 1. Information processing, performed by a connected set of boxes.
Easy 2. Neural, performed by connected areas, such as in figure 4.16.
3. Hard unknown, both neural and information-processing aspects are expected to be necessary, plus flexibility in developing new styles of processing.

As we noted earlier, neither class of easy models contains the obvious seeds of a solution to the hard problem, most crucially that of explaining why such and such a set of boxes or neural modules *must* generate consciousness as part of its activity. These models have no direct relevance to the hard problem. Nor are there any solutions yet proposed to the hard problem, which is therefore not considered further in this chapter but delayed until later chapters, where it is discussed in some detail.

We can set out approaches to the easy problems under the following more detailed headings:

1. Functional/information processing
2. Genetic approaches to monolithic neural networks
3. Learning approaches to monolithic neural networks
4. Direct approaches to neural networks through computational neuroscience
5. Other "runners" (nonneural, e.g., by quantum mechanics or quantum gravity)

It is clearly appropriate to start our survey with information-processing/boxes models; I earlier noted that these are logically prior to neural network models and should allow us to discover what the components of the neural models should be doing as part of a global plan. We then consider approaches 2 and 3, which use a single amorphous mass of neurons. Next we turn to item 4, composed of connected but separate regions, as in figure 4.16, and relate them to the information-processing ones of item 1 whenever possible. Finally, we give a brief account of the nonneural approaches, in particular considering whether or not either quantum mechanics or quantum gravity could provide a suitable framework from which to explore consciousness.

Functional or Information-Processing Models

Models of the functional or information-processing class of type 1 were popular in the 1970s and 1980s as part of the artificial intelligence approach to thinking and mind, and can be seen as emphasizing and developing the psychological side of the brain-mind duo. The development of understanding of the mental side of brain and mind is as important as developing that of the physical side, and can help bring the two closer together.

Strong and exclusive claims were made originally by the functionalist approach to mind (Pylyshyn 1984; Fodor 1975). The thrust of the argument was that the detailed implementation of information processing that occurred in the brain was unimportant, and only the functions that were performed had to be emphasized. Such a claim was useful since it removed extraneous detail from the analysis of thinking processes. By this strategy considerable progress was made in developing computer programs that implemented well-defined domains of knowledge and allow inferences to be deduced from them. These expert systems are now in use in various machines and processing systems throughout the world.

The functional approach is unconcerned with detailed neural underpinning of how the mind might be supported by the brain. Fodor, in particular, posits a three-fold distinction among sensors, input analyzers, and central processing modules, in close analogy to the distinction in a computer, where the sensor would be the input terminal and the input analyzer might be akin to a compiler, although Fodor is keen to avoid confusion with a standard compiler. He goes on to state, "Central systems look at what the input systems deliver, and then they look at what is in memory, and they use this information to constrain the computation of 'best hypotheses' about what the world is like. These processes are, of course, largely unconscious, and very little is known about their operations."

Strong and important claims are made in the analysis of central systems. These analyses are in two forms: by modules that are relatively domain specific, and by central processors that are relatively domain neutral and call on knowledge or memory representations from across all experience. The former are involved with input analysis, latter with the fixation of belief. Owing to the amorphous character of the latter, Fodor is pessimistic about useful analysis of a neural underpinning of thought. As he states, "The moral is that, to the extent that the existence of form/function correspondences is a precondition for successful neuropsychological research, there is not much to be expected in the way of a neuropsychology of thought."

We must take these pessimistic conclusions seriously; the separation of processing into local and global, with the former assigned to input analysis and the latter to belief, is of considerable value. However, EEG, MEG, PET, and fMRI are providing increasingly detailed pictures of the way the modules of the brain combine at a global level. Those involved with belief or other higher-order thought process are accessible to more detailed mapping and analysis. Thus Fodor's pessimism should be dispelled by these developments, and his insights used to help move us past the barrier he recognized. The distinction between local processing and more

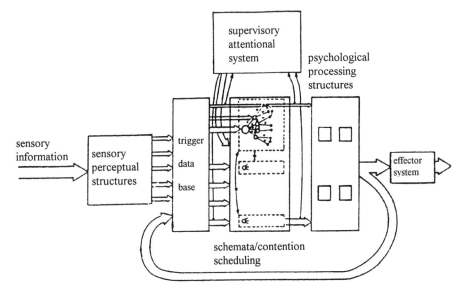

Figure 5.1
Norman and Shallice's model (Norman and Shallice 1980; Shallice 1988). The psychological processing structures unit represents the bulk of the online operation of the control systems that give output to effector systems. The supervisory attentional system exerts its action on the schema/contention scheduling system when the latter is unable to handle automatic decision making between opposing schemata triggered by the trigger database module by incoming information. (Reprinted with permission from Shallice 1988)

global, higher-order thinking will become apparent later as the conscious mind emerges in our discussion.

A more detailed information-processing approach is that of Norman and Shallice (1980); they proposed an overall system to describe the manner by which the frontal lobes are involved in controlling motor actions and how deficits in this processing in persons with frontal lobe disruption can be explained. The most crucial aspect of this theory is the division of higher-order processing into two parts, as shown in figure 5.1. One of these is the set of automatic response sequences or schemata, between which a choice is made by contention scheduling, which does not require conscious activity and decides among alternative schemata by their relative salience to the organism. If contention scheduling fails, owing either to equal preferences between two or more schemata or lack of a suitable schema at all, the supervisory attentional system is brought into play. This is a control structure that is used to attempt to solve the resulting problem by various creative strategies, such as analogy, memory search for suitable schemata, and so on.

The model gives valuable insights into the nature of control structures used in higher-order thought. It led to suggestions for successful experiments on working memory (Baddeley 1986) and increased our understanding of psychological deficits (Shallice 1988). The model is undoubtedly an important step forward in understanding and characterizing the psychological variables involved in thinking and decision making; it is possible to begin to develop a neural model of some of the detailed parts of the processing (Bapi et al. 1998).

Finally, in the category of functionalist-information processing is the global workspace model of Baars (1988). This fundamental and important theory consists of three entities: specialized unconscious processors, a global workspace, and contexts. Its two processing principles are competition through the global workspace lowering activation levels of global messages, and cooperation raising it. There is also local processing within the specialized processors, which are regarded as unconscious and not requiring access to the global workspace.

The main structure of the global workspace model is shown in figure 5.2. The most important feature is, according to Baars, "as . . . a system architecture in which conscious contents are globally broadcast to a collection of specialized unconscious processors. Furthermore, the main use of a global workspace system is to solve problems that any single expert cannot solve itself—problems whose solutions are underdetermined." The global workspace is also used to update many specialized processors concurrently; it was extended more fully recently (Baars and Newman 1993, 1994; Baars 1994a,b).

The model is complementary to that of Norman and Shallice, both giving more precision to the insights of the functional account of Fodor. All in all these approaches give us a framework on which to build a bridge to neural activity from psychology. Interesting attempts have been made to map the global workspace and some of its principles, such as competi-

**Competing
Input Processors:**

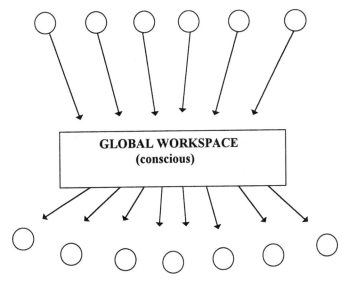

Receiving Processors

Figure 5.2
The global workspace distribute system of Baars. The input processors compete and cooperate for access to the workspace. Once there, the message is broadcast to the system as a whole.

tion, onto neural modules in suitable interaction (Baars and Newman 1993, 1994; Baars 1994a,b).

It is appropriate to mention that Freeman (1995) has experimental support for the global processing mode involved in consciousness. Thus he states, "From my analysis of EEG patterns, I speculate that consciousness reflects operations by which the entire knowledge store in an intentional structure is brought instantly into play each moment of the waking life of an animal, putting into immediate services all that an animal has learned in order to solve its problems, without the need for look-up tables and random-access memory systems." This fits very well with the global account of Fodor and the global workspace model of Baars. It is also in strong support of my relational consciousness model.

An interesting recent development using hierarchies of control structures is the humanoid "COG" project of Rodney Brooks and his group (Brooks and Stein 1993) that attempts to build a cognizing robot using eye-catching insectlike robots controlled by what is termed subsumption architecture. The insect-robots are able to learn, for example, to walk over comparatively rough terrain or search through a building to collect discarded cola cans. The subsumption architecture has higher-order control modules to issue control signals to lower-order ones in order to achieve suitable goals; this corresponds to having higher-order control structures imposed on lower-order ones. It has some relation to the model of Norman and Shallice mentioned above, although it has clear differences, such as that the executive is thought of as having only one level, whereas a subsumption architecture can possess an arbitrary number. However, COG is an important program to watch, especially since it leads to a basis of control actions for lower-order responses, such as those arising in spinal and brain stem systems. It is essential that our mechanical models of consciousness ultimately have an action basis, so COG would be a valuable platform for such developments.

Another important information theoretic approach to consciousness is "Oscar." Pollack (1989) attempted to construct a conscious machine by building the software system of Oscar to have three levels of sensors. The first-level sensors are perceptual or input ones. At the next level are introspective sensors, which can detect and track the "thoughts" of Oscar arising from the first-level sensors. At the third level are second-order introspective sensors. Pollack suggests, "Qualitative feel is the output of the introspective sensors. One may protest that the 'feel' of the qualitative feel is being left out of the picture. . . . But let us be careful to distinguish between having the qualitative feel and experiencing the qualitative feel. To have the feel is for one's first order introspective sensors to be operating, but to experience the feel is to attend to the feel itself; and that consists of the operation of the second order introspective sensors sensing the operation of the first order introspective sensors. . . . In essence my proposal for understanding the phenomenal feel of a sensation consists of distinguishing between the sensation and the feel of the sensation." This ambitious but clear structure equates self-awareness with second-order introspection.

The program seems to have been somewhat damaged in a detailed analysis (von Stubenberg 1992). According to Pollack, Oscar would not be able to modify response that was automatic. However, it is known that blindsighted persons are able to learn to perform, yet they appear to have no self-monitoring capabilities and have total lack of visual awareness. This is different from Oscar's abilities, as he would require a conscious level of processing before he could modify his response by learning. Thus the dissociation between awareness and learning in blindsighted subjects must be an important criterion in the construction of a model of consciousness. Self-analysis as a higher-order process on lower-level activities undoubtedly is an appropriate way of introducing self-recognition. The problem of learning at an automatic level need not be too difficult to include in Oscar.

It is important to use these insights and those associated with the more detailed processing by the modular global workspace and supervisory attentional system models as part of our guiding principles to construct more detailed neural models. Modular "boxes and arrows" styles also were developed and can add to our understanding of the mind's functional architecture.

Adaptive Models

There are two different approaches to building neural models of the mind. The first uses an amorphous network that is as large as possible, and attempts to train the net to function with ever greater intelligence to solve a set of tasks (given by the modeler). The other uses guidance from information-processing approaches to design a more sculpted set of neural modules so as to perform detailed information-processing tasks supposedly carried out originally by a set of boxes; it may be seen as trying to give a neural filling in of the boxes. The first method, comprising items 2 and 3 in the list of easy approaches to the mind, seems to be harder since it uses less information and also seems to attempt to do, it is hoped in a few years, what evolution took hundreds of millions of years to achieve. Yet the method is important as it gives insights into the grand scheme of development of mind in the animal kingdom.

The CAM-brain project (de Garis 1994) uses *genetic algorithms* (modeled on the manner in which evolution changed the genetic make-up of living things) to develop a cellular automaton model of a kitten's brain, containing up to a billion "nerve cells," by the year 2005. A cellular automaton is composed of a set of simple decision units, each connected to its nearest neighbors. The rule by which the system's activity is updated at each time step is simple because it calls on only nearby activity. The genetic algorithm allows for modifications of local connections between nerve cells. An assembly of identical cellular automata has random changes (mutations and crossovers between connections of pairs of cellular automata) made to each of their nerve cell connections, and the resulting descendent sets of cellular automata are tested for fitness according to how well they succeed on a certain set of tasks. Automata that are fittest are kept for breeding by further mutations and crossovers at the next generation. After a suitable number of generations, it was found that cellular automata can be evolved that are suitably successful over a range of simple tasks. These are the bases of the genetic approach to building artificial brains. The method is based on genetic principles that appear similar to those in action during the evolutionary development of life on Earth. By analogy, sooner or later it would be expected that, through mutations and interbreeding over generations, artificially created brains would arise that developed consciousness as the best way of solving the tasks used in selecting them in the first place. That was claimed in chapter 2 as the manner in which living consciousness arose over the eons. What better and guaranteed way to model how it evolved than attempting to duplicate the evolutionary process itself?

All very well, and all success to the CAM project. But important differences exist between artificial and real evolutionary brain building. There is an enormous difference between the nerve cells of the two approaches, with real neurons being highly complex, whereas artificial neurons are as simple as possible. Although the principles on which consciousness depends may not require "all-singing, all-dancing" nerve cells, complex neurons may be essential in an evolutionary approach to allow conscious artificial brains to be created in a realistic time. It may be in the complexity of the nerve cells or their connections that a large enough pool of neural networks is available from which to select the fittest candidates.

If the pool of nets is too small, it would just not be possible to find suitable "conscious" solutions. Increasing the number of nerve cells, if they are simple ones, could make up for their lack of complexity, but would make the genetic search take even longer.

Furthermore in his stimulating and wide-ranging neurobiological discussion of brain and mind, Freeman (1995) suggested that consciousness evolved in three different phylogenetic trees of brains, based on mollusks (e.g., as octopuses), arthropods (e.g., as spiders), and vertebrates, all of which possess "laminated neuropil" or cortex. It would therefore seem necessary for the artificial genetic evolution of the CAM-brain project to produce at least cortexlike structures before it could be accepted that cognitive abilities have evolved.

Turning to item 3 on the list, a more direct adaptive approach is one in which a suitably large neural network is trained by standard neural network learning methods to solve tasks similar to those considered under genetic algorithms. An example is the Hebbian learning law, described in the previous chapter, in which synaptic weights are increased if the neurons that they join are simultaneously active. This is part of the general program that I have been advocating so far and will develop further in this book. However, it will not be easy for us just to use an amorphous neural network along the lines of the feed-forward nets advertised so effectively in the "bible" of neural networks written in 1986 by McClelland and colleagues (McClelland et al. 1986). The number of possible connections between nerve cells is enormous for networks of only a reasonable size, say a million neurons, whereas our brains have at least a hundred thousand times more. The staggeringly large number of connections in our brains is a hundred thousand billion; however, the number of possible connections among those cells is even more awesome: ten thousand billion billion! The possibility for consciousness to somehow emerge by training such an enormous net is incredibly remote.

Explanation of brain function through neural network models should also incorporate details of brain structure and other information. In other words, not only neurophysiology but also neuroanatomy must help guide us in this enormously difficult task.[2] We started exploration of such structure, at a preliminary level, at the beginning of the previous chapter; later we develop it further and use it to probe deeper into the neural substrates of consciousness. At the same time it is important to use the insights that functional-information processing boxes give into possible modular decompositions of the brain.

Neural Models

Let us now move on to some recent neural models of consciousness. The closest of these to the functional approaches is that of Aleksander (1994a, 1994b, 1995, 1997), who tried to construct what he called a theory of artificial consciousness. He made the strong claim, "A mathematical theory of the mind that would solve the mysteries of consciousness is within grasp, thanks to the advances being made in computing." His general method is based on the automaton approach to artificial neural networks in which an automaton is defined by a set of inputs and outputs and the "space" of all of the states of the neurons. Thus each element of the "state space" is specified by which of the neurons are firing and which are not. The manner in which the inputs cause the state of the neurons to change and what output is then produced are part of specifying the automaton.

The general approach is based on feedback to develop attractor states (mentioned in chapter 4). It is suggested that when the network has relaxed into a particular perceptual state it is having the "artificial" conscious experience of the corresponding percept coded by that attractor. Similarly, if there is no sensory input, relaxation into a different state will lead to artificial consciousness of the corresponding percept, but now as part of imagery or dreaming. However, it was pointed out, "The description of oscillations between those (relaxation) states as the machine 'dreaming' is just anthropomorphic gloss" (Tarrasenko 1994). Yet the approach is important to build on. Attractors in neural networks (introduced in chapter 4), with their long persistence, may be one of the cornerstones of consciousness. We humans could use them in one way, machines in another. Both could be the basis of the emergence of different forms of consciousness.

The automaton approach must ultimately be able to describe consciousness and mind if a neural network method is expected to do so. It is possible to show that any artificial neural network can be reduced to the action of an automaton, and any automaton can be implemented by

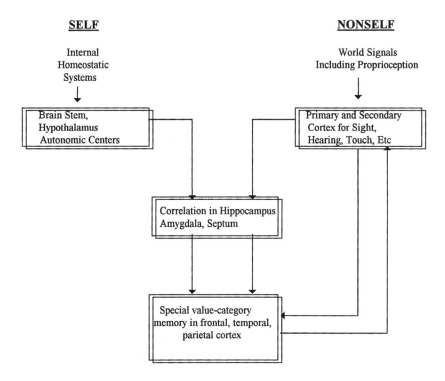

Figure 5.3
The reentrant model of consciousness. Past signals related to value set by internal control systems and signals from the outside world are correlated and lead to memory. This is linked by reentrant paths to current perceptual categorization. This results in primary consciousness. (From Edeleman 1992)

a neural network. So it is relevant to attempt to build an automaton-theoretic approach to mind as an alternative way of looking at the problem. This may help elucidate the overall dynamics of the system, and it is one I developed independently elsewhere.[3]

In a less formal system developed by Edelman (1989, 1992), the main feature is that primary or phenomenal consciousness arises from feedback from higher processors to a more primitive area (called reentrance; figure 5.3). He described it as follows: "A third and critical evolutionary development provides sufficient means for the appearance of primary consciousness. This is a special reentrant circuit that emerged during evolution as a new component of neuroanatomy. The circuit allows for continual reentrant signaling between the value-category memory and the on-going global mappings that are concerned with the perceptual categorisations in various sensory modalities." Moreover, "This interaction between a special kind of memory and perceptual categorisation gives rise to primary consciousness."

The approach to attempting to build neural models of the conscious brain has a deeper principle, termed by Edelman the "principle of neural Darwinism" or more specifically the "theory of neuronal group selection." This was expressed recently as

the idea that selection operates in the nervous systems of individual animals upon diverse, developmentally established repertoires of interconnected groups of neurons to provide working circuitry that is adapted to the needs of the particular individual in a particular econiche. (Reeke and Edelman 1995)

It is through such selection processes acting on a wide range of neural structures and connectivities generated by genetic and epigenetic processes that neuronal groups can be generated. The continued interaction among these groups by means of reentrant signaling is proposed to carry out perceptual categorization and other mental functions. In particular, the interaction and comparison of categorized responses to present input with signals of internal bodily levels, through hippocampus and temporal lobes, are supposed to lead to primary consciousness, whereas reentrant signaling of this comparison activity leads to conceptual primary consciousness.

This hypothesis is close to the relational mind model I suggested over twenty years ago and recently made more precise (Taylor 1973). However, Edelman's model suffered considerably from a too general notion of reentrance. Thus Crick commented (1989), "The problem is that it is difficult to find a path that is not re-entrant in the brain."

An example of a well-connected reentrant structure is the hippocampus, yet it can be lost with amnesia that, although highly debilitating, has no concomitant loss of phenomenal or sensory consciousness. Even so, the concept of reentrance is important in understanding activity in the brain supporting both conscious and nonconscious states, since a wealth of feedback exists to send information from higher areas back to lower ones almost simultaneously with feeding forward of inputs from lower areas to higher ones. This feedback in early vision was probed by PET studies of the human brain, and important features began to be recognized. The basic view of neuronal group selection is one of considerable processing power that has close similarities with ideas developed in the artificial neural network community concerned with the development of topographic maps of the external world in a manner that preserves their spatial layout (Kohonen 1982).

The next neural model of consciousness was proposed by Crick and Koch (1990) and discussed more recently by Crick (1994). It is based on the roughly forty cycles per second (or Hertz) oscillations observed in visual cortex in anesthetized cats (Gray and Singer 1987, 1989; Engel et al. 1989; Eckhorn 1988). These oscillations are synchronized among nerve cells in visual cortex encoding for similar features of visual inputs, such as the same orientation of edges in a picture, even though the cells may be separated by several millimeters of cortex or even be in opposite hemispheres. They are suggested as giving a solution to the binding problem, which arises from fragmentation in the brain of visual input from an object into several separate visual codes, such as shape, color, texture, motion, and so on.

The binding problem is how these separate codes are combined to give a seamless percept of the seen object. Brain defects cause slippage in the binding of object codes so that, for example, the color of a woman's dress may be seen by a patient after a stroke as a red patch partly covering her face, although the dress actually covers her body. So-called illusory conjunctions can also be brought about in a normal subject by a very rapid glance at a set of different-colored objects (Treisman and Gelade 1984); a picture of a red square and a green circle may be reported as a red circle and a green square if seen for only a very brief time.

Crick and Koch propose that 40-Hz oscillations support an attentional mechanism that temporarily binds the relevant neurons together by synchronizing their nerve impulses at the oscillatory frequency. They go on to postulate that

These oscillations do not in themselves encode additional information, except in so far as they join together some of the existing information into a coherent percept. We shall call this form of awareness "working awareness." We further postulate that objects for which the binding problem has been solved are placed into working memory.

It appears that two postulates are being made here, one about the manner in which the binding problem is solved (by 40-Hz oscillations in common across neurons encoding different codes for an object), and the other about the subsequent deposition of the bound object representation into working memory.

The more complete discussion in Crick's 1994 book seems to withdraw support for the relevance of 40-Hz activity to consciousness: "When the oscillations are seen they are usually transient. . . . On balance it is hard to believe that our vivid picture of the world really depends entirely on the activities of neurons that are so noisy and so difficult to observe." Instead, Crick proposes, "Consciousness depends crucially on thalamic connections with the cortex. It exists only if certain cortical areas have reverberatory circuits that project strongly enough to produce significant reverberations."

Considerable debate still surrounds the relevance of 40-Hz oscillations to conscious processing. One problem is that the oscillations are observed in both anesthetized and conscious animals, so they are relevant to all preattentive processing and not just to that concerned with consciousness. A second problem is that there is little evidence that the oscillations are present in awake monkeys. The situation was summarized by Koch as follows:

The vast majority of electrophysiologists are extremely sceptical that 40 Hz oscillatory neurons perform any significant function, such as binding, etc. And, indeed, the evidence for 40 Hz performing ANY function in the awake and behaving monkey—which is after all what we should be concerned about (besides human data) is slim, very slim. (Koch 1996)

The jury is still out on this question.

An alternative way of achieving binding was suggested some years ago by Christoph von der Malsburg (1986) by means of synchronized activity of a set of neurons over a short time window. The simultaneous activity of various sets of neurons gives the "tag" as to what overall object belongs to each of the separate features coded by various neural activities. Such binding by simultaneity was more specifically argued to occur in what are the multimodal regions of the brain, called *convergence zones*, by Antonio Damasio (1989a,b). However, it is uncertain whether binding occurs at a preattentive level or only on emergence of an object into phenomenal consciousness, so its relevance to consciousness is still unclear.

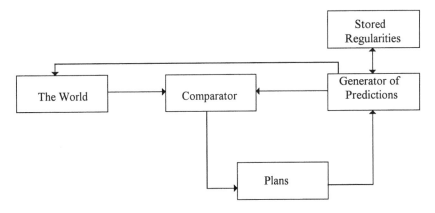

Figure 5.4
Information processing required for the comparator function of the septohippo-campal system. (From Gray 1995)

A further neural model of consciousness is that of Gray (figure 5.4) (1995). A comparator is central to the neural machinery of mind, being fed both by continuing predictions from the world and by internally generated predictions from past world inputs on the basis of a planning or predictor system. In particular, the area devoted to generating prediction is conjectured to be the hippocampus. This is an organ in the emotional or limbic circuitry of the brain, and along with its nearby companion system the amygdala, plays an important role in reward memory for inputs. As Gray suggests,

A neuropsychological hypothesis is proposed for the generation of the contents of consciousness. It is suggested that these correspond to the outputs of a comparator that, on moment by moment basis, compares the current state of the world with a predicted state.

Evidence supports the hippocampus being involved with memory tasks (Cohen and Eichenbaum 1993). Its removal or loss in patients with otherwise intractable epilepsy leads to serious memory loss. No new memories can be laid down (antegrade amnesia), nor can earlier ones for some years before the operation be made accessible (retrograde amnesia). Yet these individuals certainly are not unconscious. In fact at first meeting it may be difficult to discern that anything is wrong with them. It is only at a later meeting that massive memory loss becomes apparent. They have no conscious content derived from the earlier meeting, yet their awareness of present surroundings seems normal enough and they are able to respond sensibly in conversation, barring lack of recall of prior meetings.

It is clear that prediction and mismatch are important parts of the machinery of mind, with mismatches being both at automatic level (as certain EEG signals observed in audition show) and at the level of conscious thought (as in the model of Norman and Shallice). However, examples of amnesics with no hippocampi but apparently normal awareness indicate that the hippocampus is not necessary for consciousness. Gray's analysis must still be regarded as an important component in the search for the total machinery supporting consciousness and especially of self-consciousness.

It is fitting to conclude this description of neural approaches to consciousness with the tour de force of Dennett in *Consciousness Explained* (1991). This well-known professional philosopher incorporated numerous valuable neural features of the brain in a powerful attempt to give a broad brush explanation of consciousness. His main thesis is that there is no place in the brain where it all comes together, so to speak, to produce conscious experience. There just is no "Cartesian theater" where this might happen (Descartes claimed wrongly that such a site was the pineal gland), because memory can play tricks by changing recollections of recent experiences.

Instead, "multiple drafts" circulate "something rather like a narrative stream or sequence, which can be thought of as subject to continual editing by many processes distributed around the brain, and continuing indefinitely into the future. This stream of contents is only rather like a narrative because of its multiplicity; at any point in time there are multiple 'drafts' of narrative fragments at various stages of editing in various places in the brain." How this multiplicity is combined to produce an impression of unity is, Dennett suggests, by means of some competitive process.

This theme of multiplicity of sites of consciousness, with such sites carrying drafts that are continually being revised, is similar to one we will develop later. The nature of brain activity is now being recognized through brain imaging as involving several candidate sites for supporting awareness. However, some parts of the brain are more likely than others for the initial emergence of consciousness. So although there may be multiple drafts, these are not distributed throughout the whole brain, as Dennett seems to suggest. Thus the question of how consciousness is added by activity in those special sites where the drafts reside is still unanswered.

Other Models?

In addition to AI and neurally based methods outlined so far, several other avenues toward understanding consciousness were pursued with considerable vigor in the last few years. Some used concepts from quantum mechanics and quantum gravity, which have proved attractive to many physicists. It is curious that the need to go outside the standard cognitive and neural frameworks arose partly from the "proof" that the mind is even stranger than we thought. It is supposed to possess a crucial element of noncomputability that renders its understanding possible only in completely different frameworks than those considered so far. This led scientists to propose mechanisms for how such noncomputability arises from nondeterministic (but, strangely enough, not noncomputable) systems such as quantum mechanics.

The noncomputability story started in 1932 when logician Kurt Gödel (1986; Hodges 1998) showed how it was impossible to prove all true theorems in any formal system that contained axioms of mathematics. This incompleteness of mathematics was a shock to those in the formalist school, who wished to automate proof of mathematical theorems, but was realized by Gödel as being relevant to the human condition. It leads to statements that can apparently be seen by ourselves to be true but cannot be proved by any machine. Hence we cannot be a machine. Logicians now agree that this claim is wrong (Putnam 1994). In spite of this rebuttal, many scientists have searched for a quantum framework for consciousness. This occurred in the following manner.

Quantum mechanics was developed in the 1920s and 1930s to replace the classic mechanics of Newton with the crucial feature of uncertainty in the underlying description of particles and their motion: they can be said to be at a given position only to within a certain probability. However, the description of how measurements are to be calculated is quite at odds with the manner in which quantum systems develop. The problem posed by the incompatibility of measurement and dynamics has been realized since the inception of the subject in the mid-1920s.

Numerous attempts were made to solve this problem, in particular, by assuming that the consciousness of the observer brings about the crucial and nonunderstood features of the measurement process mentioned earlier. The manner in which this might be achieved is not known, but does bring together two mysterious processes: measurement in quantum mechanics and consciousness. As such it might be regarded as a step forward, since it would appear to reduce two mysteries to one. It leads to the need to investigate quantum sources of consciousness in the brain, a tack that has been followed by an increasing band of scientists.

Experimental results are clear, however: there is absolutely no evidence for a quantum basis of consciousness. The evidence has various parts, those directly against the relevance of quantum effects, those indicating how it cuts across what is known about the basis of consciousness, and those that show how the whole enterprise is unnecessary in the first place. I briefly discuss the first and second aspects here; the rest of this book develops an argument for the third. The uncertainty brought about in chemical transmission across a synapse by quantum mechanical effects can be calculated to be less than one in a million of nonquantum effects; they are therefore negligible. A further range of suggestions as to how quantum mechanical effects may in fact be of relevance to consciousness was surveyed (Herbert 1993), but they have no specific relation to the creation of particular states of mind, especially consciousness.

Consciousness has a different character from that which could be supported by quantum effects. The latter are expected to involve coherence of activity over localized regions that are in a "suitable" state. Such states are known in quantum mechanics only as long as they are at a very low temperature; this cannot be the case for regions of brain involve the firing of nerve cells. Quantum mechanics, on the other hand, indicates that consciousness in the brain is correlated with inactive regions, not active ones. This is clearly seen to be false from the fact that particular regions of brain are known to be active in humans who have the corresponding conscious experience and no defect; loss of these regions leads to the loss of the corresponding conscious experience.

Summary

Let me summarize the understanding of mind and consciousness that the models surveyed produce. First are psychological models, based on information processing and claiming independence of the underlying mechanism for their support. These (of Fodor, Norman and Shallice, and Baars) indicate the existence of a global processing style for the development of higher thinking processes associated with beliefs, and of a similar style (global workspace) available for the development of conscious awareness of inputs. Higher-order control systems, such as the supervisory attentional system, alert the mind to mismatches and the need for problem-solving modes of response, and are related to the predictive neural machinery in hippocampus and its surrounds in Gray's model.

Second, some neural models are based on automaton approaches or modular constructions. They use specialized modules dedicated to the support of consciousness, either input led or involved with imagery and dreaming. Feedback between modules coding different categories (Edelman's reafference), between a cortical module and its thalamic support (Crick), or just a relaxation attractor for a given module (Aleksander) are claimed by the authors to be crucial neural activities out of which consciousness emerges. Dennett says that there is no place where it all comes together in consciousness, but only continually changing "multiple drafts" circulating in some fashion around in the brain. Other systems (CAM-brain, amorphous artificial neural networks, COG project) attempt to create mind from much lower-level processing principles. Support for the CAM-brain project arises from the fact that the artificial mind is created by something similar to the evolutionary approach by which it actually progressed on Earth. The problem with this method is the length of time it could take for any kind of mind to emerge. A similar problem arises for the amorphous artificial neural network approach. It seems appropriate to incorporate into the methods further guidance in the form of clues from the relevant brain sciences, so that what originally took eons would occur far more rapidly.

Finally, the quantum approaches to consciousness are not effective in explaining the detailed facts of mental experience. Nor are they able to compensate for the enormously small effects expected (involving factors of at least a millionth compared with nonquantum effects).

The first two models made important advances on some of the easy problems associated with consciousness. Yet it is also transparent and admitted by most of their proponents that they made little headway on the hard problems. The inner subjective nature of consciousness is still elusive. The manner in which intentionality arises and conscious content is vested with meaning has also been relatively unexplored. The self is terra incognita in these approaches, other than for some brief statements. How can progress be made from the vantage point reached?

One of the morals we can draw from the models, especially those of the information-processing/psychological variety, is that a global view must be taken. It is clear that a global processing style must be considered more seriously to build the bridge between psychology and neural activity. Even more urgently, however, we must address the crucial processing components of consciousness; that might be helped if we analyze in more detail what consciousness actually is. We begin to attempt to answer that question in the next chapter.

6

Relational Consciousness

With dream and thought and feeling intertwined,
And only answering all the senses round.
—Elizabeth Barrett Browning

So far we have analyzed various aspects of consciousness and mind. We considered the evolution and development of human and animal minds, its character in sleep and dreams, pitfalls in developing explanations for it, new windows on it, the structure of the brain necessary to create it, and a range of models in support of it. Yet the inner and subjective nature of mind still eludes us. I suggested at the end of the last chapter that this was because we do not view the faculty of mind from a global enough perspective. Such a view was urged on us by results of pictures of the mind provided by MEG, EEG, PET, and fMRI that brought home most forcefully the global yet modular manner in which brain activity occurs. It also had support from the global information-processing approaches of Norman and Shallice in the supervisory attentional system and of Baars' global workspace described in chapter 5.

From now on we will strive for a global view, although that still appears not to be sufficient to reach the home stretch in the race for consciousness. There is something apparently insubstantial about the mind that gives strength to the dualistic model of Descartes in which mind and body were separate substances. What is required of a global model is somehow to incorporate into it a degree of apparent insubstantiality. The features of inner experience, qualia or raw feels, must somehow be seen to be present. Something more is necessary beyond the mere firing patterns of serried ranks of nerve cells in the brain. This comment is close to the folk psychological plaint, "How can the activity of a set of dumb nerve cells ever lead to my consciousness?" as Flanagan (1984) states concisely, "What is it about your qrxt-firing, for example, that makes it love of Adrienne as opposed to love of modern art?" (where qrxt denotes a specific set of neurons). This is again the hard problem of consciousness: how can we infuse the breath of awareness into an ensemble of unaware neurons?

The main thesis that we will use to guide the emergence of mind from brain was expressed briefly in chapter 2 and in the general thesis in chapter 3: it is through the *relations* between brain activities that consciousness emerges (Taylor 1973, 1991). These relations, such as how similar or dissimilar any two sets of brain activities are, are not themselves brain activities. It is this nonphysical essence of relations that opens up the possibility of incorporating a character of seeming insubstantiality into sets of brain activities (although at no point becoming dualistic). That relational feature is not possible for a single brain state on its own, so it is not possible for us to answer Flanagan's question in the form in which it was quoted. However, if the question were expanded to, "What is it about your qrxt-firing, in relation to earlier $q'\,r'\,x'\,t'$ -firings, for example, that makes it love of Adrienne as opposed to love of modern art?" I propose that we could give a more sensible answer. For this includes the person's history, thereby, the neural activities related to previous meetings with Adrienne or modern art.[1]

We have to be careful that the relational approach does not fall into a logical trap. If we consider a certain relation between numbers, such as "greater than," this is nonnumerical but exists in the same domain as the numbers, that is, in the set of mathematical symbols. For numbers can be properly defined only by means of further symbols that relate them together. Therefore any direct analogy of the relational approach of neural firings to that of numbers does not seem to be useful.

Yet the relations between neural firings are quite distinct from the firings themselves. These relations are encoded by the strengths of synapses between neurons activated by related firings. This relational coding has at least two aspects, as determined by connections set up between neurons by experience. One is by activating a set of neurons encoding for object representations by some sort of relaxation of activity in a network to a steady state by continued feedback, as described in chapter 4. This leads to recognition of the input as arising from a previously experienced and categorized object.

The second relational aspect is activation of memories "related to" the input as object, such as involved with the use of the object or of episodes when it occurred in the subject's experience. This involves activation of representations for a broader range of objects than solely given by the input itself. In total, synaptic strengths, as encoded memories of various sorts (preprocessing, semantic, procedural, episodic), allow further neural activity to be excited than given solely by initial input.

I suggest that such filling out of input gives a sense of insubstantiality to the resulting total neural activity. The important feature is that an input has triggered a whole host of related activity. The triggering process lifts the original input into what seems like a self-supporting and totally new arena. It is as if a skater has launched himself out onto the ice and glides effortlessly around, compared with earlier clumsiness as he tried to walk toward the rink in his skates. The initial clumsy walking is that of preprocessing, still hidebound to the input that caused it; only as the ice is reached—consciousness emerges—is some degree of autonomy achieved to elevate the neural activity to move as if released from the friction of clinging Earth. Such triggering of neural activity—the launching onto the ice—I suggest as being at the basis of the features of qualia, ineffability, transparency, intrinsicality, and so on. It is clearly very important to justify this possibility. I claim it as the seed of the new element that should be able to lift the neural modules from lack of inner experience to something akin to what we ourselves have in phenomenal consciousness. Such justification can follow only through careful development of a suitable model; I will do this gradually in the following chapters, culminating in a full analysis in chapter 11.

I hear you reply, "But isn't that neural activity still as brain-bound as before it became in any way elevated by being triggered to glide onto the ice; it is still neural activity, after all, so hasn't bridged the explanatory gap, as you claim?" It must still be neural activity; indeed, that is all there can be in the brain. It is the special, subtle character of this activity that is at issue. But to answer the question more fully we have to wait till later; we cannot run before we can walk. In the meantime let us continue to try to learn to walk.

The filling out I described is inherently relational in character. Relational structures have long been recognized as an integral part of brain and mind. Aristotle proposed that thinking proceeds by the basic relations of contiguity, similarity, and opposites. This idea was developed strongly by the associationist school of psychology of the eighteenth and nineteenth centuries. The manner in which ideas led one into another was considered seriously by empirical philosophers Locke, Berkeley, and Hume in the seventeenth century. The basic principle was stated explicitly by Hume (1986): "Mind is nothing but a heap or collection of different perceptions, unified together by certain relations, and supposed tho' falsely to be endowed with a perfect simplicity and identity."

Later associationists modified this concept of relations between ideas to that of relations between stimuli or rewards. Associationism was developed more recently through the subject of neural networks to allow for the learning of an association between any two neural activities. Activating one of these will always lead to the arousal of its partner activity. This is the basic mode of action of an associative memory. However, one-to-one relationships between stimuli and responses or between pairs of neural activities (and the related percepts) are not rich and powerful enough structures out of which the complexity and depth of conscious experience can arise. The relations we will consider more generally are one to many, so as to give a whole set of neural activities related to a given one. This set may be activated sequentially or produced simultaneously. The set of the related activities is to be regarded as the repository of past experiences related to input, and therefore of great importance in determining response patterns. I will attempt to put these relations to work more precisely to create consciousness in the next section.

Relational Consciousness

We are now ready to present the main thesis of the model of relational consciousness that is developed throughout the rest of the book:

The conscious content of a mental experience is determined by the evocation and intermingling of suitable past memories evoked (sometimes unconsciously) by the input giving rise to the experience.

This goes beyond Hume, with relations between perceptions now extended to include a range of past experiences entering the relation with a present one; these past experiences need not necessarily have been conscious when they were originally activated in the brain, or as they are evoked to enter the relation.

Thus the basic idea of the relational approach to consciousness is that *consciousness arises from the active comparison of continuing brain activity, stemming from external inputs to various modalities, with somewhat similar past activity stored away in suitable memory receptacles.* Past activities could include preprocessing, semantic, or episodic memories, where the first two involve no knowledge about the particular details of when or where the learning experience occurred. Episodic memory, on the other hand, always involves a record of the moment of experience, so that "I" or "me" is present. Both semantic and episodic memories are declarative, being able to be made explicitly conscious. Preprocessing memory structures are not declarative in the same manner, but their resultant neural activity is ultimately phenomenally experienced as qualia. Memory structures of a nondeclarative form are excited by a given input, such as value memory associated with earlier encounters with the objects involved in the input.

In all, then, *the conscious content of an experience comprises the set of relations of that experience to stored memories of relevant past experiences.* Thus consciousness of the blue of the sky as seen now is determined by stored memories of one's experience of blue skies. This relational expansion of experience was described most eloquently nearly 200 years ago by the English essayist William Hazlitt (1946):

The sight of the setting sun does not affect me so much from the beauty of the object itself, from the glory kindled through the glowing skies, the rich broken columns of light, or the dying streaks of the day, as that it indistinctly recalls to me the numberless thoughts and feelings with which, through many a year and season I have watched his bright descent in the warm summer evenings or beheld his struggling to cast a "farewell sweet" through the thick clouds of winter.

The indistinct recall of the "numberless thoughts" from his experience gave him his experience of the setting sun, and of other aspects of the beauty of the contryside; a relational account through and through.

Similarly, consciousness of sights, sounds, or smells may not only be of the simple records of such experiences but also of the emotions involved in them. Emotional content may have powerful effects, even though the emotional memory itself is not consciously experienced. That is dramatically brought out by the case of a woman who had gone through a strong near-suicidal experience when wearing a certain perfume. Six months later, and completely recovered, she decided to use up the perfume instead of wasting it. The next thing she was aware of was lying in hospital having had the contents of her stomach pumped out.

Besides such anecdotal evidence, support is increasing for a relational model of consciousness from experiments performed by psychologists during the last decade. In general, the thesis strongly shows the past experiences, however stored, influence present behavior. Is there a concomitant effect on present consciousness? To answer that question, consider the function of consciousness, which has been debated with considerable energy for a long time but with no clear conclusion. However, experiments support the minimal thesis that consciousness has a veto effect on our developing behavior (Libet 1982), although it is not used in determining all the details of our responses. Even such a minimal interaction indicates that consciousness is influenced by past experiences, as they themselves influence behavior and lead to a choice of responses requiring conscious intervention at appropriate times.

The community of cognitive scientists upholds the relational consciousness model when it is rephrased to state that consciousness arises from the interaction of top-down with bottom-up activities. To cognitive scientists the thesis in this form is obviously true—they would ask, "What else can there be as the source of conscious experience?"—and they therefore do not demand further proof. Moreover, the thesis is well supported by a host of evidence presented in numerous textbooks. However, it is necessary to develop independent justification for it here since you may not be a cognitive scientist and may need some persuasion. It is the basis of the present approach and will be used to build a more detailed framework with which to model both the easy and the hard parts of consciousness; it therefore must have strong grounding. Cognitive scientists have been notorious in their rejection of consciousness as a legitimate area in its own right, so I hope to redress that lacuna to a certain extent by considering the question of the justification of consciousness per se and not some other related phenomenon usually called cognition or other euphemism.

But I can hear you say, "I like the relational idea as a basis for consciousness, but you have been emphasizing the complexity of consciousness so strongly earlier that I began to believe it. Now you talk about consciousness as a single entity. Please don't confuse me; which part of consciousness are you talking about now?" This is a sensible question, but one for which I suggested an answer in the previous paragraphs: the part of consciousness considered in the relational consciousness model as being evoked by a particular memory structure is that particularly associated with that structure. Passive consciousness is closely involved with preprocessing and semantic memories; active consciousness with anterior working memories as well as planning and goal memories; and consciousness of self with autobiographic memories. The further components of consciousness that are in the wings are also handled in this manner. The thrust of the answer to the question should now be clear: memories are divided into preprocessing, semantic, episodic, and emotional categories that fit perfectly, in terms of relational consciousness, with the earlier division of consciousness. If I use the word "consciousness" on its own in further discussions I mean the whole constellation of its complexity; I will be more precise when discussing any part of it by using the appropriate terms.

Justifying Relational Consciousness

An area in which our past experiences are used to color our consciousness is categorization, which is heavily sensitive to past experience. If you were asked to name a bird, you would most likely say "robin" or "sparrow" if you live in an urban landscape, whereas if you have just been out on a hiking or hunting trip you would respond with "hawk." Studies show that context dependence of prototypes of categories is quite strong (Barsalou 1987), and "The concepts that people use are constructed in working memory from the knowledge in long-term memory by a process sensitive to context and recent experience."

The idea of working memory is one we will return to often and should be defined carefully: it involves a buffer or temporary store in one's brain to hold information, as while making a telephone call after the number has been looked up in the telephone book. It is natural to expect that such a store is the depository of various items of information one uses in solving tasks. We will call such a store a buffer working memory.

The manner in which past experiences alter responses in other situations has also been explored recently. One fertile area is memory illusions. Witherspoon and Allan (1985) had subjects first read a list of words on a computer screen and later judge the duration of presentation of additional words (including some the subjects had read the first time) presented individually on the screen. Subjects judged the exposure duration as longer for words read the first time than for those not seen before, although the actual duration of each word was identical. They misattributed their fluent perception of old words to a difference in duration of presentation of the words. Their conscious experience of the old words had thus been altered by the experience of exposure to them.

A number of similar features, including the "false fame" effect, were recounted by Kelley and colleagues (Kelley and Jacoby 1993; Jacoby and Whitehouse 1989). The false-fame effect involves two phases. In the first, people read a list of nonfamous names. In the second, these earlier names are mixed with new famous and nonfamous names in a test of fame judgments. Names that were read earlier were more likely to be judged as famous than were new names; this was especially so if subjects were tested in the second phase under a condition in which their attention was directed to performing another task, such as counting down from 100 in threes. Conscious recall of the earlier list was thereby suppressed. The authors concluded, "Past experiences affect the perception and interpretation of later events even when a person does not or cannot consciously recollect the relevant experience."

For two reasons, in spite of apparent strong support, much more work must be done to make relational consciousness acceptable. First, universal acceptance is relative only to those active in cognitive research. It is clearly not acceptable to the majority of people in a number of important categories at whom the thesis is ultimately aimed. Certain philosophers of mind, psychologists, and even some cognitive scientists do not seem to be in such agreement, as evidenced by the broad range of ideas in compendia on the mind (Lycan 1990; Davies and Humphreys 1993; Warner and Szubka 1994).

The second, more compelling reason why relational consciousness requires more work is that it gives a general structure, acceptable to most cognitive scientists and supported by the experimental evidence recounted above, on which a more detailed model of mind and consciousness can be erected. It allows us to ask further questions to determine how the model might be expanded and further features implemented. We can then test such implementations by experiment or relate them to existing experimental data wherever possible; in particular, results of the noninvasive instruments must ultimately be related to. Finally, we must instigate a much more detailed global modeling and experimental program (Taylor 1995a,b).

What, then, are the next steps that we must take to develop the model? What is lacking is specification of how the brain supports and uses the relations posited as being at the basis of the model. If we could explore how such effects were occurring, detailed modeling of crucial parts of the support and operational modules would be possible. Comparison with experimental data would also become clearer and allow us to test directly activities of the suggested modules.

Exploring Relational Consciousness

To explore relational consciousness more fully, let us return to the basic statement of the model given earlier:

The conscious content of a mental experience is determined by the evocation and intermingling of suitable past memories evoked by the input giving rise to the experience.

The key words to focus on in this statement are *input, evocation, intermingling,* and *suitable memories.* In other words, we must analyze the manner in which input is processed to excite or evoke one or more memories (of various sorts) relevant to the encoded input, and thus is seen as suitable. We should then combine (intermingle) these memories in some manner with the input. The process is shown in figure 6.1.

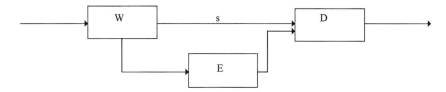

Figure 6.1
Schematic of the connectivity of a neural net with meaning in the original relational mind model (Taylor, 1973, 1991). The net W is the preprocessing net and E is the episodic net. The final net D is the decision net.

Input is encoded up to a certain (nonconscious) level in the module W. This involves us in the use of memories at the semantic level. A transformed or encoded result then excites a further set of memories from a long-term memory store E. All of these memories are intermingled in some further manner in the module (or set of modules) D, which denotes the process of a decision being taken by it. Labels W and E could be used to denote preprocessing-semantic and episodic memory, respectively, but that identification will be considered in more detail shortly. The essence of the relational structure in this more explicit version of the relational consciousness model is in two places:

1. The excitation of the memories in the modules W and E
2. The decision made in the module D

These require more careful exploration, with an ensuing extension of the model. Also we must discuss which component of consciousness arises: passive, active, or self? At the same time we should consider the manner in which intentional and seemingly insubstantial features might arise. Finally, we must relate the extended model to those discussed in the previous chapter that have a specific informational and neural basis. We turn first to memory structures involved.

Memory in Relational Consciousness

Memory in some form or other is quite extensive throughout the brain. Earlier we made a distinction between declarative and nondeclarative memory, dividing the former into semantic and episodic memory. At the same time early input is transformed by preprocessing modules, which we should also include as part of the total memory structure (with genetic effects). Nondeclarative memory includes at least skills and value, although the latter can become declarative, as when one says, "I like that (object)." Emotions and affect are important features that we will consider in more detail later; in the meantime we must accept that value memory is used to make decisions and should be included in E. Thus the memory structures initially to be used in figure 6.1 are W; preprocessing-semantic memories (in a given code), and E, episodic and value memory.

These identifications do not solve the binding problem as to how the different codes for an object, in general activated in different regions of the cortex, are combined to give the unified experience of the object. In particular, they leave open the manner in which outputs of preprocessing-semantic memories across given codes (say, color, shape, texture, and motion, for objects) are integrated to give a satisfactory bound representation of an object to be used as input to the episodic and value memory stores E. This last we initially assumed to be independent of separate codes, but based on unified objects representations. One potential manner in which binding might occur arises from two further features: the temporal character of memory, and the nature of the decision system.

For the manner in which time enters in memory, it is clear that there are two sorts of memories. One, that of buffering, involves continued activity without necessarily any concomitant structural changes (e.g., as increase or decrease of synaptic weights). Such activity has been observed in various parts of the brain, but especially and most predominantly in the multimodal regions of the cortex (inferotemporal, parietal, frontal) and in related subcortical structures. These are where nerve cells are found that have a relatively persistent response to inputs in a number of different modalities. The length of time such activity can persist itself seems modifiable, especially in frontal lobe (up to about 30 seconds), as shown by experiments in monkeys. On the other hand, the posteriorly sited phonological store, the working memory part of the phonological loop (Baddeley and Hitch 1974), can hold activity for an unalterable period of about 1 to 2 seconds. Experimental evidence indicates the existence of both variable-duration frontal lobe memories, which we call active working memories here (Fuster 1993), and more fixed-length and more posteriorly placed buffer working memories, which are discussed in more detail later.

The other sort of memory involves adaptive change in the ease of reactivation or reduction of error rate of recall for the associated memory. In other words, it is based on structural change of the brain and not on continued neural activity. The lifetime of such changes, once they have been established in cortex, is many years, as autobiographical or episodic memories clearly show. On the other hand, shorter-term priming memories are brought about by a single exposure to an object, which could help increase the speed or ease of access to long-term memories. This increased access persists for a limited time, on the order of hours or days. Priming memory provides crucial support to earlier experiences so as to give content to consciousness, as some of the experiments mentioned earlier in support of the relational consciousness model indicate. Such effects exaggerate the strengths of outputs from the neural sites of preprocessing-semantic memory W for recently experienced inputs.

This description of the nature of memory is a very brief account of the structures that many neuroscientists are attempting to elucidate. The problem of untangling memory is proving very hard, partly because memory seems to be so ubiquitous in the brain. If there is a hard part of the easy problems, it is clear that memory should be included in it.

Competition in Relational Consciousness

Having briefly considered the various kinds of memories used in the relations of the model, let us now turn to decision module D. Of what does that consist? To achieve some level of unity to conscious experience, a form of competition must occur in D, both to reduce choice in the set of memories that has been activated, and to reduce ambiguity of sequences of inputs arriving at the preprocessing-semantic memory system W. Many words are ambiguous in their meaning, as are many visual scenes. For example, the word "palm" could refer to hand or tree. Which should be chosen at any one time? Both context and memories are of value here. Thus even in the phonological code clarification is necessary. At the same time, binding across different codes (e.g., color or texture) is required, both for singling out combinations of features as suitably salient objects for conscious awareness and for further processing.

In a particular code it is therefore useful to have a prior or lower module achieving preprocessing or semantic encoding, with no interference or competition between nodes or assemblies of nodes coding for distinct interpretations of items. All possible interpretations should be available for later processing. Such activations also have to die out reasonably fast so as not to clog up the module with traces of past activities. We will call a module acting in this manner a *preprocessing net*.

A given working memory net can have more than one preprocessing net. This is clearly so in the case of object vision, with preprocessing nets for motion, color, texture, shape, and so on. The various highest-level nets in each code are all in parallel at the same level of the early-processing hierarchy. A similar situation arises in spatial vision. On the other hand, where words are concerned there seems to be only one highest-level preprocessing net, the semantic net, although several lower-level preprocessing nets are involved in lexical and orthographic coding.[2]

I will assume parallel activations on the preprocessing module for all of the interpretations of a given input, such as for the multimeaning or polysemous word "palm".[3] These are passed forward in an excitatory manner to the buffer working memory module, which holds activity for several seconds. On the buffer site there is also lateral inhibition between incompatible representations of the same or related inputs. A process of competition then occurs on the buffer working memory. Activations of nodes are reduced by competition from earlier activations that are contradictory to some of the nodes activated later. In this manner incorrect interpretations from earlier preprocessing-semantic net are removed from active later use. However, such activities, in particular the inhibition needed to occur on the buffer module, will have effects on later processing, such as reaction times for decisions made about later inputs. Experiments support the existence of such effects from work on subliminal processing; this is discussed in more detail in chapter 9. The inhibitory interactions necessary for such competition on the buffer site are assumed to arise from inhibitory interneurons in cortex, which consist of about 15 to 20 percent of all cortical neurons. It is also possible that the binding of different features of objects to make an object percept (the binding problem mentioned earlier) is solved by competition between and among alternatives; such a solution has been put forward by a number of scientists.

The winner of this local competition on a given buffer working memory I will identify with passive consciousness. I cannot support this claim further here by demonstrating that the activity on the working memory buffer has features that allow a glimpse of some attributes of phenomenal experience. It is only later (in part IV) that some justification is made for this enormous claim by looking into more detail of the nature of the construction itself. In the meantime please bear with me. At least this activity on the buffer working memory has time, through being buffered in the first place, to possess one of the crucial features of phenomenal experience, the existence of the specious present, the temporal extension of consciousness to allow us to experience it in the first place. Without such a time window for activity to persist there could be no consciousness at all. However, that is not a proof that the resulting temporally extended activity is phenomenally conscious; a stronger justification will be given later.

In a similar manner I suggest that active and self-conscious experience can emerge from winners on the more anterior working memory sites in the frontal lobes, where activity can persist for up to 20 seconds or more. In this way the relational consciousness model is applicable to all three main components of consciousness that we have identified in detail.

Finally, I raise a question as to interactions among working memories (either posterior buffer sites or anterior active ones) in different modalities. It was suggested (Taylor 1992a,b, 1993a,b, 1996a) that this is achieved through a suitable sheet of global inhibitory neurons, one candidate for this being the nucleus reticularis thalami (NRT), that surround the thalamus. All outputs from the thalamus to cortex and vice versa give off collaterals to excite NRT. This sheet has been of great interest to neuroanatomists for several decades and is suggested to play an important role in attention.

One proposal that I made some years ago is that the NRT is the basis of a global competitive interaction among working memories of different codes and modalities (although some may combine and not inhibit each other).

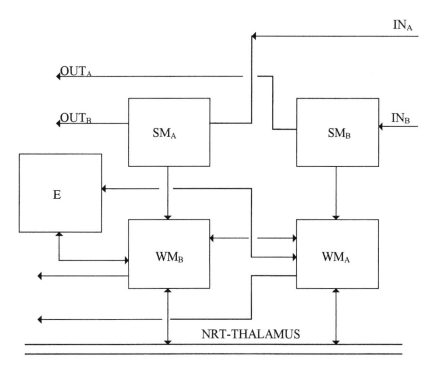

Figure 6.2
Flow chart of the relational consciousness model. See the text for details.

On extension to include the NRT and cortical inhibition, the model becomes the competitive relational consciousness model. The flow diagram of the model is shown in figure 6.2. Input IN has been processed up to a certain level before entering different preprocessing memories. Their outputs are fed respectively to their associated buffer working memories, as well as being available for direct and automatic activation (say, of frontal or midbrain system) for motor response. At the same time competition is occurring on each of the working memories, with its associated activation and support from episodic memory. This occurs both during intracortical inhibitory competition on each buffer working memory and the global one run between them by the TH-NRT-C system. Output from them is to be used to guide higher-level response.

To summarize, competitive relational consciousness involves competition among activities in various cortical sites of working memory through contact by means of the inhibitory sheet of neurons on the NRT. Competition (and combination) also occurs among activities internally on each of the working memory modules so as to take account of past context on that site. At the same time one or other of the working memory modules is supported from feedback from episodic memories activated by the input. This model applies to combinations of all three components of consciousness.

Summary and Conclusions

After some introductory remarks, I presented the relational consciousness model as a guide in developing a detailed model of the mind. I extended that to the modular system, which emphasized the need for a fuller exploration of the memory and decision-competitive systems. This was done briefly in the next section with the creation of the more explicit modular system and the associated competitive relational consciousness model.

Our task ahead is now clear. First, we must develop models of modules of the competitive relational consciousness model and compare them with known experimental data. We must obtain experimental support for the flow chart and, where necessary, modify and improve it. In particular, we must determine if and under what conditions there is triggering of activity on the sites of buffer working memory so as to support the inner experience associated with qualia.

Second, we must introduce further modules, and systems that will allow for higher-order control of the competitive relational consciousness system. Thus we will provide active consciousness and self-consciousness systems, sited in the frontal lobe. Finally, we must discuss the manner in which the whole brain coheres in health or degenerates owing to various types of deficits, on the basis of the extended competitive relational consciousness model. These tasks will be taken up in the last three parts of the book.

III

Building the Components of Consciousness

7

The Global Gate to Consciousness

O, the mind, mind has mountains; cliffs of fall.
Frightful, sheer, no-man-fathomed
—Gerard Manley Hopkins

Consciousness emerges anew against a rich panoply of context provided by previous experience. The ebb and flow of consciousness is like the tide going back and forth on the sea shore: each time it ebbs new shore is uncovered, carpeted with a whole array of flotsam and jetsam. That is similar to the contents of a conscious experience just completed—the flow of the experience is the tide, the flotsam and jetsam is the continuing experience. The tide sweeps in again, covering the now old flotsam and jetsam and bringing new material to be deposited on the beach. New content arises; it might also consist of some of the previous content; the new beach remnants often contain some of the old ones, unless the sea is so rough that it sweeps them away completely, to start afresh each time a wave pounds in. This analogy shows us some of the problems we face: the way conscious content is always changing but is seamless, how it sometimes remains similar for a period and then changes dramatically, and how it involves just one sea and one shore. It is a unified experience. This unity is especially problematic in the light of the divisions of consciousness we recognized earlier. How can I glide so effortlessly from being in a state of phenomenal consciousness, say of being moved by the play of sunlight on trees seen through the window, to turn back to the page I am working on right here in this book, and try to write down my thoughts about the subtleties of consciousness coherently? On the scientific level, how can we describe the way consciousness changes in the relational consciousness model? And where does the unity of consciousness appear as a natural part of the model, in spite of switching from one part of consciousness to another? I try to answer these and related questions in the next three chapters using behavioral responses and their related inner experiences taken from subjects in a set of key experiments. By the end of part III, I will have developed a neural framework for relational consciousness that leads me to suggest a tentative mechanism for the emergence of consciousness in part IV.

To summarize where we have come so far, basic features of the relational consciousness model are that (1) competition occurs both inside a given neural module and among local sets of neural modules in the brain; this first provides local winners and then produces an overall winner of the total competition (competitive aspect); and (2) various forms of memory (preprocessing, semantic, episodic, value assignment, priming, working) are used to help a given set of modules to win the competition. In the process inputs are integrated across modalities and among different sources to give the best interpretation of a sequence of inputs. In this way the content of consciousness arises. Through this relational filling out of initial input, the spark of life is breathed into consciousness and it gains content (relational aspect).

Various pieces of evidence were presented in chapter 6 to support the model, although I did not claim that they completely justified it. How then can the model be tested more rigorously? So far, support has been only at a qualitative "hand-waving" level. To go further we must obtain detailed agreement between predictions arising from the model and experimentally determined quantities, following the guidelines I laid down in chapter 3.

The next step is to attempt to place the relational consciousness model on a quantitative basis. I do this here by identifying neural modules in the brain that could support the two features and use these modules and their interactions to answer earlier questions: how does consciousness emerge, and how is it held together as a unified experience in spite of its constant changeability? The unity of consciousness was considered as an important part of the conscious experience in chapter 2, and without it neither you nor I is a single personality. Let us consider how we can develop such a crucial feature as part of relational consciousness.

The Global Competition

We can use two extreme methods to unify a set of parts (whatever these parts are):

1. Bundle up all of the parts to make a complete whole.
2. Throw out all of those parts but the best (chosen by some criterion).

The first of these, which we can call the greedy approach because it never reduces the set of parts, can produce very large wholes, rather like producing obese people. There is no survival value in obesity and nor is there in information overload, which would certainly occur if all the sensory inputs you or I experienced were kept and combined together. The opposite extreme appears to be the case for humans when the "parts" are objects we are observing, since we can attend to about only one object at a time. So it is the second extreme, the sparing approach, that we will follow.

The basic idea behind this is simple: unification of a set of activities is achieved by some form of competition among them, ending in the largest or most salient winning. The victor holds sway until it is unseated in turn by a new competitor with greater energy. That winner then is displaced by another newcomer. As the saying goes, "The king is dead. Long live the king!"

For the competitive aspect of the relational consciousness model, when each winner has won the battle it, together with its associated "supporters club" of memories, becomes the content of consciousness. Once displaced, it slides back into oblivion, and the new winner achieves consciousness. The content of consciousness associated with each winner is the set of activities involved with whatever input (or internally generated activity) one has consciousness of: appropriate semantic and episodic memories, as well as involvement of emotional and priming memories. All of these give a rich color and depth to consciousness that lead to its complexity and to our having an apparent inner world completely separate from the dross matter of our brains.

To test this idea we must develop a more quantitative model to carry out what we earlier termed intermodule competition; that will be between sites on cortex that are quite well separated. For example, the buffer working memory for objects is down in the lower more forward part of the temporal lobe, quite far from the buffer working memory for word sounds, which is up at the back of the temporal lobe. How could this competition be achieved over such distances?

The most natural form of competition is by one competitor trying to decrease the activity of another. That is what happens between boxers, when one tries to knock out his opponent. A similar method could occur between nerve cells. As we noted earlier, some cells send out signals that excite their recipients, others decrease that activity. These reducing or inhibitory signals play a crucial role in setting up a competition in the brain. For example, let us consider three inhibitory cells, each connected to the other two, and each trying to reduce the activity of its colleagues. As an example of how this occurs, think of three men standing with their arms on each other's shoulders, each trying to push the other two down to their knees but standing up as strongly as he can himself. They are functioning in exactly the same way as the three mutually inhibitory cells; in the end the strongest man will win and remain standing. For nerve cells, the weaker two will cease firing while the winner will fire as strongly as it can. If each cell is multiplied a million-fold to make sheets of cells, we have an idea of the size of the modules; the principle remains the same.

The Site for Competition

It is all very well talking about three competing men playing the strong-arm game or three nerve cells inhibiting each other in a somewhat similar manner, but the brain is composed of separate modules of cells. Each module is composed of cells that are only excitatory, with only a small minority of inhibitory cells. If these inhibitory cells can exert strong control over their excitatory companions, the disparity in their numbers need not be a problem. But how can competition between modules be run effectively when they are, as noted earlier, some distance apart in the brain?

The natural answer, which I have already made, is by inhibitory signals between the regions, so that each tries to destroy the other by playing the strong-arm game. Since the active regions are expected to be relatively distant from each other, as might arise between inputs in different modalities, we must discover neural circuits that produce long-range inhibitory interactions among different localized cortical activities. The solution will be the basis of the experienced unity of consciousness.

Competition is supported in several places by inhibition between cells. One of these is the outer layer of cells in the retina. Light falls onto the back of the eye and is absorbed by photosensitive nerve cells there. They signal the intensity of the light falling on them, which is then fed to cells of a special retinal outer layer, where it spreads over long distances across the retina; the cells of this outer layer end up calculating an average of the light signal across the whole retina. The resulting averaged activity is then subtracted, by inhibition, from that falling on a particular site in the retina. If only a constant light signal were falling on all parts of the eye, this averaged signal would be calculated by the outer layer and removed from the input. Since the two (outer layer average signal and input) are the same, no output signal is produced.

It would be useful to have a similar mechanism in the cortex but one is not immediately apparent. It is possible that an equivalent to the well-connected retinal outer layer could be composed of the dense "feltwork" of connections existing in the uppermost layer 1 of cortex. These could average all inputs and then contact cells in lower layers in a suitably inhibitory manner. However, we presently have no evidence for such a possibility.[1]

Other circuits might exist in the cortex that carry inhibitory effects between different separated cortical areas (LaBerge 1990). However, only the excitatory pyramidal cells of cortex have long-range axons, so direct long-range inhibitory messages of the desired sort cannot exist. The problem does not have an obvious solution. Yet we must not neglect the inhibitory cortical cells; they will play an important role in the competition between different activities on one and the same site of working memory, which we consider in detail later.

The ideal candidate to achieve the long-range competitive effects we require is a network of well-connected nerve cells that mutually inhibit each other; they play the strong-arm game with their nearest neighbors. It is similar to rugby, in which members of scrum try to pull each other down. In that case the strongest man survives standing upright with the others scrabbling on the ground at his feet. There may be a particular very strong group who are close together; they would surely pull all the others down.

In neural terms, excitatory inputs being fed to different regions of the net (keeping the "men" on their feet) would damp down activity aroused elsewhere. This would produce an effective competitive system among sources of input to the net; the net would signal only the strongest input.

Several candidates are available for regions of inhibitory neurons. The first is a sheet about two or three cells thick that covers the surfaces of the two thalami, the NRT. Another is clumps of cells in the basal ganglia and known to be crucially involved with motor and higher-order cognitive control functions. Damage to either region produces defects in cognition and motor action, although effects on consciousness seem more subtle.

Candidate 1: The NRT

Since all sensory inputs passing through the thalamus on their way to the cortex pierce the NRT, this is our ideal candidate neural network for supporting the competition for what was called passive consciousness. It has a primary character in the sense of being first evinced by input. Later, as in the case of needing to solve hard problems not previously encountered, the frontal control system is called into play.

I postulated earlier that passive consciousness arises from activity in certain portions of the posterior cortex, sites of buffer working memory. I now conjecture that NRT can support competition among different buffer sites as they fight to gain ascendancy over each other and their activity emerges as the content of consciousness. I must emphasize that at present this is purely a working hypothesis.

The NRT has been an object of great interest to neuroscientists for the last thirty years. Figure 7.1 is an illustration of this nucleus and related thalamic nuclei. All inputs to the cortex from the relay nuclei of the thalamus pierce the NRT, and descending axons from the cortex back to the thalamus also penetrate it. Both sets of axons give off connections that make synaptic contact with cells on the NRT.

The NRT has been regarded as a set of gates controlling access of information into and out of the cortex. Over a decade ago one of the experts on this wrote:

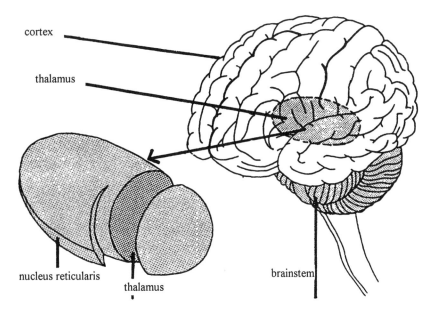

Figure 7.1
Thalamus and nucleus reticularis thalami (NRT). (From Kandel and Schwartz 1985; redrawn with permission in Taylor 1993c)

Situated like a thin nuclear sheet draped over the lateral and anterior surface of the thalamus, it has been likened to the screen grid interposed between the cathode and anode in the triode or pentode vacuum tube.

Physiological studies show that stimulation of parts of the thalamus or the subcortical white matter lead to high-frequency burst discharges in the reticular nucleus. Early ideas that the NRT projected widely and diffusely to the cortex have now been discounted, and the only output from it is back to the thalamus. How specific this return is is hard to determine, although it is well documented that certain parts of the nucleus are dominated by inputs from a particular sensory system. However, there appears to be a great deal of overlap in terminations of axons from thalamic nuclei onto it. Since dendrites of NRT cells may extend over considerable distances, even more than 1 mm, a single NRT cell receives input from several thalamic nuclei.

The structure of the NRT was gradually unraveled by painstaking probings over many years by a host of neuroanatomists, such as

Americans Scheibel and Scheibel (1966, 1972). Its form as a sheet hanging over the thalamus, and even the geometrical shapes of its nerve cells, have been carefully catalogued. Added interest in the NRT arose because it was discovered to be the source of global waves of electrical activity spreading over the whole cortex during sleep. This shows that it plays an important role in global control of cortical activity, a feature we require to explain the unity of consciousness.

How might such global control be achieved by the NRT? To answer that we have to know how well its cells are connected to each other; the better connected they are, the easier global waves of activity will flow over the NRT, and the more effectively it will exercise global control. Normal nerve cells send connections to other cells by long smooth axons. These connect to the cell body or its extensions, the dendrites, shown in figure 4.1. So cells normally connect by way of:

cell → axon → dendrites or body of other cell.

Something special happens in the NRT. Careful studies, some using million-fold magnification of the electron microscope, showed that NRT cells have additional connections directly between their dendrites. These are the dendrodendritic synapses, which also exist in the outer layer of the retina, thereby enabling the average of light falling over the whole retina by this sheet of cells to be calculated effectively. In other words, dendrodendritic synapses are good for long-range communication of nerve cell activity by smooth passage of this information from cell to cell, and not by patchy axon outgrowths of cells. The synapses cut out the axon "middle-man" and allow the cells to be more uniformly and closely coupled to each other. It is interesting that these connections occur in some species including cats and primates, but not in rats (Deschenes et al. 1985; O'Hara and Lieberman 1985). If suggestions about the importance of the NRT for supporting various characteristics of consciousness are valid, we can begin to uncover species differences in conscious experience. Table 7.1 examines such differences in properties of NRT.

Not only are NRT cells extremely well connected to each other, thereby inhibiting each other, they also provide inhibitory feedback to the thalamic sites that feed them. These features have long been recognized as being an important source of cortical control. In sleep it was noted earlier

Table 7.1
Species differences in properties of NRT

Property of NRT	Rat	Cat, primate
Dendrodendritic synapses	No	Yes
Inhibitory neurons in nonsensory thalamic nuclei	No	Yes
Inhibitory interneurons in lateral geniculate nucleus (thalamic nucleus devoted to visual input)	Yes	Yes
NRT connected to anterior thalamic nuclei	Yes	No

that the NRT acts as the generator of global waves across cortex. What is its role in the awake state?

Experiments with MEG support the possibility of the global influence of the NRT on the human cortex when awake. On human subjects hearing an auditory "click," it was found (Llinás and Ribary 1991) that a wave of neural activity traveled from the front to the back of the auditory cortex. A similar wave was observed traveling in a similar direction subcortically, but preceding the cortical wave by about 3 msec. That is exactly the amount of time it takes for activity to travel from the thalamus up to the cortex. The only well-connected subcortical region that would seem able to support such a traveling wave is the NRT. This suggested a model for the observed activity waves in which the NRT is given importance as being critically involved in the production of such a wave (figure 7.2).

Further evidence about the importance of the NRT for global cortical activity comes from work in dogs and rats (Skinner and Yingling 1977; Villa 1987) showing that current fed into electrodes stuck into the frontal lobes can cause strong activation on the rear part of the NRT. This is best understood if the NRT is acting in a global manner, with activity over its whole surface coordinated by its internal connectivity.

How effectively global control is exerted by the NRT over the whole cortex could be discovered by destroying the NRT with a selective chemical and observing changes in behavior. So far that has not been done because it is difficult to destroy the NRT without at the same time causing damage to nearby areas; in the future it is hoped that such a selective experiment will be performed.

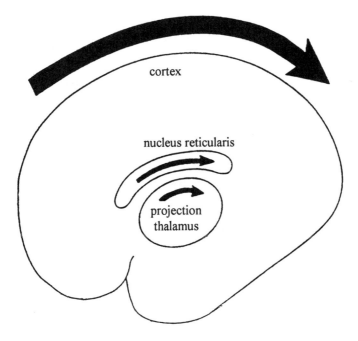

Figure 7.2
Wave of nerve cell activity observed by MEG techniques, and explained as involving cortical, thalamic, and NRT correlated activity. (From Llinas and Ribary 1993)

An alternative is to observe changes in behavior in transgenic mice in which a crucial gene has been modified so that NRT no longer functions properly. Steps have been taken along this path, although NRT has not yet been knocked out completely. But such a possibility is not far away; the NRT hypothesis is close to being tested.

In summary, the NRT is a thin, continuous sheet of mutually inhibitory cells lying over the top and sides of the thalamus. It exerts important global control over the cortex at the beginning of sleep by synchronizing oscillations over it, and has global action in the waking state, when it is involved in generating waves of activity that spread form the frontal region backward. It can support competition in activity among different sites of cortex, although we have no direct experimental evidence for that as yet.

We can now develop a detailed neural model for producing the experience of the unity of consciousness using the NRT.

The "Conscious I"

The next step is to construct a specific neural model to test the conjecture that, through global competition on itself, the NRT can indeed achieve global control of cortical activity. What are the principles, based on the simplest known features of the NRT, that would be behind any such model?

Simulation studies carried out by a number of research teams indicated that, in terms of a simple model, the NRT can function as a supporter of competition among activities at nearby cortical areas (LaBerge, Carter, and Brown 1992). This competition allows the largest of the activities to destroy that of its neighbors. These local competitive abilities of lateral inhibitory nets was analyzed more fully by mathematical tools (Hadeler 1974; Taylor and Alavi 1995). The present problem is to determine if the thalamic-NRT-cortex system can achieve global competition right across cortex, and not just support competition at a local level. In other words, can some localized activity on cortex battle against other activities at distant cortical sites so as ultimately to destroy them? Furthermore, it is important to find out if the thalamus-NRT-cortex system could support a traveling wave of activity commencing, say, at the front of the NRT sheet and moving steadily backward; such a mode of action would agree with experimental results I described in the previous section.

My research colleague Farrukh Alavi (then a research student) and I constructed a simplified model of the thalamus-NRT-cortex system using underlying neural network ideas (Taylor 1992a,b; Taylor and Alavi 1993, 1995; Alavi and Taylor 1995) and explored it both mathematically and by simulation. The wiring diagram of the neural network model is composed of three layers of cells, those of the cortex, NRT, and thalamus (figure 7.3). The cortical and main thalamic cells are excitatory (so exciting colleagues to which they signal) and the cells of the NRT are inhibitory (clamping down those they gossip with). The connections among these cell groups are shown in the figure, with NRT cells feeding back inhibition to both inhibitory and excitatory thalamic cells. The output of each of the neurons is assumed to be a smoothly increasing function of the total activity arriving on it from other cells.

The only connection not specified completely in the model is that on the NRT sheet itself. There are well documented normal lateral connections

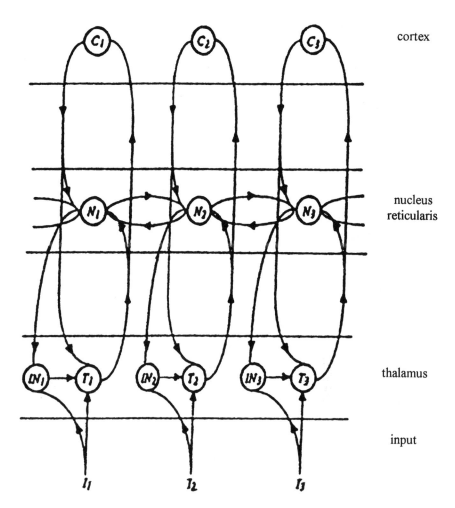

cortex

nucleus
reticularis

thalamus

input

Figure 7.3
Wiring diagram of the main model of the thalamus-NRT-cortex system. Input I
is sent to both the thalamic relay cell T and the inhibitory interneurons IN; the
latter cells also feed the thalamic cells. Output from the thalamic cells goes up
to the corresponding cortical cell C, which returns its output to the same thalamic
cell. Both axons TC and CT send an axon collateral to the corresponding NRT
cell N. There is axonal output from N to IN as well as collaterals to neighboring
NRT cells; there are also dendrodendritic synapses between NRT cells. (With
permission from Taylor and Alavi, 1995)

between the cells on the NRT, as well as more specialized dendrodendritic synapses in cat, monkey, and human. We can relate this special structure, the dendrodendritic synapses, to that of the outer layer of the retina on the basis of these findings. I noted earlier that the retina also has such dendrodendritic synapses and functions to average over space incoming light signals arriving on photoreceptive retinal input cells. Processing by this outer layer of cells removes redundancy in the input signal, one that is constant across the retina is totally redundant (it contains almost no information) so is not transmitted, a valuable property.

The signal in the retina resulting after the outer layer has done its bit in removing redundancy from the input signal, when analyzed in a manner that emphasizes the denseness of nerve cells and their intimate interconnectivity, possesses many of the quantitative features observed in the living system. Our use of a network of interacting cells, with an intimate contact between cells achieved through dendrodendritic synapses, is both an understandable and a useful model for early vision.

For these reasons I applied a similar approach to that I used earlier for the retina (Taylor 1990) to the NRT sheet. That is why I called this model the "conscious I," with its analogy to the eye. The NRT acts like a further retina, surrounding the thalamus where all inputs enter, and inspecting inputs to ensure that only the most salient get past its watchful gaze. The NRT can also focus on various parts of the input scene, as does the eye through its movement. To understand how that is achieved, we go back to details of the NRT model.

Strong lateral connections, achieved by dendrodendritic synapses between NRT cells, are now included in the model. The most important resulting feature is that neural activity on the NRT sheet can be regarded as a form of heat that flows along the sheet as heat does on an iron bar. This simple analogy allows us to transfer ideas and understanding from the flow of heat to the flow of activity in a neural network.

The rate of heat flow is determined by a diffusion constant. If you heat one end of an iron bar the other end will gradually heat up as a wave of heat flows from hotter to cooler regions. The bigger the diffusion constant for the material of the bar, the more rapidly heat flows along it. In the case of the NRT something surprising occurs: the diffusion constant is negative. In other words, flow is in the opposite direction to that of the flow of heat from hot to cold. Neural activity flows from cold to hot, or more precisely from regions with low neural activity to those with higher activity! Clumps of high neural activity therefore form.

This reverse flow of activity is explained by a similar feature of what we might call negative diffusion observed in a number of physical systems (Iguchi and Langenberg 1980; Berggren and Huiberman 1978). Formation of global structures of patterned activity was studied in pattern formation and growth on animal surfaces (Cohen and Murray 1981; Murray 1989), such as spots on a leopard or stripes on a zebra. The appearance of illusory visual shapes in drug-induced states was explained by a global wave of neural activity on hyperexcitable visual cortex (Ermentrout and Cowan 1978). The plane wave excitations of cortex expected in this case are shown in column b of figure 7.4; the corresponding retinal image is composed of spiral shapes shown in column a. Of interest, they are the same shape as those experienced by drug addicts on a "high." So a whole range of physical phenomena can be explained by means of a common idea—the reverse flow of heat in a suitable medium.

The flow of neural activity from regions of low to those of higher excitation values leads to the break-up of constant neural activity covering the whole NRT sheet. Waves of neural activity then arise, similar to those observed in the physical systems just mentioned. For large enough values of the strength of lateral inhibition among different NRT cells, such waves can be proved to arise by mathematical analysis.[2] They can also be observed in simulation; the result of one of these by Faroukh Alavi and me is shown in figure 7.5. The global wave pattern on the NRT is clear, and arises from a steady localized input onto a selected set of thalamic relay cells.

How the NRT supports cortical competition in a global manner in the model can be seen from the wiring diagram of figure 7.3.[3] Inputs fight their way to cortex through the relay cells of the thalamus. As they pass up through the NRT they give extra support to whatever activity is there. These NRT activities battle against others over long distances to produce a global wave of activity over the whole NRT, whose shape is determined by the strongest activity coming onto the NRT; thus the largest activity sculpts and dominates all others. The inhibitory controlling action the NRT exerts turns off the inhibitory interneurons in thalamus, and does

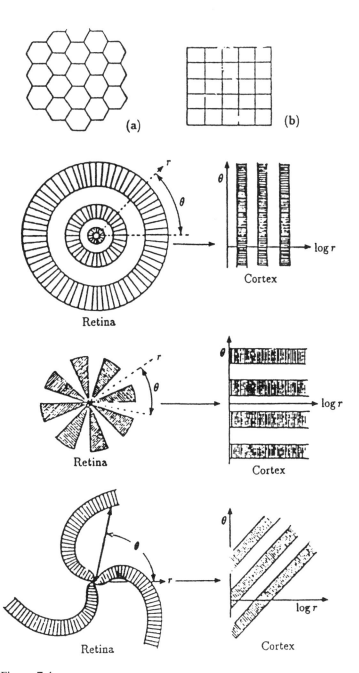

Figure 7.4
Corresponding patterns expected in (a) cortex and (b) retina when plane waves are excited in cortex due to drug-enhanced synaptic strengths. (Reprinted with permission from Ermentrout and Cowan 1978)

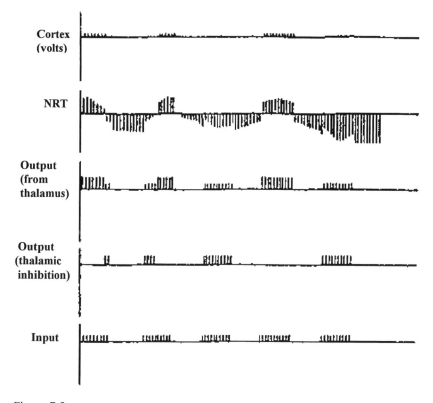

Figure 7.5
Simulation run showing full global control with short-wavelength periodic input.
Note the removal of parts of the input in cortex, governed by the nature of the
NRT wave it has created. (Reprinted with permission from Taylor and Alair,
1995)

so most effectively for those NRT cells at the peaks of the wave created
on the NRT; the related input can flow in even more strongly. This, then
is a global competitive control action over cortical activity.

By analogy a large enough scrum will create a wave of activity over the
heaving mass of men. It would be an interesting phenomenon to observe!

Candidate 2: Inhibitory Neurons in Cortex
To be thorough, we must consider other alternatives to the NRT as the
global controller for posterior consciousness. These can provide further
support to the long-range competition to give unity to consciousness. Our

second neural candidate is in the cortex itself. Excitatory neurons in the cortex send long-range axons to other areas of the cortex. If these cortico-cortical excitatory connections directly feed to inhibitory cortical neurons, they could spread their inhibitory influence around them to damp down the excitatory activity. In this way they could support long-range inhibitory influence of one cortical region on another. More pictur-esquely, a lot of different gossips, telephoned by a distant (exciting) gos-sip, could damp down activity effectively around themselves as they spread their news in their inimitable (inhibitory) manner and in the best of all possible taste (so whoever they talk to becomes silent for a while).

Some clues indicate that the direct corticocortical route is important. For example, global oscillations of neural activity were observed at about 40 cycles per second, which are common across a number of brain regions (Bressler 1994). These could be explained by the effects of such long-range action of excitatory cells onto inhibitory ones, an excitatory cell sending its activity to an inhibitory one that then damps down the cell activating it. The activity in this cell then dies away, so it no longer supports the inhibitory cell, which itself dies away in turn. But then the excitatory cell regains its strength, and the cycle starts again. That leads to oscillatory activity as the cycle of activation, inhibition, dying away, reduction of inhibition, and regaining of activity repeats itself over and over again.

Evidence coming from brain imaging indicates the suppressive action of various regions on others. Consider, for example, solving tasks that require holding concepts in mind over tens of seconds. Increased brain activity was observed in frontal lobes for times longer than about 10 seconds, with a related reduction of activity in other regions (which may otherwise interfere with the concepts being held in mind). This reduction of activity in one set of areas by another could be caused by the first areas sending activity most preponderantly to the inhibitory cells of the second areas. These cells would then reduce the activity in their own locales by local inhibition, in which they are well versed.

Why isn't such a mechanism more important than that using the NRT? We have no answer at this juncture. More experimental information is needed, and so for the present we should consider both candidates.

There is also a third candidate that we should not discount, involving inhibitory cells in the basal ganglia.

Conclusions and Summary

I suggested the NRT as a possible candidate for the site of global control of cortical activity. Suitably coupled to cortex and thalamus, global waves of activity on it are able to suppress some thalamic inputs and enhance others. Cortical inputs are similarly supported and enhanced, or reduced. The resulting model leads, by analysis and simulation, to global competition between inputs to cortex and between resulting cortical activities. The global activity predicted is expected to be observable by MEG measurements. Presently, only one supportive result (Llinás and Ribary 1991) demonstrates a backward-going wave of activity brought about by a click played into the ears of a conscious subject. At single-cell level, correlations among activities in distant portions of the NRT have been observed (Skinner and Yingling 1977; Villa 1987). The present prediction is that such long-range correlations will be crucially related to the emergence of consciousness supported by the winning activity.

We have another possible neural candidate for producing consciousness, by spreading inhibition locally from inhibitory neurons being accessed from afar by excitatory neurons. This is a strong contender, and may contribute in addition to effects from our first candidate.

At present we must include both the NRT and corticocortical effects to build a complete model supportive of the unity of consciousness. So far we only have a simplified model of the first. Let us put it to work, not forgetting that the other candidate may have ultimately to be involved in the activities for which we presently consider only the NRT. In particular we have two possible neural candidates for unifying consciousness.

In a remarkable series of experiments Benjamin Libet and colleagues (1964) created consciousness on demand, so to speak, by applying electrical current to the bare cortical surface of awake subjects while they were being operated on for various movement defects. Patients felt as if the backs of their hands had been touched. The results of these experiments showed that it takes time for conscious awareness to be created. The particular way that the time required to create consciousness depends on the strength of the current being used is amazingly simple and specific, and a feature that our models of control and coordination of consciousness must face up to. That is considered in the next chapter.

8

Winning Control

That spoke the vacant mind.
—Oliver Goldsmith

A lot of machinery has to whir away behind the scenes before consciousness can emerge full-blown the way it does. This emergence is the most critical phenomenon on which theories of consciousness must be based. For it has to bridge the explanatory gap between neural activity and inner experience; the neural activity that corresponds to a nonconscious state is somehow transformed into that which miraculously supports consciousness. We meet the hard problem yet again: how does this miraculous transformation occur?

That this is a good level on which to attack the problem of consciousness was suggested by the distinguished neurophysiologist Lord Adrian over forty years ago:

I think there is reasonable hope that we may be able to sort out the particular activities which coincide with quite simple mental processes like seeing or hearing. At all events that is the first thing a physiologist must do if he is trying to find out what happens when we think and how the mind is influenced by what goes on in the brain. (Adrian 1952)

Investigation of the emergence of raw feels is appropriate, since they are unencumbered by a number of extra factors that complicate the features of consciousness when raw feels are transmuted to ever higher levels of consciousness. Provided a subject is in an environment that is neutral and tranquil, and he or she is accustomed both to that environment and to the experiment being performed, creation of awareness at its most primitive level can be analyzed experimentally without too many added complications; its deeper secrets should thereby be exposed. We must, however, be prepared to do some preparatory spade work before we can hope to have even the briefest glimpse of these secrets. We will start to do that now, but we have to develop a strong enough neural framework in this part of the book to allow us to enter the final lap and approach the winner's post in part IV.

We are helped in our quest by a series of beautiful experiments performed initially over thirty years ago by Libet and colleagues (Libet 1987; Libet et al. 1964) that give amazing clues as to the detailed manner in which brain activity is related to the emergence of sensory awareness. They used the response of conscious subjects to electrical stimulation applied directly to the bare surface of their somatosensory cortex. As electric current applied to an electrode on the cortical surface was increased, the subject would report a sense of a touch experienced on the back of one hand; the corresponding current at which that awareness emerged was then noted.

Libet's experiment has the essential features necessary to bridge the gap between brain activity and awareness: the report of conscious subjects and detailed control of the experience by the experimenter. These subjects, in preparation for an operation to help cure Parkinson's disease, spasticity, or head tremor, had become accustomed to the operating room environment, so the experimental set-up was ideal to probe the mysteries of the mind. The results led to some remarkable and far-reaching conclusions about the manner in which normal awareness is attained, and they will help guide our further search for the brain mechanisms at the basis of consciousness. Simultaneously, in terms of their detailed quantitative character, the results support the competitive mechanism for the emergence of consciousness proposed in the previous chapter.

These are not the only experiments in which the human brain has been subjected to the probing gaze of the researcher. Many people have had thin electrodes inserted deep into the brain to determine where massive bursts of neural activity are causing them to have epileptic seizures, thus enabling a map to be made of the regions to be removed surgically. During these operations Canadian neurosurgeon Wilder Penfield tested the effects of electrical stimulation of various regions near the disturbed cortex. He, and others since then, found amazing localization of function:

past memories were brought back and past scenes relived by patients while conscious. These results proved of great importance in building up the picture we now have of the location of function and memory in the brain. But only Libet and his colleagues were brave enough to attempt to determine details of how consciousness was created by injecting carefully measured amounts of current into the bare brain from the outside. The results are astounding.

The first questions we will ask about Libet's results are:

1. What are the characteristics of the stimulating current applied to the patients' somatosensory cortex that bring about sensory awareness and nothing else (e.g., no muscular contractions)?
2. What is the neural activity that could explain these characteristics?
3. Why must it take about 300 to 500 msec to develop awareness by applying external electric current?

In particular, the most intriguing aspect is the time during which directly injected electrical current must persist for awareness of the stimulus to be experienced at all. The necessary 300 to 500 msec found by Libet and co-workers is considerably longer than normal reaction time, which is only about 150 msec or so in most people. What is the need for consciousness if it occurs only after response has been made to an input signal? Such a result made some psychologists claim (Velmans 1992) that consciousness has no use, and it is purely an epiphenomenon. We must return to that later when other aspects of consciousness have been explored.

It is surprising that Libet's results have not been analyzed earlier, although data were available in the mid-1960s. However, as I indicated previously, the prevailing atmosphere during the 1960s, 1970s, and 1980s was much against exploration of conscious awareness as a part of science. Some even denied the existence of consciousness. The atmosphere has undoubtedly changed enormously, not only in psychology but also in neural modeling. We can even recognize the beginning of the race for consciousness. It is timely to go back to earlier work that has been neglected and explore its implications.

Another feature is worth mentioning that might help explain the delay in bringing physically based notions to bear on Libet's work. The study was performed by neuroscientists and surgeons appropriately concerned for their patients, but curious to explore sensory awareness during operations on them. In the 1960s and 1970s the physical sciences kept more to their own backyard. "Matter" in increasingly ordered states was easier to probe and understand than the messy wet-ware of the brain. With increasing interest in the subject, the need for interdisciplinary endeavors that move across traditional subject boundaries grew. Such movement is now clearly strong and here to stay, as evident from investigations into the brain and mind presently under way.

A considerable body of work could be of great relevance to our quest— psychophysics, the study of physical stimuli and their relation to sensory reactions (Stevens 1968; Graham 1989; Geisler 1989). However, it is clear from reports of work in this area that the important emphasis in psychophysics has been placed on low-level analyzers, with little concern for the nature of the experience of the subject being experimented on. It is almost as if the subject were unimportant and only the response to stimuli were relevant. Yet again the dead hand of antiawareness ruled the day, as in other areas of psychology. But the experimental results of Libet do not allow that easy way out, for the experiencing observer is now where the buck stops.

Creation of Awareness

The experiments of Libet (Libet 1987; Libet et al. 1964) were performed in cooperative patients being treated for movement disorder, mainly Parkinson's disease. After the relevant portion of the skull was removed to expose the cortex under general anesthesia, the patient was given time to recover. Tests were then carried out on the awake patient, each lasting for from 30 to 90 minutes; the sessions were terminated when the patient demonstrated reluctance or the responses became unreliable, which was often associated with fatigue. In all, ninety-nine tests were carried out in ninety-two patients.

The procedure was to place a flat stimulating electrode on the exposed area of cortex in the primary somatosensory region (at the top of the brain). Pulsed current, usually with 60 or so pulses per second, each lasting for a fraction of a microsecond, was then fed into the electrode; its position was varied so as to require the least amount of current to cause the patient to report the sensation of a slight touch on some portion of the hand on the opposite side of the body or, less frequently, on the wrist or forearm.

Before therapeutic stimuli were given to the deeper cortex as part of the treatment to destroy damaged or incorrectly performing brain regions, tests were performed to determine the stimulus characteristics that produced conscious awareness. Various forms of these were carried out, both at and above the minimum threshold for the onset of conscious experience of the brief sensation of touch.

The experiments had two parts. In the first, the minimum current was determined that would result in persistent awareness of the sensory experience caused by the current, such as a tingling sensation on the back of the hand. Current below this value caused no sensory awareness, however long it was applied; that somewhat above it might cause more complex sensations and even movement of the hand.

The second part of the experiment determined the shortest time for a given current and at a given frequency to produce sensory awareness of being touched. This shortest-onset time decreased only if the strength of the current was increased in a suitable fashion.

The manner in which the threshold current varied with the frequency of pulsed current was one of the most important results of the experiments. Figure 8.1 indicates somewhat similar results for seven patients. The curve of the threshold current is plotted against the frequency of the current pulses applied to the stimulating electrode. The resulting variation of threshold current against pulse repetition frequency over a broad range led Libet to the conclusion that "threshold current is roughly proportional to the pulse frequency raised to the power −0.5."

We expect a decrease of the current required to produce conscious awareness as the frequency is increased, since there will be more electrical power to activate suitable brain areas as the frequency of the current pulses is increased. However, the detailed form of the relationship (increasing the frequency by a factor of 4 reduces the threshold current by a factor of 2) was not explained by Libet. We can deduce by simple algebra a simple result from Libet's statement that consciousness requires a minimum amount of electrical power to be switched on. In other words,

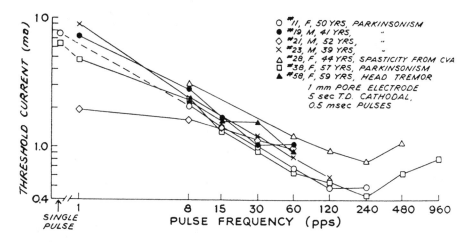

Figure 8.1
Threshold currents required to elicit a sensation using 5-second train durations
at different pulse frequencies. Each curve represents a set of determinations made
at one session for each of the seven subjects of the graph. (With permission from
Libet et al. 1964)

consciousness has a highly lawful "turn-on"; it is not loosely coupled to
material processes but is controlled by a precise formula.

Libet further discovered that once the sensation had been experienced
it continued as long as the minimal current was still applied. He and his
colleagues concluded: ". . . threshold current is relatively independent of
train duration, when this is greater than 0.5–1 second."

These experiments led to the simple rule that, provided just enough
electrical power achieves the turn-on of awareness, continuing to supply
the same amount of power enables that conscious sensation to continue
almost indefinitely.

We need not really be too surprised by such a result if the electrical
character of brain activity is taken into account. The brain is composed
of electrically charged nerve cells passing pulses of electricity among each
other. As we should expect from this electrical activity, it must come
under the control of the laws of electrical circuits. Nevertheless, it is remarkable, since it indicates an absolutely essential role in the creation of
consciousness, and not just of any form of neural activity. To explore
even more precisely the emergence of consciousness, it is necessary to
turn to the second part of the experiments.

The minimum time for the applied current to achieve awareness is about 0.5 to 1 second when set at the minimum threshold value. To attain faster breakthrough to awareness, it was found necessary to inject an increased current into the patient's bare cortex. The results are summarized in the curve of figure 8.2 (B. Libet, personal communication, 1995).

As we see, each curve is composed of two parts. The flat portion (region II) is for large enough durations of the applied pulse trains of electricity, and corresponds to current values independent of the pulse train duration. These satisfy the quotation from Libet as the pulse frequency is varied, and they are the results of the first part of the experiment. It is the curved portions of the curves between the train duration and the applied current, at a given pulse frequency, that are new (region I). As noted by Libet (Libet 1987; Libet et al. 1964), "When the train duration of the applied current pulses (denoted TD) are reduced below the level of about 0.5–1.0 seconds the threshold current values begin to rise rather sharply." It is in this regimen of increased current to create awareness that a new feature arises. This curved portion of the curves is region II.

Analysis of the summarized curves (Taylor 1996a) indicates that they are fitted by an extension of the rule we deduced earlier by changing electrical power to electrical energy. Again this is reasonable; power is the rate of use of energy. Continuing to supply energy at a given rate corresponds to supplying power at that rate, allowing the changeover from the regimen described by region I in the curve to region II.

The above rules may be summarized as two beautifully simple laws for the creation of consciousness.

Law 1: to achieve reportable sensory experience at a fixed frequency, a critical amount of electrical energy must be supplied to a primary cortical region by a stimulating electrode.

Law 2: To continue a reportable sensory experience once it has been achieved by a stimulating electrode, it is necessary to continue to supply a critical amount of electrical power to the primary cortex.

The laws are similar to those of electrical circuit phenomena, emphasizing once again the remarkably concrete physical support by the brain for consciousness. Furthermore, this is specified quantitatively by simple electrical laws related to the minimum energy requirements to turn cortical activity on and keep it on. The laws indicate a strong "lawful" aspect

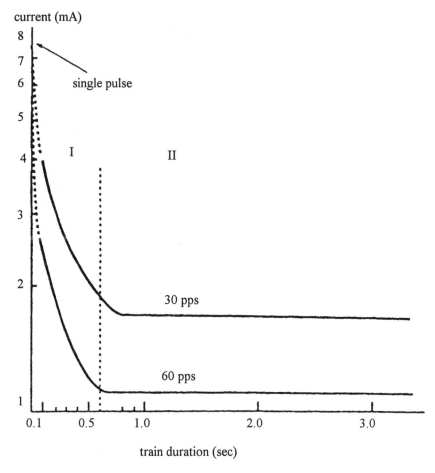

Figure 8.2
Intensity/train duration combinations for stimuli just adequate to elicit a threshold conscious experience of somatic sensation when applied to somatosensory cortex. Curves are for two different pulse repetition frequencies. (Reprinted with permission from Libet 1966)

of the emergence and continuation of consciousness, which has important implications for its effective physical grounding and modeling.

Competition for Consciousness?

We can interpret the various experiments of Libet and co-workers in terms of the manner in which higher-level processing modules (both cortical and thalamic) are used in analysis of sensory input. Libet did this experimentally by leapfrogging certain low-level analyzers, especially peripheral ones such as on the surface of the skin and in the spinal cord. Stimulating electrodes were inserted directly into higher level thalamic and cortical modules to reproduce similar sensory awareness to that arising from peripheral stimulation.

To explain the phenomenon of detection of a stimulus with or without awareness we need high-level analyzers (say at thalamic and cortical levels) that have access to suitable neural circuitry that will produce awareness. They must be some of those being activated in Libet's experiments. These ultimately activate the neural circuits for awareness (figure 8.3). Direct throughput from high-level analyzers activated observers' responses for detection without awareness, which also occurred in later experiments, whereas activation of the highest-level awareness circuits produced observers' responses with awareness.

The patients in Libet's experiments were aware of their surroundings. A particular awareness circuit, that for touch, was activated by directly injecting current into their cortex in a more "effective" manner than another one for which there was previously awareness from peripheral input; this could have been from, say, the visual scene of the operating room sent to the higher-level visual analyzer. The basic question, then, is how a choice is made between these various modalities, so that input to a single one, in this case for touch, gains awareness and at the same time awareness of visual input must be destroyed.

At the level involved with emergence of consciousness we face the problem of combining inputs so that the output from the neural awareness module contains only information of one input. It seems difficult to consider methods of combining inputs to achieve such an output other than through a competitive or winner-take-all strategy; the strong-arm game

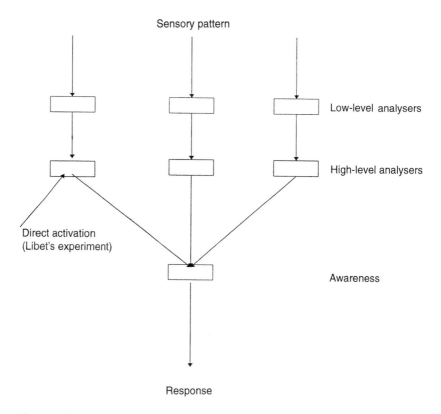

Figure 8.3
A general framework for the models of pattern vision discussed in psychophysics.
(Adapted from Graham 1989)

again! Evidence exists for such a form of processing in visual cortex as
well as in inferotemporal cortex (Salzman and Newsome 1994; Desimone
1995). This supports some of the comments we made in the previous
chapter about competition as a source for the unity of consciousness.

In all, it would appear that some form of competition is most appropriate for the final selection of access to awareness.

The Competitive Gate

We can now return to one of our candidates for the global competition
for consciousness, the thalamus-NRT-cortex system, and consider in

Table 8.1
Nature of stimulus necessary to produce consciousness

Site of stimulus	Nature of stimulus
Skin	Single pulse
VPL or LM thalamic nuclei	Train of pulses
Cortex	Train of pulses

Data reported by Libet et al. (1979, 1991).

what manner it can help support competition between inputs in different modalities to explain the data of Libet et al. How might the NRT, acting as a net in which clumping of activity occurs by means of lateral inhibitory connections described in chapter 7 (playing the strong-arm game), enable such a competition to be run? An important aspect of Libet's results helps answer that.

Cortical activity needs a long enough time to gain final access to awareness, for either peripheral stimuli or the more directly applied electrical pulses to thalamus or cortex. This is one of the most important messages we can take from Libet's work: consciousness must have a long enough duration of neural activity to emerge; this was emphasized in the previous section. The properties of the required length of time of these impulses are summarized in table 8.1.

Entries in this table support the more detailed figure 8.4, in which input first goes to a set of preprocessing-semantic modules. These give a higher-level analysis of the inputs without necessarily any competitive interaction between alternative interpretations or consciousness of their contents; they have not yet reached awareness. The more highly encoded material is then fed to buffer working memories, which can hold activity over several seconds. It is conjectured that such holding of activity is important to allow competition between modalities to be run. The short-lived activities on the lower neural sites will have disappeared before the competition has run its course, so only the buffered activity will count. In the strong-arm game those who leave early will not win. And it is only of the winner that consciousness emerges.

This suggestion is supported by the results of Libet and co-workers shown in table 8.1. We can understand the need for the pulse duration to last at least half a second for a somatosensory cortical stimulus to

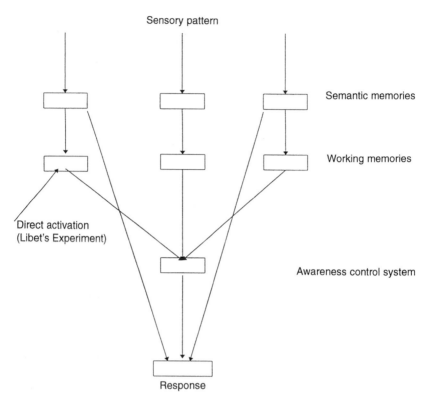

Figure 8.4
An extension of the decision model of figure 7.3 extended by addition of high-level buffer working memories, an awareness control module, and motor response systems.

reach awareness as arising through the artificial creation of a buffer working memory module by the persisting injected current. The extended pulse train creates an artificial buffer working memory to function in an inter-modality competition, especially to compete against activity already in control of consciousness, such as visual awareness of the operating room. I must emphasize the importance of Libet's results again: an artificial buffer site must be created to beat any previously existing winner of consciousness and turn on awareness of the neural activity related to the site. Consciousness takes time for activity to enter it, one of its most important features.[1]

A theoretical explanation of the two laws summarizing Libet's results can be given by means of a mathematical analysis,[2] but I will spare the reader. It is also possible to model them by simulation of a simple neural network model (Taylor and Alavi 1993; Taylor 1996a). This consisted of 400 neurons arranged to model the human cortex, NRT, and thalamus in a very simple manner, as shown in the model in figure 7.3. An initial input was given to the cortical model neurons to correspond to activity of which the model was initially "conscious." An additional input was then imposed at a later time on the cortical layer to correspond to the current applied to the bare cortex of one of Libet's patients. The time it took for this input to destroy the first (and so become conscious in its turn) varied with the strength of the input (corresponding to the strength of the current applied to the patient's cortex; figure 8.5). It is similar to the variation of current against time as measured by Libet and colleagues in humans (as shown in figure 8.2).

Our simulation and our mathematical analysis support my claim that the artificial working memory site, created by the continued electrode activation of patients' cortex, can tap into the thalamus-NRT-cortex system. In particular, the NRT acts as a competitive arena. Activity in one region of the NRT being fed by nearby cortex can be used to control and even turn off activity in another area of cortex.

A similarly successful explanation of Libet's results has not been forthcoming in terms of the second candidate of the previous chapter—inhibition being run internally in the cortex—but that may be possible. It has just not been attempted.

Summary and Discussion

I made various conjectures in trying to answer the questions raised at the beginning of the chapter, in particular, as to the nature of the neural activity underlying the artificial creation of consciousness by Libet and colleagues.

Certain laws that summarize the process of consciousness creation were deduced from Libet's data. These laws can be expressed very simply: first, a requisite amount of electrical energy is necessary to capture the

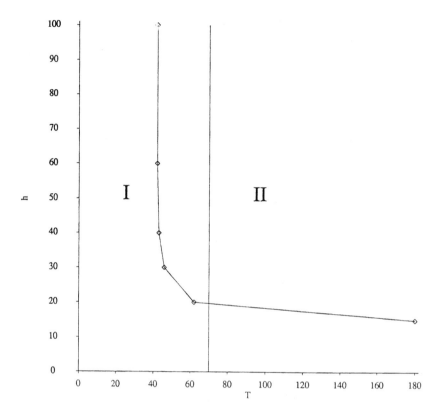

Figure 8.5
Results of simulation on the competition for an input to gain cortex. After an input on a set of neurons in the circuit of figure 6.4 was established, a new input, of height h, was set up on another set of neurons. The time T for this new input to destroy the first one is plotted against h. It is similar to the curve of figure 8.2, with the division of the dependence of h on T being split into two parts in each case.

consciousness of a patient, and second, enough electrical power is required to keep that consciousness turned on.

Additional experimental data were then used to support a competitive model for consciousness in which different sites of long-term holding of processed activity (the buffer working memory modules), compete among each other for access to consciousness. Libet's method of using a sequence of injected pulses of electrical activity of long duration created,

I suggested, an artificial buffer working memory module that could enter effectively into competition against other sites of buffer working memories, one of which was supporting the activity determining previous consciousness.

I made two crucial assumptions to be able to use the thalamus-NRT-cortex model (or any other one) of competition for consciousness:

1. Consciousness arises by competition among different neural activities, each preprocessed to a suitable level before accessing suitable neural modules (buffer working memory modules) between which competition takes place.
2. Consciousness emerges when activity in any buffer module reaches a critical value.

I discussed the first assumption at length in this chapter. It is to the second that we now turn.

I can give various reasons to support this assumption. The detailed simulation in figure 8.5 shows how long-distance effects across the NRT can achieve destruction of inputs of which consciousness had already occurred. However, it is not at all clear how the winning activity, on an artificially created buffer working memory site, would actually lead to the experience of consciousness of the correspondingly encoded activity. It is possible to consider the context of the conscious experience, the whereabouts on the body surface from which it was thought to have arisen, as having been specified by the position of maximum electrode activation, to be encoded by the topographic representation of the body surface at that point. But what is the actual module to which access is obtained by winning the competition assumed under 1 and reaching the critical value given by assumption 2? We have no clear answer to this question from the experiments of Libet et al. They looked for special sites where it might be said that consciousness arises owing to special sorts of electrical activity observed there, but they could not find them. To obtain an answer to this question we have to develop the competitive model in more detail. Experiments that can help us do that will be evaluated in the next chapter before answers can be conjectured as to the nature of the awareness modules.

In the meantime let us turn to an important question we can answer: what is the response to the claim that "consciousness does not enter into human information processing" in the sense that it does not "enter into or causally influence the process"? Is consciousness purely an epiphenomenon, as concluded in that quotation, from the external objective point of view?

The answer, which we discuss more fully in chapter 9, is definitely no. It has the important role (among others) of singling out which interpretation of a given input appears the most correct from many alternatives available. This selection process (involving the binding together of various possible combinations of features to make object representations at a nonconscious level) may be unsuccessful if inputs are seen for only a very short time or are degraded. Illusory conjunctions of features— awareness of a red square and a green circle when briefly shown a red circle and a green square—may then lead to percepts of objects that were not actually present (Treisman 1988). So consciousness is not always accurate during the time it acts as a binder of different codes for an object.

It is natural at this point to ask a second question, namely, which is more accurate, the nonconscious level of processing or the conscious one? That question we begin to answer in the next chapter when we turn to the manner in which consciousness emerges from nonconscious activity. The nature of that activity is of great relevance here; it will be found, perhaps a surprise, that nonconscious activity may activate many interpretations, only a few of which may be consistent with the total context. This is efficient, since it will be valuable to have consistency imposed once only, and that at as late a stage as possible. It seems that consistency is achieved when consciousness emerges. That is explored in the context of word processing in the next chapter.

9
Breakthrough to Awareness

No, my mind baulks at it.
—Ivy Compton-Burnett

How can awareness break free from the cortical areas of unconsciousness? If we were smaller than a nerve cell we could voyage into these areas of the brain and try to break out ourselves through the starting gate. Would there even be any such gate, or would we find, as we traveled to ever higher regions in the brain, that imperceptibly the nerve cells interact with each other ever more efficiently and faster? We cannot make such an impossible voyage, so we will have to content ourselves with investigating more indirectly. We must probe from outside so as to disturb the brain in subtle ways that uncover enough clues for us to understand how to plan the break-out; the mind will balk no longer!

Our plan is to continue as before, to try to build a neural framework for consciousness. Such a framework should ultimately allow us to erect the bridge over the explanatory gap—if it can ever be done. We want to build as simple a model as possible that is also consistent with the crucial experimental features of the phenomena. If we can encapsulate the data in this manner we should have a much simpler set of features to attempt to understand and extend to cross the gap. The constant drive toward neural models is an attempt to simplify and codify the wealth of brain data relevant to consciousness, and so make the task more amenable to analysis. A word on notation: throughout this chapter consciousness means the passive part, although I drop the word "passive" for ease of reading. We discuss active consciousness in the next chapter.

One important feature is time: nonconscious activity must have a suitably long time to emerge into consciousness, as shown by the work of Libet et al. described in chapter 8. I developed two basic suggestions for the subtle but powerful creation of conscious awareness based on specialized buffer working memory modules, in which neural activity persists for a suitably long time. Let me restate them in a more compact and digestible form:

1. The competition for consciousness: awareness arises from competition between activities on different buffer modules.

2. The emergence of consciousness: the moment of emergence of consciousness occurs when the activity on a buffer site reaches a critical level, so winning the global competition.

These working memory sites must be fed with activity that has been preprocessed at a suitably high level in preprocessing modules to give the polished texture and feel of consciousness. They are the neural modules of working memory, which I discuss in more detail shortly.

Hypothesis 1, that consciousness arises from competition between activities on different buffer sites, I developed in the previous chapter in terms of the thalamus-NRT-cortex neural model of competition among different modalities. In the present chapter I want to construct a neural model for hypothesis 2, that consciousness emerges when the neural activity on a given buffer site reaches a critical level. In the process we will probe more closely the manner in which an input that has reached the semantic level of processing can influence activity from later input and change the speed with which the latter can burst forth into awareness.

The preprocessing module we will consider is one that codes for the semantics or meaning of words. The word "semantics" is a complex one, with numerous meanings. It must be considered especially carefully when we analyze the creation, by learning, of neural modules able to encode the semantics of objects. However, we will start simply. A semantic module for words is one for which words are encoded in some suitably organized neural module, with words that have similar meanings represented by neurons close to and excited by each other. The module acts thereby as a dictionary: inputting a word leads to the lighting up of nearby neurons representing similar words. This is exactly what happens when we look up a word in a dictionary—a set of words of similar meaning. Only nouns are considered here, so that a site for such a module is Wernicke's area in the temporal lobe, as shown by many studies in which loss of that area of the brain caused humans to lose the meanings of words.

We considered in chapters 7 and 8 a candidate neural model to change awareness from one modality to another. This change also occurs, although more smoothly, in a single modality alone. As you read these words you are continually changing your experience. It may be from a single word to the next, or it may be in phrases or sentences. But change occurs and must be understood. We will develop a neural model that will help us understand some of the features of how this change could occur.

Subliminal Priming

You experience the interesting and controversial phenomenon of subliminal processing when you are shown a stimulus very rapidly or faintly so that awareness of it does not quite occur. Rapid stimulus presentation can be achieved by masking the stimulus soon after it has been shown, such as by shining a jumbled array of lines onto a screen right after a word or a single letter has been shone briefly onto it. Although you say, "No, I didn't see anything," your later behavior can be changed by the exposure; you will have gained subliminal knowledge.

By carefully changing subliminally processed input, such as showing different letters or words, it is possible to demonstrate that modifications in the emergence of consciousness depend on previously subliminally processed words. For example, changes in reaction times to a decision as to whether or not a string of letters is a word (a lexical decision) can be brought about by changing a prior subliminally processed word. If it is similar in meaning to the later letter string, a response is faster than otherwise; knowledge is acquired in this manner even if one has no awareness of it. Such data are important grist to neural modelers' mill, and are used here to develop a neural model of the initial emergence of consciousness.

The phenomenon of subliminal perception has been explored actively over the last thirty years or more and has caused some to conclude that it does not even exist, in spite of anecdotal evidence to the contrary. Also at issue is the question as to what level the subliminally processed input attains; is it at letter, word,[1] or sentence level, for example?

The approach we take here follows the conclusion of American psychologists Cheesman and Merikle (Cheesman and Merikle 1985) that the phenomenon of subliminal perception does indeed exist, but that it is necessary to be careful in defining the threshold that is set for how long an input is experienced before it is masked. There appears to be both a subjective threshold and an objective one. The subjective threshold is set by ensuring that, below it, the subject reports no awareness at all of the input. The objective threshold arises if a forced-choice decision about the presence or absence of the input is just above chance level, even if the subject admits to absolutely no awareness on which to base the decision but was only guessing.

Under this separation of thresholds, below the objective threshold no information whatsoever about the input is acquired by the subject during exposure, whereas above that threshold, but below the subjective threshold, some sort of knowledge is obtained and biases response to later inputs. The subject has no awareness of the input.

The important experiment performed by Marcel in 1980 (Marcel 1980) showing that such bias occurs, required subjects to give a decision as to whether or not two strings of letters were actually words. He set the scene by shining a subliminally processed word just a second before the letter string. This subliminal word affected the reaction time to the next "word," even though subjects were not aware of the first word. But even more surprising, all possible meanings of the subliminal word were accessed, since they affected later words that had a similar meaning. For example, for the word "palm" both tree and hand meanings were subliminally activated.

This has an important relation to the broader nature of conscious experience. Earlier I claimed that the inner content of consciousness arises from those activities in appropriate memory structures that are activated by the input; these memories were proposed to consist of preprocessing and episodic memories. When there is data-driven awareness, with correspondingly little self-awareness, preprocessing memories and their relations are preponderant. It is these we are exploring here, and in particular the effect of previous activities, residing in buffer memory sites, on later inputs. We wish to discover if and how these earlier inputs can help nudge later ones through the consciousness barrier just a little faster (if they have similar meanings) or slower (if they disagree in meaning). Marcel's results are of crucial importance to help us understand that nudging and discover more about the barrier.

The model we can develop from Marcel's results is shown in figure 9.1. It has input first going to all possible meanings of words in a semantic memory module. The output is then sent to a buffer working memory, the phonological store. Good neuroanatomical support exists for this simple model. We have to incorporate the details of the workings of the separate modules to extend the model beyond the bare wiring diagram and relate it to the facts of subliminal processing.

The form to be taken for the semantic memory net has been outlined. It is assumed to be activated by inputs of the experiment under discussion. The net is considered to be composed of nerve cells, each dedicated to a particular meaning of a word. That is an assumption whose correctness depends on what semantics means. We can divorce such a deep problem from the final representation of the semantics, say, of words, for which a more distributed representation, involving many nerve cells representing a given word, is more natural; we will try to keep our model as simple as possible.

We made a strong claim in the model of figure 9.1 that information can be processed right up to and including the meanings of words before consciousness of it occurs. This is indeed a high level of processing, and different from the proposal that consciousness emerges at a very low level. We have more to say about this for vision later; for words, good evidence supports the model besides the work of Marcel. Let us consider three forms of it. First, there are experiments on what is called parafoveal viewing (Di Pace et al. 1991; Fuentes et al. 1994). The fovea is that region in the retina with the highest density of cells and so the greatest acuity. We move our eyes so that we can look at an object through the foveae if we want to see it in detail. Farther out from the central region scanned by the fovea is the parafoveal region, which extends from about 1 to 5 degrees of visual angle from the center of view; this has a somewhat reduced acuity

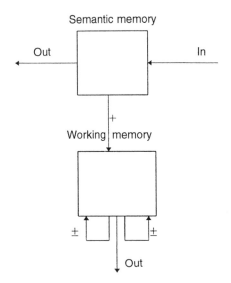

Figure 9.1
Information flow used in the analysis of subliminal-conscious processing. Input is coded in the semantic memory module SM and accesses the working memory net on which there is a competitive process between different interpretations of the same input.

compared with the fovea. If a subject fixates on a word shone foveally, a word shone simultaneously but briefly (too short for an eye movement to it) on the parafovea is not experienced consciously. However, the parafoveally presented word can be processed up to the level of its meaning.

This can be demonstrated by shining another word on the foveae to which the subject has to answer as rapidly as possible as to whether or not it is, for example, the name of an animal. If the test word has a similar meaning to the parafoveally presented word, the subject's response speeds up. That is so only provided that the period of time between the two presentations of words is no longer than 200 msec; any memory of the parafoveally presented word lasts, at the semantic level, only for that short length of time. This is considerably shorter than the time activity can persist on the buffer working memory, which is about 1 to 2 seconds, ten times longer.

This result shows that processing can occur up to the level of the meaning of words without awareness of them. It supports the model of figure 9.1; it also indicates that lifetime of activity on the semantic module is much shorter than that on the buffer working memory.

The second type of evidence is from experiments to probe the time course of word processing by using distractors input at different times during the processing of a given word. Subjects were shown a picture of an object, such as a sheep, and asked to respond with its name. At different times while they were responding a distractor word, such as "sheet," was spoken into their ears. If the distractor had a similar meaning to the object word, such as the distractor "goat," the speed of the subject's response was delayed only if the distractor word was presented before the picture of the object. On the other hand if the distractor sounded the same as the object word, like "sheet," it had to be presented at the same time as the object. This and similar evidence led Dutch linguist William Levelt (Levelt 1991) to claim, "This result supports the notion that semantic and phonological activations of the target word are strictly successive." Moreover Levelt stated that many meanings of a word are activated, but only one phonological interpretation is activated in its turn. This is the bare bones of figure 9.1.

The third type of evidence is from patients who suffer from what is termed neglect. This occurs usually after a stroke in the parietal lobe, and causes a person no longer to be aware, say, of one side of a visual scene. Recent studies show that, in spite of no awareness of the left half of what they are viewing, they still have knowledge about it at a higher level. For example, they displayed knowledge up to category level of objects in their neglected side. This was shown by shining a priming stimulus in their neglected field of view, such as the picture of a hen. Subsequently the picture, say, of a mouse, was shone in that field, and subjects had to state as rapidly as they could whether it was an animal or a fruit. A number of patients gave a more rapid response in this case than if they were shown the picture of a car or other object in an unrelated category; they truly displayed knowledge they had acquired from the priming stimulus at a categorical level. As the experimenters wrote, "the stimuli do not reach consciousness even when processed to a semantic level."

In all, evidence shows that a two-stage system is at work in the brain, the lower one working up to semantic level but not involving awareness, and the further one mandatorily bringing consciousness onto the scene.

What can we conclude about the properties of the higher-level system where awareness first emerges? This level I posit as the buffer working memory module. The critical need for temporally extended activity on a buffer working memory-type of structure for that activity to become conscious has been proposed ever since the time of William James (James 1950). He suggested the term "primary storage" to refer to a form of temporary storage that was at least in part responsible for what he called the "specious present" experience. This storage can be explained only by considerable extension of neural activity underlying consciousness from, at most, the few tens of milliseconds of duration of isolated nerve cell activity to the order of seconds, a hundred-fold increase. This fits in well with the experimental results of Libet and linguists such as Levelt, with competition for the unique phonological representation taking place on the buffer working memory. However, we are jumping ahead of ourselves and must go more slowly. To develop the action of the buffer working memory module in more detail, I now describe its various features.

Working Memory

London schoolmaster John Jacobs first discovered in the 1890s the existence of a specialized short-term memory system. He devised a simple method for measuring the mental capacity of his pupils by presenting a sequence of numbers and requiring the subjects to repeat them back in the same order. The resulting digit span is defined as the maximum length of sequence beyond which perfect recall is impossible. In the late 1950s it was shown that even small amounts of information are rapidly forgotten if the subject is prevented from rehearsing it, say by having to count down in threes from 100 in the interim. This was so for words and patterns of tactile stimuli, and was interpreted as the gradual fading of a short-term memory trace. Further support for a fading trace in short-term memory arose from the method of free recall: subjects were asked to recall as many words as possible from a string of unrelated ones just previously seen. Given a list of, say, fifteen words, about half will be remembered. The probability of remembering early words is low, but the probability of correct recall for the last few is high. This is called the

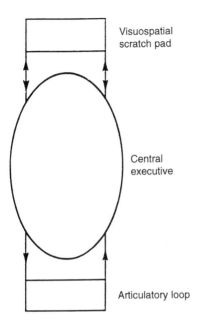

Visuospatial
scratch pad

Central
executive

Articulatory loop

Figure 9.2
A simplified representation of working memory. (Adapted from Baddeley 1986)

recency effect, and is thought to arise from the operation of short-term memory.

But there is no all-encompassing short-term memory. Earlier models of a limited capacity unitary short-term memory system (Atkinson and Shriffin 1968) that held information before it was recorded in a long-term memory store had to be discarded. This was due to the discovery of patients with amnesia but satisfactory short-term memory storage (Baddeley and Warrington 1970), and othes with normal long-term learning but a digit span of only one or two items (Shallice and Warrington 1970).

Such problems facing a unitary short-term memory model were resolved by the multicomponent working memory model of British psychologists Baddeley and Hitch (Baddeley and Hitch 1974; Baddeley 1986). Three components were proposed for this model, as displayed in figure 9.2. The central component, the central executive, is a control system for attention. The short-term memory trace resides in two slave subsystems: the phonological loop for words and the visuospatial sketchpad for spa-

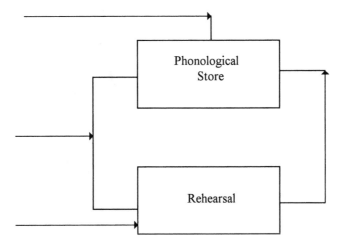

Figure 9.3
A schematic of the phonological loop. Details are given in the text.

tial vision. More recent evidence (Farah et al. 1988) indicates that the latter is divided into a system for holding object representations and one for buffering spatial maps. As expected, a similar slave short-term memory exists for touch and possibly in other codes such as for hearing (Burani et al. 1991).

We will consider only the phonological loop in this chapter. It comprises two components, a store that holds auditory verbal traces for about 1.5 to 2 seconds and a subvocal rehearsal process (figure 9.3). The system shown there, with unavoidable access by unattended speech into the phonological store and visual input of words to the articulatory rehearsal process, explains a number of well-attested phenomena:

1. The phonological similarity effect. For items that sound alike, such as the letters G, C, T, P, and V, the memory span is much poorer than for letters that are dissimilar, like X, K, W, R, and Y. An explanation of this is that storage, in the phonological store, is based on an acoustic code; acoustically similar letters have more overlapping neural activity representations than dissimilar ones, and so the former are more confusable than the latter.

2. The irrelevant speech effect. When the subject has to ignore irrelevant spoken material it reduces the span of memory, since the irrelevant

material automatically inputs the phonological store and degrades whatever is already there (figure 9.3).

3. The word length effect. Memory span is decreased for longer words since more time is taken to rehearse them than short ones. Memory span is determined by the decay time of the memory trace on the phonological store (roughly 1.5–2 seconds) and the speed of subvocal rehearsal. The moral of this is to speak a language with short compact words for most efficient thinking!

4. Articulatory suppression. Continued utterance of an irrelevant sound such as "the" is assumed to prevent rehearsal and also recoding of visually presented material into a phonological code.

5. The existence of patients without short-term memory (Burani et al. 1991).

6. The "dislike of mobile phones" effect. Owing to the irrelevant speech effect you cannot avoid listening to the usually vapid conversation of someone on the other side of the train or bus. Loud, continued conversation can also be intrusive; on a long train journey I had to explain the irrelevant speech effect to a pair of especially irksome businessmen before they would tone it down.

My research student Simon Hastings and I developed a simple model solely of the phonological store.[2] It fits data on short-list learning quite well so was used for the working memory module of figure 9.1. The basis of the model is that there are continued activity traces on dedicated nerve cells in the buffer working memory. We make the simplification of taking a single such nerve cell to represent each specific input word (although the model can easily be extended to be more realistic). The phonological store is thus composed of what are called leaky integrator neurons. Any activity arriving on such neurons decays away in a time in agreement with that found by psychological methods, namely, a value of 1.5 to 2 seconds. The nature of the model is shown in figure 9.4 (Taylor 1992a,b; 1994; 1996a,b).

Words with Many Meanings

The important experiment of Marcel in 1980 showed in what manner subliminal perception of a word with many meanings can influence the processing of a later word. We noted this experiment briefly earlier, but

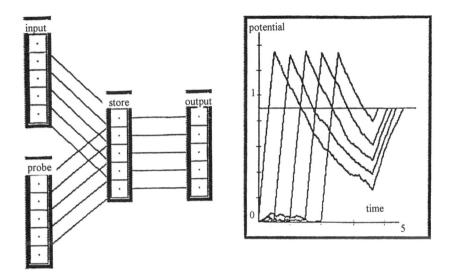

Figure 9.4
On the left is the neural architecture to model short list buffering; input goes directly to a dedicated node in the store, where it is held until a probe activation attempts to obtain a response by means of suprathreshold activation of the store node. On the right is the activation level of different nodes in the store. (From Hastings and Taylor 1994)

must now spend a little time explaining how it supports the model. I will not go into all of the details but only those that are important for our purpose.

Subjects were asked to decide, as rapidly as possible, whether or not a letter string shone on a screen in front of them was a word; they had to make this decision and then press one of two switches, the first if they thought the word actually was a word, the second if they thought it was not (called a forced-choice decision for obvious reasons). A second or so before they saw the letter string a word was shone on the screen in such a way that subjects were either aware of it (in one part of the experiment) or they only had subliminal knowledge of it (in another part). The word was below the awareness threshold of Cheesman and Merikle mentioned earlier but above the objective one. They were also exposed to an even earlier word whose further influence gave extra information.

The influence of the subliminally processed word on the decision on the later word turned out to be of crucial importance. Let us consider this word to be "palm," which can mean both tree and hand. Which of those meanings was activated at the subliminal level? In some tests the next word, whose character had to be responded to as rapidly as possible, was "wrist." Marcel discovered that the reaction time to wrist speeded up when palm was subliminally shone on the screen, compared with a longer delay when there was actual awareness of palm. The conclusion he reached was that the speed-up could only have been caused by both meanings of palm being active at the subliminal level, compared with only one, that nudged by previous word (such as "tree"), when awareness of palm occurred. To quote from Marcel (1980): "It would thus appear that on each trial the polysemous word is accessing both lexical/semantic entries." This agrees with results from psycholinguistics mentioned earlier, and is an important feature of our model: all possible meanings of a word are activated below the level of awareness. It also requires two modules, one at semantic level and the other for awareness at a later stage, with nodes on both coding the same words.

The basic problems that we face in modeling the experiments are (1) the nature of the modules that make up semantic memory and achievement of awareness in the flow pattern of figure 9.1, and (2) the manner in which these modules are connected together.

We will assume that the semantic net is constructed of different nerve cells activated by the different meanings of words. In the case of palm, separate nodes will be chosen for the hand and the tree meanings. Thus the semantic net has both a palm/hand and a palm/tree node. Moreover both these meanings are taken to be accessed by the input palm to an equal extent.

The nature of the module for awareness is of central inportance: it is assumed to be the buffer working memory module. It is taken to be almost a duplicate of the semantic module discussed above, but with a somewhat different structure as far as the time for decay of activity on a nerve cell and connection weights between them are concerned. In particular it is assumed to be composed of neurons with much longer decay times than the semantic memory module. That such a difference is required is clear from the modeling of short-term list memory by the buffer working memory by Hastings and me, discussed in the previous section, as well as the need for neurons with long time decays of their activity to support the lengthy activity necessary to lead the emergence of consciousness, as determined by Libet et al.

Awareness of a certain word input in a person is assumed to occur when the activity of the node, corresponding to that word on the awareness net, first reaches a certain threshold value. There are alternative choices, such as the node in question winning the competition among all of the nodes on the awareness net, setting the activities of the other nodes to zero. Our choice appears most natural when the more complete competition among modalities is considered, as discussed in the previous two chapters. When there is only subliminal experience we assume that only the appropriate node on the semantic module is active, sending its activity on to the working memory module but not causing the relevant node there to be active enough to reach the awareness threshold.

The Model of Consciousness Emergence

In the formulation presented here, I will model only the most important features of Marcel's experimental result. The flow of information involved in the emergence of consciousness is:

INPUT → SEMANTIC MEMORY (= Subliminal Knowledge) →
BUFFER WORKING MEMORY(= Consciousness)

The main points of the model are as follows:

1. Semantic memory excites only the buffer working memory, and has no excitatory or inhibitory connections on itself.

2. There are only feed-forward connections from the semantic to the buffer module, so that no feedback from the latter to the former exists that could otherwise cause the supposed rapid processing on semantic memory to be upset and confused by longer-held activity from the buffer site feeding back.

3. Lateral inhibitory connections are present within the buffer working memory as well as excitatory ones. These cause competition to arise among different nodes on the buffer working memory, to achieve the supposed breakthrough to consciousness. The lateral connections (as well as those feeding forward from the semantic memory) are taken as

hard-wired, not learned. Any learning necessary to set up the nets in the first place is assumed to have already taken place.

4. Awareness arises on the buffer working memory when the activity of a neuron is above some threshold.

I assume the manner in which the buffer working memory nodes achieve awareness to be by the value of the activity on the winning cell rising above a certain threshold. This possesses the ability to go ahead and win the more general competition among activities on various buffer memories, as outlined in the global approach considered in chapters 7 and 8. Such a more general competition involves both corticocortical and thalamus-NRT-cortex contributions, as discussed in some detail previously. The competition occurring on the working memory can thus be regarded as local, or as a heat for the final race to be carried out globally.

Some sort of threshold occurring as a barrier to awareness is evident from investigations in patients with prosopagnosia, in which they are no longer able to recognize faces, even of their loved ones. This can be caused by a stroke or brain injury. One such patient was able to recognize faces provided several of them were in a similar category, say of film stars. She was very surprised at being able to regain her lost ability. In a summary of this, British psychologist Andrew Young wrote

Such findings in blindsight and prosopagnosia show that the boundary between awareness and lack of awareness is not as completely impassable as it seems to the patients' everyday experience. The fact that certain types of stimulation can trigger experiences they no longer enjoy routinely fits readily with a model of the type in which *activation must cross some form of threshold before it can result in awareness.* (Young 1994)

The need to cross a threshold before awareness occurs is exactly that incorporated into the model.

Data on changes of reaction time brought about by Marcel's experiments can be analyzed using the above model of expression and figure 9.1. It can be done quite simply from the model, without going through detailed analysis or simulation, by using the small effects of the lateral spread of activity among different nodes on working memory, and from spread of activity from a dedicated semantic memory node to a differently

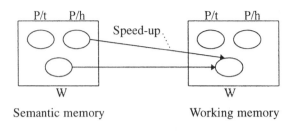

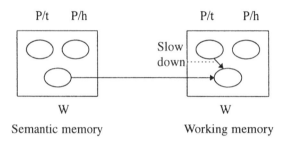

Figure 9.5
The coupling between the two nets (semantic and buffer working memory) to explain the data of Marcel and others on word processing. Activity from the palm/hand (P/h) node on the semantic memory, if not experienced (so not activating its working memory companion appreciably) can speed reaction time by gently exciting the buffer wrist (W) node by assumed lateral connection; if the palm node (P) is experienced, it fires on the buffer net, but when preceded by experience of "tree" it excites the palm/tree (P/t) node on the buffer net, which inhibits activation of the wrist node there, so delaying reaction time.

dedicated working memory node with a compatible meaning. The reaction times are defined by the value of the time when the activity of a particular node on the working memory module has reached the critical value for awareness. They are obtained by equating the activity of the node, evaluated at that time, with the requisite critical threshold value. If the value of the time to reach consciousness is evaluated, the small changes it undergoes due to lateral effects can be obtained in a straightforward manner. This is shown in figure 9.5; the excellent agreement between model and data is shown in table 9.1.

Table 9.1
Comparison of predictions and experimental results

Condition between words	Level of awareness of second word	Reaction time change predicted	Reaction time change measured	
Initial	Any	0	0	
Unassociated	Any	0	0	
Congruent	None	t_1	11	13
Separated	None	Same	8	11
Same	Subliminal	Same	6.5	13
Same	None	Same	8	18
Incongruent	Subliminal	t_2	28.5	28
Unbiased	Same	Same	23.5	30
Congruent	Same	$(t_1 + t_2)$	36.5	37
Same	None		0	6
Incogruent	Same		−13	−14
Unbiased	Same		2	13

In the experiments, Marcel (1980) presented three words in order, with relations between them described in the first column; congruent, unassociated, initial, separated, and unbiased indicate, respectively, that they all have similar meanings, no relation between their meanings, only the first and second have similar meanings, only the first and third have similar meanings, and there is no relation between the meanings of the first and second words. In the right hand columns the first is for time between the second and third words (ISI) of 1.5 secs, the second for ISI of 0.6 sec. The entries in the column for predicted changes in the reaction time involve the free parameters t_1 and t_2, which determine seven changes in close agreement with their measured values. The last three lines of the table involve further parameters of the model and may be used to show, from the incongruent case, as seen by the negative times entered there, the presence of lateral inhibition between the incongruent nodes on the buffer working memory module.

Predictions from the model were quantitatively consistent with experimental results, giving even further insight into some of the patterns that might be discerned in them, such as equality between some reaction time changes.

Conclusions

The main conclusion we reach is that it is possible to explain Marcel's results on modification of the reaction time in lexical decisions brought about by subliminal priming by earlier polysemous words, in terms of a simple model. This is based on the existence of a pair of modules, one for semantic memory, the other for buffer working memory activity. The latter acts by prolonging the activity fed to it by its semantic memory module, leading to competition among different buffer nodes for attaining a critical threshold and thereby reaching awareness. The model is also supported by qualitative effects in processing words in the parafovea and in probing the time course of word processing. One crucial feature I want to draw attention to is that the decaying activity of previous winning nodes on the buffer module allows context to be included in the competition. A decay time of about 1 to 2 seconds on the buffer working memory allows for context to be effective over the observed short-term memory span of about five to seven items.

The resulting system was analyzed for the modification of reaction time to the third in presentation of strings of three letters under a variety of conditions on the letter strings, and on the level of awareness used for the second. Various predictions on relations between the modifications of reaction times were satisfied experimentally.

Does consciousness, therefore, occur exactly when the winning node reaches a special threshold value, or is it only necessary that the winning node should actually win the competition, whatever the value of its firing rate? What happens to the activities of other nodes on buffer working memory? That they can be reduced may be part of the phenomenon of inhibition of return, in which prevention of response to a given input causes a slower response to it later, although it may be necessary to include anterior attentional nets to analyze such a phenomenon more properly (Jackson et al. 1994).

One interesting conclusion is that all meanings of a word, even a word with contradictory meanings, are activated in semantic memory, and can be distinguished only by further processing on the associated buffer working memory. In that situation various contradictory hypotheses can be subconsciously entertained simultaneously, but only one or other of them comes to awareness according to its most effective agreement with criteria imposed by anterior control systems. This can be seen as a simple model of the creative process. Creativity could not then be encapsulated in a standard logical structure, as required in the debate on the computability of thought processes mentioned in chapter 5 (Lucas 1960; Penrose 1989, 1994). We can also see how to model some of the unconscious processes central to various psychological theories; these features are considered later.

In this chapter we discussed only the passive component of consciousness. We must now look at active consciousness to expand our neural framework and erect a more powerful scaffold.

10

Active Consciousness

I have striven not to laugh at human actions.

—Baruch Spinoza

We are acting all the time, not necessarily in the theatrical sense but with purpose and intent to achieve desirable goals. People and other animals without goals are involved in neither the goings on around them nor, even more crucial, those inside them. Normally, then, we obey the pragmatic transformation of Descartes' famous dictum "I think, therefore I am" into "I act, therefore I survive."

The actions we make are often laughable, as Spinoza observed, but we make them nevertheless; the ones least likely to cause laughter are those that are carefully planned. Through planning, possibly many steps ahead, we can foresee the consequences of our actions and, if good, make them, if not, do something else. Planning and reasoning are abilities we possess in abundance, together with creativity, far above other animals.

The complexity of the structure of passive consciousness leads us to expect similar or even greater complexity for the active part, since it must incorporate the additional features of attention, drive, control of action, planning, reasoning, and creativity. These processes go beyond the sole involvement of the preprocessing, semantic, emotional, and episodic memory systems discussed thus far in the relational consciousness model. Some functions of active consciousness that we also consider involve the construction of action-perception sequences, which are used at an automatic level in so many of our goal-seeking endeavors after initial

conscious learning. We also have the unresolved question of where episodic memory is involved—is it only in posterior consciousness, or does
it also, or even mainly, contribute to its anterior companion?

Action and thought occur mainly in the frontal lobe of the cortex: motor actions are controlled by the motor cortex, which is just in front of the
posterior half of the brain at the beginning of the frontal lobes. Thinking,
reasoning, and planning are all crucially tied up with the most forward
part of the frontal regions, the prefrontal cortex. I analyze here some
of the action-based functions that can be supported by frontal cortex.
Subcortical structures, which are closely coupled with the frontal lobes,
especially the basal ganglia and thalamus, must also be considered as part
of the brain structures supporting frontal functions.

What do the frontal lobes do? In general, they act as an intermediary
between output from posterior cortices (for content) and from the limbic
regions (for emotional value of the input) to activate the muscles. As we
can see from figure 10.1, the frontal cortex is involved in controlling response to inputs from posterior cortex. Yet the right-hand side of the
figure shows that the frontal lobes have a hierarchy of their own, from
the motor and premotor cortices directly involved in modulating and ini-
tiating motor acts up to the most anterior regions of the dorsolateral
prefrontal cortex (figure 10.2).

We can learn about the frontal lobes from a variety of sources: wiring
diagrams, measurements made by noninvasive instruments, and other
more direct neurophysiological approaches. Thus we can uncover the
general nature of motor control by the lower levels of the frontal lobes
and their accessory subcortical modules. Later in the chapter I describe
a simple neural model, the ACTION network (Monchi and Taylor 1995;
Alavi and Taylor 1995), to explain how such actions and action sequences could be generated and learned by underlying neural architectures; the manner in which actions contribute to semantic memory is also
discussed. Throughout the discussion we will constantly meet the theme

Figure 10.1
Schematic diagram of cortical information flow in the perception-action cycle of
the primate. On the right, the frontal motor hierarchy and its subcortical connec-
tive loops are illustrated. (From Fuster 1993)

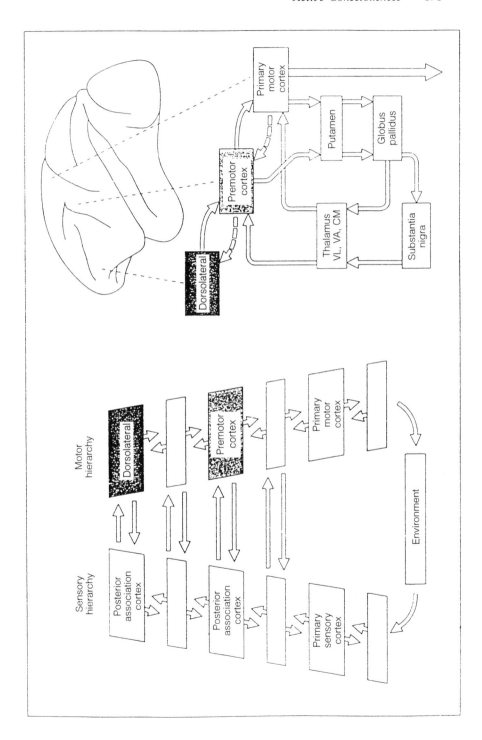

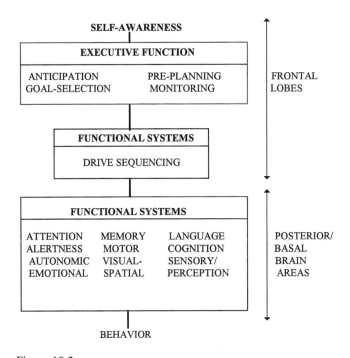

Figure 10.2
Hierarchy of brain function with the frontal lobes occupying the top hierarchy. (Reprinted with permission from Stuss and Benson 1986)

of the difference between the abilities of posterior and anterior cortex and what it tells us about the battle-collaboration between passive and active consciousness. Finally, we consider how this approach can help us understand active consciousness.

Frontal Structures

Up to the close of the first half of the nineteenth century it was uncertain whether or not some parts of the brain did one thing and other parts another, that is, differentiation of function. In spite of the observation that brain-diseased patients often had localized brain damage, clinicians had not been able to discover consistent relations between deficits and places in the brain where they could see damage. This was especially true for the frontal lobes, with fairly extensive frontal lesions failing to produce clear symptoms. The prefrontal region was therefore called silent. No one knew what it did.

This was changed by medical reports in 1848 about Phineas Gage, a young man who had suffered an accident while working on the railroad. As the result of an explosive blast that went off prematurely, he was in the path of an iron bar, 1.25 inches in diameter and 3.5 feet long, that shot through his left frontal lobe and emerged from the right frontal bone of the skull; the bar destroyed his left frontal lobe and the anterior temporal region, as well as some right frontal tissue. Despite this injury, Gage was able to be moved in a conscious state some miles from the scene of the accident to receive treatment. His memory and other intellectual powers did not seem to suffer in any remarkable way, and he was sufficiently competent to be self-supporting until his death thirteen years later. However, his personality changed to such an extent that he was constantly in danger of losing his job. Before the accident he had been considered by others to be honest, reliable, and deliberate and a good businessman; afterward he became "childish, capricious, and obstinate," used strong language, and was inconsiderate. Such considerable change of personality was later noted in others with prefrontal damage; we mentioned similar examples earlier.

Many detailed experiments in animals and further investigations in humans supported the conclusion that the frontal lobes are involved in personality. For example, British neurosurgeon David Ferrier believed that prefrontally injured monkeys were partially demented and had personality changes. With more careful analysis of humans, both from the study of behavioral deficits and from observation of brain damage at autopsy, it became clear that different areas of the prefrontal region modulated different aspects of behavior. This analysis was greatly aided by the introduction of surgical prefrontal leukotomy in the late 1930s, and injuries produced by the two World Wars. Injuries suffered by soldiers improved knowledge of disabilities produced by damage to the front of the brain, and the importance of the connectivity between various prefrontal regions and the nearby thalamus, limbic system (hippocampus, amygdala, and hypothalamus), and basal ganglia. In general, the middle and underside regions of the prefrontal cortex were found to participate in emotional and autonomic changes, whereas the sides and the top are related to planning, preparing muscles for motor actions, holding attention, and related high-level cognitive tasks. The divisions of the various parts of the frontal (and other parts) of the brain are shown in figure 10.3.

To understand the magnificent power of the frontal lobes we must look briefly at their structure. They are divided into three regions: precentral, premotor, and prefrontal. The precentral region is the classic motor cortex that produces motor signals going to the spinal cord. In front of that lies the premotor region, which includes areas with different functions, such as the supplementary motor area, frontal eye fields, and Broca's area. The supplementary area is involved in programming and initiation of movement sequences, frontal eye fields participate in controlling eye movements, and Broca's area is involved in voluntary speech.

The prefrontal cortex is especially important. It increased in size as species evolved, and occupies about 30 percent of the total cortex in humans (Fuster 1989). The prefrontal regions, which are the last to develop in infants, degenerate first as a result of disease.

The prefrontal cortex works on inputs that have already undergone considerable processing, as is evident from its inputs from the higher cortical areas involved in vision, audition, and somatic sensation. Primary sensory cortical areas are not directly connected to the prefrontal region, but only indirectly through higher-order sensory areas. The area is also connected to sites for the emotions in the limbic areas, so knows about the feel of inputs.

The important subcortical region, the basal ganglia, needs some discussion. The basal ganglia are crucially involved in the control of movement, although they have no direct output to the spinal cord or direct input from it. The way they are involved in movement has become clear from clinical observations; postmortem examinations of patients with Parkinson's and Huntington's diseases revealed pathological changes in the basal ganglia. These and similar diseases are accompanied by characteristic motor disturbances:

1. Tremor and other involuntary movements
2. Changes in posture and muscle tone
3. Poverty and slowness of movement without paralysis

For a while the basal ganglia were thought to be involved only in movement control, as in patients with Parkinson's disease. It is now realized

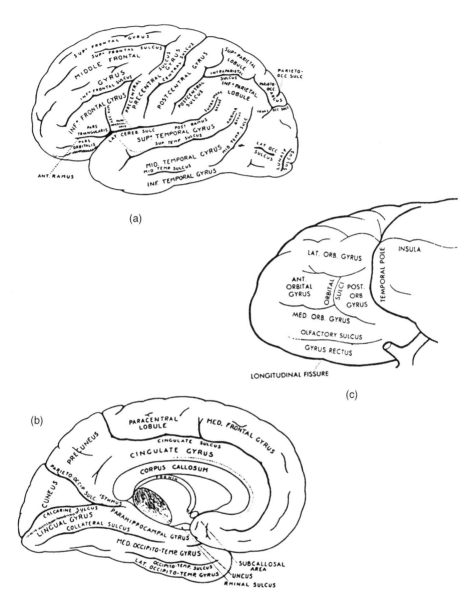

Figure 10.3
Differentiation of various regions of the brain, with emphasis on (a) frontal lobes, sulci and gyri of the cortial surface as seen laterally, (b) as seen medially, (c) as seen from under the frontal pole. (Reprinted with permission from Stuss and Benson 1986)

that cognitive disorders accompany later stages of these diseases, as would be expected, given a linguistic aspect to the cognitive processes that require motor action. More general cognitive activity of any form requires action-based processing: the total cortex-basal ganglia-thalamus system is crucial in achieving that.

So how does the system do its amazing work of allowing us to learn actions, plan and reason, and even be creative? The answer must be in terms of how frontal cortical activity is controlled by the basal ganglia, an influence absent from the posterior cortex.

The connectivity of the frontal cortex, basal ganglia (stratum and pallidum), and thalamus has a looped structure:

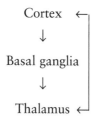

where the directions of the arrows indicate the flow of neural activity. A powerful feedback loop between the thalamus and cortex is controlled by the side effects of disinhibition (inhibition of inhibition) feeding down from the cortex through the basal ganglia. This is known to be a general feature of the frontal architecture (Alexander, DeLong, and Strick 1986). It is supported by many experiments, such as the beautiful demonstration of disinhibition of eye movement shown in figure 10.4.

There are five such loops: motor, orbitofrontal, frontal eye fields, and two involving the dorsolateral prefrontal area (figure 10.5). It is amazing to see so much similarity of overall structure across these loops combined with such a variety of functions. These loops, I claim, are the major features of the difference between frontal and posterior cortices; the posterior cortex has no such loops.

A simplified form of this connectivity in what I call the ACTION network is shown in figure 10.6. The basal ganglia are simplified as a single region. The essential feature of this network is that activity in cortex is controlled by feedback from activity going from cortex to thalamus and its return to cortex. The basal ganglia can act like the fulcrum of a lever

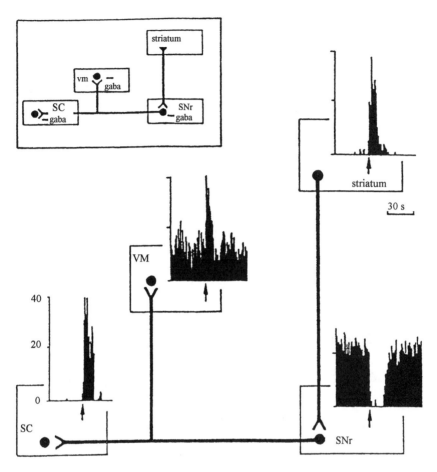

Figure 10.4
A striatal spike discharge, evoked by local application of glutamate, readily in-
duces a clearcut silencing of tonically active nigral neurons. Released from this
inhibition, collicular and thalamic cells are vigorously discharging. (Reprinted
with permission from Chevalier and Deriau 1990)

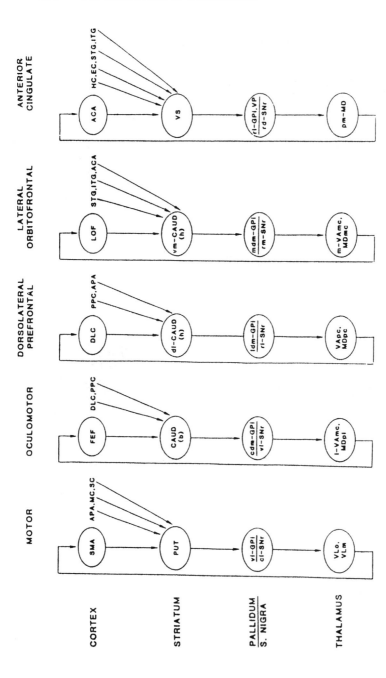

Figure 10.5
Proposed basal ganglia-thalamocortical circuits. Parallel organization of five such circuits. Each circuit engages specific regions of cortex, striatum, substantia nigra, and thalamus. (Reprinted with permission from Alexander, Delong and Strick, 1986)

The ACTION Network

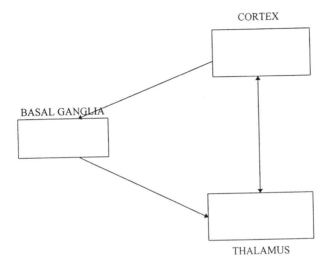

CORTEX

BASAL GANGLIA

THALAMUS

Figure 10.6
General structure of the cortical-thalamic-basal ganglia loops, as used in the connectivity of the ACTION network (for details see text).

for this cortical activity; a given cortical site can send activity to the basal ganglia, which then spreads sideways to affect other frontal cortical areas. This, I suggest, is the source of active processes of a sequence of output motor responses as well as the action of one cortical region internally on another (e.g., mental rotation of an image of an object one can hold in the mind).

Feeding back and forth of neural activity between cortical cells and between cortex and thalamus leads to activity of long duration. It is of interest to note that this reverberation of activity between thalamus and cortex, including that laterally between cortical sites, is a type of working memory. It has a special active character that I remarked on earlier, since it can alter neural activity in other frontal sites by means of connections to regions of the basal ganglia associated with these other sites. I use the term "active working memory" to describe it, to emphasize the active nature of the representations involved; they can be used to perform either external actions by activating muscles or internal actions on other frontal brain activities. These frontal active working memory systems, I claim, are able to support reasoning and thought at the highest level of the processing hierarchy; they will be where neural support for active consciousness is expected to be sited. Moreover, these frontal sites have access to various sorts of memories; posterior semantic memory as well as episodic memory sites are well connected frontally. The frontal lobes also store implicit memories involving various sorts of skills, especially, it is thought, in the connections form cortex to the basal ganglia. So the relational approach to active consciousness has a good anatomical basis.

Besides possessing the evidently useful neuroarchitecture of the ACTION network, the frontal lobes have an important neurochemical property: they are sites for flooding by the chemical dopamine. This acts as a signal of reward, and helps learning by amplifying the strength of special synapses on cells in the cortex thought to be modifiable. It was even suggested that the critical difference between the frontal lobes and posterior regions of cortex is the far greater dopamine supply to frontal sites. However, the distribution of dopamine over cortex seems roughly the same. The supply to the basal ganglia is threefold that to the cortex, emphasizing again the importance of the basal ganglia to functions supported by the frontal lobes.

In summary, the networks of the frontal lobe are a set of active memories, each represented by the ACTION network model. They can hold activity over many seconds, and can use such memory to make desired actions either on the outside world or on each other. We consider next how external actions can be controlled.

Actions

The motor cortex has long been regarded as a key area in the generation of motor outputs, based on observation of patients with motor seizures and results of studies employing lesions and electrical stimulation. Many experiments have also been performed on monkeys to determine the detailed character of motor cell activity as the animals make a movement. Cell activity is highest for movement produced along what is called the cell's preferred direction, and decreases gradually with movements in direction farther away from the preferred one; typically there is a broad tuning of sensitivity, as shown in figure 4.6, for carrying out two-dimensional movements.

Single cells (neurons) are the atoms of the brain; however, a single cell may die or misfire. Any coding of brain activity that depended only on single cell activity would therefore be highly vulnerable to degradation. Suppose you had a "grandmother" cell, whose firing indicated you were seeing her. If the cell died, you would lose all knowledge of a loved one. This is a very fragile way of remembering. To obtain more robust neural representations we must consider aggregates of cells and not just single ones. This leads to population coding: the partial information carried by a single neuron is combined with similar information from a population of others to give an output for motor control more secure against loss or misfiring of a few neurons. A unique way the net direction of movement is represented neurally was suggested by the American Georgopoulos and colleagues in 1983 (Georgopoulos et al. 1983; Georgopoulos 1994) as the sum of preferred directions of the neurons, each weighted by its present activity. The resulting population vector was shown experimentally to point in the final direction of reaching made by an animal; the activity of cells over a distributed region of motor cortex determines the signal sent from motor cortex to muscles.

As a monkey waits for instructions to move in a remembered direction, the population vector in its motor cortex grows dynamically during the delay. This growth is shown in figure 10.7, where the population vector in motor cortex of a monkey waiting to make a movement in a memorized direction is plotted every 10 msec. When the direction of that movement is commanded to be changed by an external signal (for example, by a bright light, which the monkey has learned is a signal for such a change), the movement direction is seen to rotate steadily. Rotation rates were similar to rates in human studies, in which the similarity of two objects projected on a screen could be assessed by a mental rotation of the image of one of them in the subject's brain, and measurement made of the resulting reaction time to a decision about the degree of similarity.

This is an amazing result, and is of fundamental importance in all sorts of cognitive processing—reasoning, thinking, planning, and so on. This most primitive cognitive act is now seen to be performed by a population

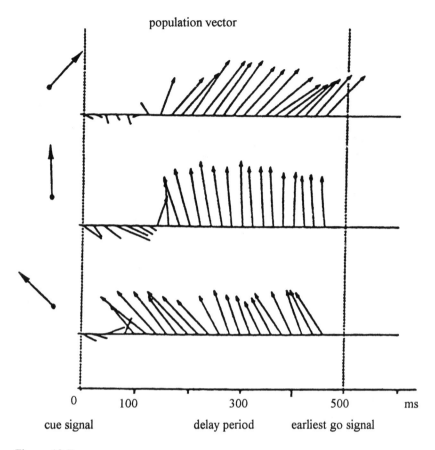

population vector

0   100   300   500   ms

cue signal   delay period   earliest go signal

Figure 10.7
Time evolution of the neuronal population vector during a delay period. Three
movement vectors are illustrated. (With permission from Georgopoulos 1994)

of nerve cells active in frontal cortex. Agreed, it was initially observed in
monkeys, but from the similarity between the rotation rates of the two
species it can be inferred as also occurring in humans. When you next
reach out for that glass of wine or beer at the dinner table, remember it
is your population vector that is doing the work, rotating steadily and
surely—there goes the vector—there your hand—and ah—what a good
drink!

The curiously slow growth of the population vector in figure 10.7—
it takes several hundred milliseconds to reach its maximum—can be

understood in terms of the ACTION net as follows. A signal enters cortex and triggers a build-up of activity in motor cortex (see figure 10.6) by reciprocal connections between the cortex and the thalamus. The signal shuttles back and forth between the areas, acquiring a little bit more activity each time it bounces back from one to the other. The time taken for this build-up to reach maximum as activity reflects back and forth between cortex and thalamus can be determined by the amplification factor involved at each bounce and the time it takes for one bounce each way. The activity continues to persist at the same level of activity determined by the original input, even though the input itself has disappeared. This is truly a "blackboard" type of neural system, where activity from elsewhere can be "written" on the blackboard and first grows and then persists until it is erased; shades of the global workspace, and surely sited frontally!

Thus the ACTION network is a simple model into which may be incorporated some of the main features of coding of movement by motor cortex. Other similar maps of the surface of the body (in other words, of its musculature) are involved in higher-level motor control in the premotor and supplementary motor cortex. Cells in those areas indicate generation and control of sequences of movements and direct where actions are to go (aided further by activity in parietal areas).

To summarize, motor and premotor-supplementary motor cortex control movement and sequences of movement generation through population coding. The ACTION network is a neural model that incorporates the observations in a simple manner.

What is the relevance of this to higher cognitive processes—thinking, planning, and consciousness? Have patience; we require more training before we can jump hurdles of the great race. To move to a slightly harder jump than that of single actions, consider sequences of actions. How can they be understood in neural terms?

Scripts and Schemata

Sequences of actions and percepts, at different levels of detail, are recognized as forming units of information for encoding efficient movement in the environment. They are called scripts at high level and schemata at a lower or more specific level of detail. For example, a car script specifies how the sequence of activities for driving a car is carried out: starting, stopping at a red light, steering, and so on. A shopping script for a young child consists of "you buy things and then you go home"; a script for making cookies is similarly terse: "Well, you bake them and you eat them." Schemata are more specific in their details and in their use of processing modules to carry them out.

Thus a schema such as word dictation (by which spoken words are transformed into written form) uses a word-form system involving phonemes and a variety of systems for producing the shapes of letters (Shallice 1988).

Developments in artificial intelligence leaned heavily on the notion of schemata and scripts (Schank and Abelson 1989), which are considered fundamental in early learning of categories (Fivush 1987). In the eating script of figure 10.8 various objects are involved: a child has its bib put on, is placed in a high chair, eats from a plate, drinks from a cup or a bottle, is cleaned up, and is removed from the chair. The food could be cereal, bread, or banana; the liquid could be milk or juice. A number of objects can be substituted at a given point in the schema, leading to the possibility of functional categories being formed based on objects collected together according to their function. Objects are also encountered sequentially, allowing the formation of thematic categories collected by the themes they are involved in. At the young age of six months, infants collect objects together when playing with them along one of these two ways, rather than by using the more classic features of the objects (e.g., squareness or color) to create categories. Thus scripts provide an important insight into the construction of concepts and even of their semantics.

Developing Scripts and Schemata

But we do not yet know how these action sequences—scripts and schemata—develop. Are they innate or are they learned? If learned, how? It is becoming increasingly accepted that scripts and schemata are learned on top of underlying, innate sensorimotor reflexes; they piggy-back on them, so to speak. A particularly important figure in this area is Swiss child psychologist Piaget (Piaget 1945) who used schemata to understand

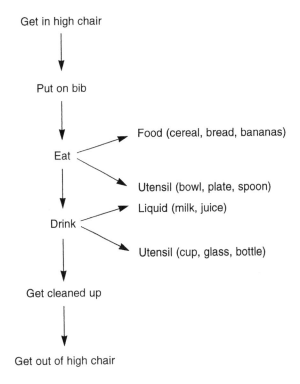

Figure 10.8
The structure of the eating routine script. (Adapted from Fivush 1987)

cognitive development. He introduced the concept of assimilation, by which an infant or child makes sense of a situation in terms of the schemata available to it, and accommodation to describe the creation of new schemata if no suitable one is available. These two features, use of available schemata and creation of new ones, are highly relevant to processing of information by the frontal lobes. We start this section with a more detailed presentation of these ideas before indicating briefly how they can be implemented neurally.

Piaget had a major impact on theorizing how children develop their understanding of the world. His central concern was with equilibrium: humans achieve their persisting identity through dynamic interaction with the environment so as to reduce disequilibrium and maximize satisfaction. The process can be seen as an attempt to attain equilibrium points for drives through assimilation and accommodation with the environment. As he stated, "Equilibrium is not an extrinsic or added characteristic but rather an intrinsic and constitutive property of organic and mental life."

For Piaget, a built-in property of a living organism is its ability to persist in self-maintaining equilibrium. However, this cannot be achieved without a battle; the environment is always changing and can be hostile. The living organism can be seen as comprising a set of structured systems of self-regulating cycles enabling the struggle for dynamic equilibrium with the environment to be fought and, it is hoped, won. These structures can be organic, psychological, social, and so on. The schema is the simplest type of substructure to aid the survival process; it is a structure, originally of action that, through repetition and variation, becomes generalized and is built on reflexes.

A typical example is the sucking schema. Originally a built-in reflex schema that causes the very young infant to give an automatic sucking response to the nipple in contact with the mouth, it generalizes to sucking on other objects. It can be further enlarged when seeing and grasping are coordinated through assimilation into the existing schema as the infant matures. This allows extension and ultimately control, by accommodation, of objects in the field of view attempting to be grasped. Large unsuckable or ungraspable items also have to be accommodated, and the child has to adapt to a situation in which no reward ensues and disequilibrium may arise.

The infant or child is driven to find a resolution, or equilibrium, through a series of definable developmental stages. As part of his research, Piaget discerned stages in which development is roughly incremental in a given stage, with behaviors of a given type being extended but with no radical increase in representational complexity.

In the first stage, in which schemata for objects are developed, that takes place form birth to about eighteen to twenty-four months (onset of language), the following stages can be observed:

1. Reflex activity develops by becoming spontaneous, then it generalizes, and later comes under voluntary control. For example, the sucking reflex generalizes to objects other than the nipple, such as a finger or toy.

Sucking may also occur with no object present in the mouth. Objects may later be brought to the mouth to be sucked.

2. Coordination of reflex schemata, in which increasing control is obtained over the use of reflex schemata, and of the use of several of them to achieve a desired end.

3. Repetitive actions to reproduce accidental events, with behavior becoming object centered.

4. Coordination of preexisting schemata for new purposes in new situations.

5. Experimentation with objects.

It is possible to see how to model some of the stages of development outlined above, say in the case of the sucking and rooting reflex (Ogmen and Prakash 1994). For stage 1 this appears to be composed of three substages:

1. Development of spontaneous (nonreflexive) response
2. Generalization of the reflex to a broader range of inputs
3. Learning to control the response so it is no longer a pure reflex

These substages require separate modules to perform the input and response stages as well as those to act as memories of motor actions. This allows the relevant actions to be available, to be rewarded at some later time. Multimodular neural networks can be suggested to perform these substages.

Learning Schemata

How do we learn schemata? We have no explicit rules that tell us; we must do so by some form of reward learning. But how? Some parts of schemata have to be learned ab initio, without use of reflexes as starters. Coordination of existing schemata is also required to build larger ones. For example, learning to drive a car uses low-level motor action sequences, but coordination and sequencing these actions has to be learned with conscious attentive processing in a somewhat painstaking manner, as any student driver can tell you. Learning such action sequences initially involves deliberate attentional control, but ultimately the actions become automatic. Moreover, learned schemata can be "sewn together" to build up more complex schemata. I briefly describe how the ACTION network can be used to model schema learning, on the basis of which I develop a neurally based theory of object semantics.

Various suggestions have been made for sequence learning in frontal lobe using known structures (Arbib and Dominy 1995; Houk, Adams, and Bart 1994). The correlated loop structures, especially their active memory systems, are proposed here to be the sites of the learning. One model of this was composed of an ACTION network and is shown in figure 10.9 (a) (Alavi and Taylor 1995; Taylor and Taylor 1996). The result of simulation of this process is shown in figure 10.9 (b). It produces neuronal responses closely similar to those shown in figure 10.10 observed in behaving monkeys (Tanji and Shima 1994). The architecture of figure 10.9a indicates the principles behind "chunking," in which certain nerve cells are taught to represent sequences of actions; these chunking nodes can be developed by learning (Arbib and Dominy 1995; Houk and Wise 1993; Taylor and Taylor 1996).

In conclusion, a variety of neurons code for the generation of temporal sequences in premotor cortex and the associated basal ganglia and thalamic regions, and they can be created by suitable learning processes.

Learning Semantics

Now we turn to the difficult problem of semantics. No one knows what it is, although numerous suggestions have been made. We start with an alphabet of highest-order features into which inputs have been split up. This alphabet we assume to have been represented in coupled semantic-buffer working memory modules in posterior cortex. How this is achieved is not our present problem, but we expect that the alphabet of higher-order features is composed of combinations of lower-order features (e.g., oriented edge and slit detectors in vision being combined to make lines and shapes, and these to make parts of objects, like legs or arms).

Evidence for such a coding by highest-order features comes from studies on monkeys (Wang, Tanaka, and Tanifuji 1996). Dyes that change color when the electrical activity around them increases were applied to exposed areas of a monkey's cortex. When pictures of objects were shone onto a screen in front of the animal, clusters of electrical activity were

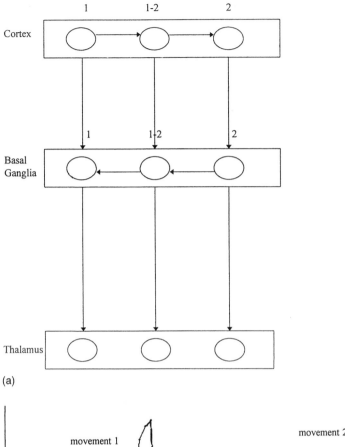

Figure 10.9
(a) Structure of the modules used to achieve sequence generation. (b) Results of the simulation to be compared with measurements of figure 10.10. (Adapted from Taylor and Taylor 1998)

The cortical cells 1 and 2, together with their basal ganglia and thalamic colleagues, produce the movement 1 and 2 activators. The first of these sets of the transition cell (labeled 1–2 in (a)) which turns off the cells 1 and then, when it has grown active enough, turns on the movement cell 2.

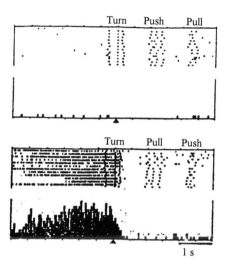

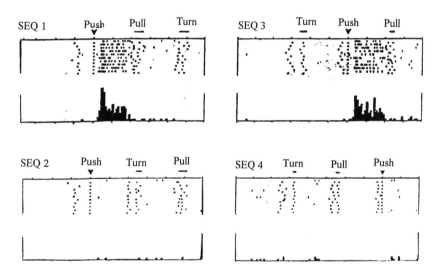

Figure 10.10
Activities of cells in the supplementary area specific to the initiation of a sequence, and to the transition between a pair of movements. The second recording shows a cell involved with initiation of the action sequence Turn-Pull-Push. The third and fourth recording shows the transition cell for Push to Pull in two different sequences (SEQ1 and SEQ3); it is inactive in the fifth and sixth recordings (SEQ2 and SEQ4). (Reprinted with permission from Tanji and Shima 1994)

noticeable. These clusters shifted slowly as the pictures had their form altered gradually by the experimenter. The objects activated separate regions for different letters of the alphabet of which they were composed, and as these letters changed slowly so did the regions that they activated.

Activations for the set of letters of which a word is composed somehow have to be glued together so as not only to function as a unified representation of the word, but at the same time be able to be activated in parallel and not in series (the binding problem again!). Moreover, the semantics of the word must be obtained as part of this binding, so we come back again to our original question: what is semantics?

Attempts to define semantics from linguistics (by using purely the relationships between words) and philosophy (defining the meaning of a proposition as the situations in which it is true) have failed. For linguistics this is due to lack of words of the language being related to objects in the external world (failing to give them significance in guiding actions on these objects); for philosophy it is because propositions can be constructed with different contents that have the same meaning.

A variety of evidence shows that meaning has its ultimate basis in actions (Johnson 1987; Lakoff 1987). Numerous experiments were carried out to compare the nature of knowledge gained when an animal can use actions for exploration compared with when it cannot. They showed that action-based knowledge is far superior to that acquired passively. Furthermore, analysis of the active mode of exploration for the development of a knowledge base in the growing infant, started by Piaget, showed different stages of development, as mentioned above. Psychologists (Rovee-Collier 1993) showed how actions made by an infant achieve categorization of visually seen inputs. Work in infant development is continuing to determine how knowledge is transferred between vision and touch, and how it is related to the use of movement in the acquisition of knowledge (Streri 1993).

There are fMRI results on the most active brain regions when meaning of words is processed. In one particular result[1] subjects compared how close in meaning a test word was to a set of three words they had just seen and were asked to remember. Strong brain activity (compared with when they were not making such a comparison but just looking at words) was observed in exactly those regions suggested earlier as being at the root of semantics—the basal ganglia and the front part of the thalamus, as well as certain frontal cortical regions.

So a close relation exists between the development of effective actions and a store of knowledge (Logothetis and Sheinberg 1996). Perhaps that is to be expected, since active exploration leads to better acquisition of knowledge simply by enlarging what can be experienced by moving around. Such an interpretation, however, misses the point, as results of active versus passive exploration mentioned earlier shows. In all, we can be fairly sure of the existence of at least an important component, especially before an infant achieves language ability, of the development of semantics through action-based perception.

The first stage in constructing the neural system for learning semantics on an action basis is to develop neural networks for actions to be taken as part of the recognition process. Let me first summarize what the ACTION network can do for frontal functions.

The reciprocal corticothalamo-cortex loop, along with more local cortical connections, can preserve activity for an extended time once the correct connections are set up. The frontal system stores and retrieves patterns in the cortico-corticothalamic loop. This loop activity can be altered by activity from other parts of the cortex being sent to the regions of the basal ganglia where the original activity is persists. The new activity thereby helps stabilize the persisting loop activity or causes it to alter, such as by generating a sequence of activities, so extending the model of sequence generation of figure 10.9. Alternatively, comparison of two different activities in separate cortical regions can be achieved by lateral inhibition between the activities on their relevant parts of the basal ganglia—the strong-arm game again (since basal ganglia cells are nearly all inhibitory). The ACTION system can also bring about attentional control by holding an activity template, which prevents inputs from arousing different activities than the template (again by lateral inhibition on basal ganglia). In all, the frontal system appears to have a considerable degree of flexibility, enough, it would seem, for the some of the superior powers of the frontal lobes.

How can the frontal system learn an action-based semantics? Input from an object in a given modality activates the representation of a feature of the object (which was previously coded in the highest

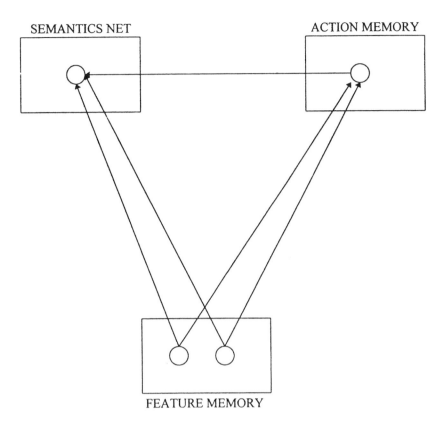

SEMANTICS NET   ACTION MEMORY

FEATURE MEMORY

Figure 10.11
The coupled ACTION network system for learning semantics (see text for details).

preprocessing semantic-buffer working memory system) in posterior cortex. Further feature representations are successively activated by input sensors. These are actively brought to focus onto further features of the object by a sequence of actions by the subject. The heart of the system proposed here is the learning of this sequence of actions by neural connections between the module on which the features are active and the sequence of actions necessary to bring about input of the next feature. This sequence, when learned by chunking cells in the frontal lobes (as in figure 10.9), reactivates the cells at a low level so as to create a "virtual" action, ready to support any real action if one has to be taken. The outline of a neural architecture to achieve this is shown in figure 10.11.

This action-based approach to semantics provides a high-level solution to the binding problem raised in chapter 6. Chunked nodes in the semantics net, representing sequences of actions taken during recognition of features of objects, can be used by feedback to lower areas to search for the best hypotheses binding together these low-level features into higher-level objects. This gives possible implementation of various ideas proposed for the use of feedback projections to lower-level feature-detection areas in order to achieve good object-recognition systems (Kawato 1993). The observed close relationship between the neural activities in posterior and anterior regions during the solution of cognitive tasks (Bressler 1994), all oscillating in unison at about 40 cycles per second, is experimental support for such a mode of action.

At this juncture let me relate this virtual actions approach to semantics to the simplified notion of it, and the very simple semantic modules used in chapter 9, to model the phenomenon of breakthrough to awareness. My position is based on the facts from lesion and PET studies that visual or auditory representations of the meanings of nouns are encoded in posterior cortex Wernicke's area in the temporal lobe, whereas verbs are encoded in Broca's area in the left frontal lobe. Verbs, having a frontal representation (where the action is!), can be consistently represented by action-based chunks associated with their semantics considered above. The posterior representations for nouns in Wernicke's area, as used in the model in chapter 9, are therefore symbolic codes of visual and auditory inputs to which the full action-based semantics is attached only by extending the symbols to the action-based perception sequences just described. These correspond to sets of verbs that can act on them. The semantics of nouns is then only a pale ghost of the more full-bodied version in which virtual actions are also incorporated.

Executive Function

We now approach the highest function of the frontal lobes—where the buck stops. Executive function was discussed briefly with relevance to the model of Norman and Shallice. We now explore this notion in a little more depth to appreciate what sort of control system might exist at the highest cognitive level and, in principle, in what way it can be modeled by neural networks.

A danger about the buck stopping anywhere is that we might suddenly come face to face with the dreaded homunculus, the ghost in the machine (although I do not believe in ghosts, having spent time looking for them in my enjoyable youth and always being disappointed). If the homunculus is there after all, we will have to extend the number of laps in our race to include the homunculus as one of the entrants, developing homunculus brain imaging techniques, and all that. Inside that homunculus will be another homunculus . . . and our race to consciousness will never finish! Let us move forward cautiously so we do not fall into that trap. A model of executive function must be constructed that is its own executive in some manner, or avoids the task by suitable delegation. We can proceed with that idea in mind.

We agree that two important components of the executive function of the frontal lobe are (Bapi et al. 1998) multilevel schema formation and associated decision making, and the support of active memory. The first of these involves the development of schemata in the frontal system as observed in various experimental paradigms; I proposed that the creation of schemata was achieved by suitable holding and correlated learning of activity in the ACTION networks of the frontal system. The manner in which schemata are decided among involves the emotional concerns brought about by the set of inputs (which led to the problem of choice of responses in the first place). This uses emotional values, coded initially in suitable parts of the limbic system, in particular the amygdala and the orbitofrontal cortex.

The second feature of executive action, active memory, has been explored in some depth in association with the ACTION network. The only aspect I wish to emphasize here is that the ACTION network structure allows the frontal cortex to act as a form of mental blackboard on which can be written items initially encoded in posterior cortex and then passed on to frontal cortex for active manipulation. This blackboard mode of action allows an activity to be held on it until an erasure occurs, at which point new activity can be written. Such notions are well established in computer science and were imported into consciousness modeling by

Baars with his fruitful idea of consciousness as the global workspace. This is especially helpful in its use of the frontal lobe as the blackboard playing an important role in anterior consciousness, and leads us to consider anterior consciousness as based on the structure. The nature of the interaction between it and posterior consciousness will be made easier by considering the manner in which the corresponding circuits are connected; we will do that shortly.

To summarize, the manner in which executive function works is in terms of the various features able to be supported by the ACTION network:

• Active memory, especially of plans and goals
• Temporal sequence storage and chunking
• Competition and monitoring
• Manipulations of activities on some ACTION modules by activities on others.

However, as we noted earlier, the forntal lobe has at least five ACTION networks, each performing different functions among those listed above, so we would not expect a single executive function but a number of dissociable ones. The way in which these combine is relevant to the construction of anterior consciousness.

Active Consciousness

As summarized by neuroanatomists (Petrides 1994; Carmichael and Price 1994), the relevant working memory regions in posterior cortex, the site of emergence of posterior consciousness, are well connected to appropriate regions of frontal cortex. The parietally sited buffer working memories are connected to the dorsolateral prefrontal cortex, whereas the inferotemporal ones are connected to the ventral frontal cortex. The former connection supports the manner in which active spatial processing may be achieved by the frontal cortex, whereas the latter provides both object representations and their values being fed to the ventral regions of the frontal cortex.

I proposed in chapter 2 that anterior consciousness is supported by the frontal lobe active working memory; the process of holding in mind observed in continued activity of frontal neurons in monkeys is a feature of it. This persistent activity can be achieved by two mechanisms. The first is through the creation of long-lasting neural activity set up by recurrent cortical connections in those sites with the highest density of cells in upper layers. The extra feature, giving flexibility to frontal lobe persistence, involves the more powerful ACTION type of neural network architecture in which a particular cortical region can affect another by means of activity it sends to the relevant region of the basal ganglia to achieve its aims. The dopamine reward signal floods into the basal ganglia to help oil the works. In any case, the relevant regions of frontal cortex are well known to support long-lived neural activity, over many seconds, so are good candidates for sites of active consciousness.

To understand how such consciousness can arise, we can now apply the relational consciousness model to the appropriate ACTION network. As in posterior cortex, a hierarchy has been recognized by various methods in various frontal areas. Regions in the lower areas of the frontal lobes (areas 10–15, 44–47) are to be regarded as lower than those more toward the sides, such as areas 46 and 9. Loss of these sites through brain injury causes most damage to the highest abilities of planning and reasoning. I noted above that there are good connections between posterior high-level sites of preprocessing-semantic memory and lower-level sites of the frontal cortex; there are similar good connections between the highest-level sites of posterior and frontal cortices. It would therefore seem that frontal knowledge of whatever is occurring posteriorly at a comparable level is present. At the same time the frontal lobes add their value to the knowledge they receive. In total, posterior memories feed their activity frontally to similar although more flexible sites.

Active consciousness has therefore a fertile knowledge base from which to be constructed. Altogether, both the posterior preprocessing-semantic memories and their frontal counterparts, together with buffer working memory activity, lead to active conscious content through competition on the highest frontal sites. That content also has additional material from limbic sites giving emotional value memory and goal memory coloration. Frontal consciousness has a greater range of knowledge giving its content, as well as having material already digested at posterior level. The value of a further apparent duplicate of the posteriorly based passive consciousness can now be recognized; it has at least three extra features beyond passive consciousness of:

1. Strong contributions from emotional and goal memories
2. Ability to be used to act on neural activity in other regions (either frontal or posterior) to achieve a goal
3. Allowance of choice to be made among response strategies so as to be more effective in achieving a goal

This is how active consciousness has greater richness than its posterior companion of passive consciousness. Such richness is necessary, since it must contain greater complexity to solve its tasks. Without it we are far less effective, as humans such as Phineas Gage who lose their frontal lobes show.

Fusing Consciousnesses

So far I claimed that two components of consciousness, the posterior or passive and the anterior or active forms, are important constituents of overall consciousness. How can we fuse these two components or, if we cannot, how can we understand the experience of unity of consciousness that we all possess? To resolve this puzzle, let us look at the connectivity that exists between the posterior and anterior regions.

The strong connections between posterior and anterior cortical regions indicate a probable high correlation between these two activities, and thus a strong correlation between posterior and anterior forms of consciousness. However, it is still an open question as to whether or not we should conclude that these two components of consciousness are in fact one, and that waking consciousness is not really divided into two parts described in chapter 2.

From analysis of cases relating to loss of frontal lobe, which I discuss more fully in the final part of the book, it would appear that it is possible to have posterior consciousness with little contribution from the anterior component. It does after all appear that a dissociation exists between the putative components. Moreover, people without working memory in one or other modality have little apparent deficit in typical frontal functions (although they have some learning deficits).

Results of brain imaging support such an antero-posterior separation of functions in the normal brain; the frontal sites of working memory are active only when processing demands are heavy. For example, in the "n-back" experiment a subject had to respond if a letter in a sequence being looked at is identical to one seen earlier. The frontal regions were activated only if n was two or more; at the same time the posterior regions had their activity reduced. This distribution of activity over the cortex— strong at the front, weaker at the back—reversed itself when n was one, so a shorter time is necessary to hold the information in memory (Cohen et al. 1997; Courtney et al. 1997). In a different experiment when a number of words had to be held in mind over many seconds, prefrontal cortex was again the most active. A similar distribution of activity was observed during recall of words from a previously learned list when it exceeded the normal short-term memory span of seven or so words.

A powerful brain imaging study (Grasby et al. 1994) showed even more precisely that not only are the frontal components of working memory brought into the act when the processing load is too large to be handled posteriorly, but they also suppress the posterior ones as they come on stream. This was a clear demonstration of the limited capacity of posterior cortical components of working memory in comparison with their frontally sited colleagues, and of a balance between frontal and posterior activities: if one is very active (and effective in solving a task), the other is much less active.

We conclude therefore that there are two components of consciousness, and that in certain states of mind activation of one component is much greater compared with the other, as observed by brain imaging studies in attentive tasks. Understanding the detailed manner in which the two interact involves unifying by the control action of the NRT, which was considered earlier with respect to posterior consciousness. It also has a role in anterior consciousness owing to the similar connections of frontal cortex to NRT and the appropriate part of the thalamus.

An example of possible loss of control in anterior over posterior consciousness arises in the case of the excessive production of intrusive thoughts in persons with depression. These patients have reduced power to inhibit the production of such thoughts, perhaps due to inability to suppress denigratory remarks generated from the medial orbitofrontal loop, suggested in the next chapter as containing autobiographic memory representations. These remarks may be produced by one or all of the following possibilities: increased noise in the loop, reduction of inhibitory control systems involving basal ganglia, or increased strength of feedback in the loop carrying them. Broadcasting the remarks to the phonological loop then leads to intrusive thoughts. A similar mechanism is at work, although more strongly, in the hearing of voices by schizophrenics.

From the evidence so far, I conjecture that the two forms of consciousness have a range of correlated activity levels, from the case when the anterior form is large and the posterior one small to the opposite. The former is expected to occur when hard mental work is being done (using the ACTION network style of active processing), the latter when a more passive state exists. In a range of in-between states of mind, the anterior and posterior forms are well correlated to give the experience of unity of consciousness but both at a medium level of activity.

This leads naturally to the division of anterior consciousness into the blackboard component and an ACTION network component. The first passively receives outputs of posterior working memories following the analysis of the connections mentioned earlier (parietal to dorsolateral, temporal to ventral), and after suitable learning, allows itself to be written on. The second component is the controller brought into action when motivation is roused by emotional concerns. It either rehearses and refreshes the frontal blackboard (and the associated posterior one, as part of the same process) or transforms activity on it to achieve a suitable goal activated from limbic circuitry.

I introduced five ACTION loops as part of the frontal architecture; does this mean that anterior consciousness has at least five components, any of which might be combined with its posterior companion? The answer is no, since these loops involve cortical regions at various levels in the frontal hierarchy. The expected conscious components of anterior consciousness should be identified with those recognized as equivalent to posterior cortical sites of working memory. According to neuroanatomists (Mesulam 1985; Petrides 1994) the frontal cortex has two different sites, each of which is well connected to a corresponding posterior site. One of them is the dorsolateral area of frontal cortex, with its associated region in the posterior parietal cortex (with evidence for working memories for somatosensory and visuospatial information). The other is the ventrolateral frontal cortex, with the associated posterior region being the various sites of visual and auditory information in the temporal and inferior parietal lobes. Thus separate posterior "what" and "where" cortical information pathways feed to separate frontal regions, although these frontal regions are well interconnected. There appear to be at most two components of anterior consciousness with correlated activities.

Do two independent components of consciousness, anterior and posterior, exist, each of which is composite in the manner just described? Perhaps the anterior form of consciousness is used only for rehearsal of the posterior form to extend its lifetime. A doubling up of consciousness would occur in this manner, so the posterior form would indeed be a "slave" of the anterior one. Only one consciousness would be required in that case. However, earlier evidence from brain lesions and imaging shows that the anterior form is not identical to the posterior one, involving different activities (to allow the rehearsal process and thought and reasoning to be achieved). In addition, in the more passive state little anterior consciousness may be involved.

We know this also from our own inner experience. When we are thinking hard about something we do not want to notice outside influences; we shut them out. This is a well-known cause of friction between partners: you may be (unwisely) following your own train of thought while your partner is talking to you. Then your partner becomes very annoyed when it is obvious that you have not taken in anything that was said— "there are none so deaf as those who will not hear."

We conclude that experience consists of two independent components of consciousness (depending on the nature of the processing task) based on independent but usually well-correlated components of neural activity. Different states of consciousness can arise involving different combinations of activities on posterior working memory and anterior active memory sites. In general, the activities code different information and so are important in their own right. The overall experience is a composite arising from various competitions extending that for posterior cortex to include the relevant frontal ACTION networks.

Finally, we have met no homunculus so far as we probe the control systems of the mind, nor have we found a highest-level controller (although the anterior cingulate does stand in for hard decisions). Decisions are reached by consensus, with emotional concerns holding the ultimate sway. So the final arbiter, where the buck stops, is in the limbic system, and very likely is not even conscious.

Summary

I described the nature of, and possible neural modules for, various frontal functions: actions, generating action sequences (schemata), learning these sequences, and executive function. In all of these the underlying ACTION network gave a reasonable neural architecture to explain this broad range of functionality. Further analysis could show that many complex psychological processes, such as reasoning and creativity, can themselves be supported by a range of known neural networks, especially of ACTION network type. Active consciousness was explored from the relational consciousness framework; its richness is explicable in terms of extra knowledge flowing to candidate sites for its emergence in frontal cortical areas. Finally, the relationship between the anterior and posterior forms of consciousness was analyzed, with usually correlated but sometimes dissociated activity supporting them as having an underlying separate existence.

11

The Emergence of Self

For I am fearfully and wonderfully made.
—Psalms 139:13

The self appears to be the deepest and most difficult aspect of mind, yet it is what we as individuals each constantly experience; it is almost a truism that each of us is closest to ourselves. As William James wrote (James 1950), "A man's self is the sum total of all that he can call his own."

However, that does not help us come to grips with the subject. Dictionary definitions specify the self as "Person's or thing's own individuality or essence, personal things as object of introspection or reflexive action," or as "personality, ego; a side of one's personality; what one is." These aspects we will explore in attempting to discover which neural structures can guide us to a better understanding of self. However, the above definitions are not very insightful as to how the self might emerge from brain activity.

If we turn to the philosophers, a large amount of disagreement is found as to what constitutes the self. David Hume even claimed that it dissolves away on a deeper analysis:

For my part, when I enter most intimately into what I call myself, I always stumble on some particular perception or other, of heat or cold, light or shade, love or hatred, pain or pleasure. I never catch myself at any time without a perception, and can never observe anything but the perception. . . . If anyone, upon serious and unprejudiced reflection, thinks he has a different notion of himself, I must confess I can no longer reason with him.

For Hume, then, the self disappears on closer analysis, an interesting feature to which we return later.

To attack the subtle problem of the nature of self, several strands must be explored. One is the development of self in the infant, following the ground-breaking work of Piaget and others who followed him. Some aspects of this were explored in the previous chapter, but mainly from the viewpoint of sensorimotor schema and semantics. Such developmental aspects of self and personality must be considered further to achieve a deeper understanding.

A second strand concerns expansion of the notion of autobiographic memory, the set of memories involving the self. A clear hierarchical structure has been found in these memories, and at the same time a more specific structure has become apparent for methods of access to these memories, as described by the headed records model, described later in this chapter.

Other features of self and personhood arise in split-brain patients or in multiple personality disorders. A further strand in a neural approach is analysis of the underlying brain regions that are most relevant. I summarize each of these aspects before developing a neurally based model of self. Before commencing such a descriptive and model-building project, it might be helpful to indicate the goal I am aiming at, to explain the selection of items marshaled as a preliminary.

The main thread throughout the book has been the original relational mind model, developed more fully into that of the framework of the relational consciousness model. Creation of the multifaceted relationships of inputs to neural representations of the past is posited in this approach as the basic mode by which consciousness emerges. The relations are determined by the manner in which past memories are reactivated and used to relate to the present input and to define a response. The same relational approach is expected to be appropriate to tackle the problems of the emergence and nature of self. Neural forms of self-memories and the competitive control structures relevant to their use are at issue. The detailed form of resulting behavior and experience are facts to be marshaled to bolster and refine the relational approach to self.

The Development of Self

In chapter 10, I noted how the infant learns action sequences or schemata by what Piaget termed the processes of assimilation and accommodation.

Initially, the infant acts in a manner driven by its basic reflexes arising from subcortical stimulus-response circuits. As increasing cortical power becomes available through maturation, value and object representations are created to give ever greater content and complexity to response and exploration patterns. Consciousness emerges as part of this growth, initially with increasing semantic memory and later with episodic memory. Consciousness of self is also observed to emerge gradually.

Piaget described the periods of development subsequent to the sensorimotor stage as concerned initially with preoperational, then concrete, and ultimately formal operations. In the first of these stages the child begins to manipulate the truth of propositions, just as the previous stage involved manipulation of objects, and begins to think and speak of past or distant events, of cause and effect, of number, of time, and of the perspectives of others. The next stage sees development of reasoning powers, and in the final period, beginning approximately at adolescence, the capacity to represent abstract truth instead of just the current state emerges. Hypotheticodeductive reasoning appears, as does the ability to generate systematic permutations of sets of objects. Relations between objects themselves become the objects of formal reasoning. These cognitive aspects of the emerging mind are clearly of importance in development of personality and the notion of self.

Piaget considered early childhood to be egocentric, with the child not understanding the views and thoughts of others as different from its own. However, this characterization was seriously challenged in the 1970s and 1980s, with suggestions from a theory of mind emerging at about two and one-half to four years of age to the claim that infant-parent interactions led to intersubjectivity in the first year of life. In particular, it seems that by two to three years of age a child can imagine having a mental state of belief or desire; for example, she can imagine wanting to drink milk when she is not thirsty.

A child also develops the ability to engage in pretend play (Leslie 1987). Piaget knew that pretence undergoes elaboration between twelve and forty-eight months. Initially, for a very young child, a doll is a passive recipient of ministrations; by age three or four years, the doll is granted beliefs related to pretend facts as designated by the child (e.g., having one doll unaware of the presence of another hiding behind a tree).

Now that we have briefly reviewed the processes of cognitive development of the young child, we can extend it to include that of personality. This involves interactions with the mother, which acquires social significance at an early age; this relation is an important affectional tie that promotes a sense of security and trust, as well as the development of internal controls in the infant in response to the demands and reinforcements of the mother. Apart from effects on the child of the style in which he is reared (levels of permissiveness versus authoritarianism) a crucial genetic influence also exists.

In general, personality traits emerge from the genetically determined substructure of neural connections, glandular makeup, sex, physique, and physiological constituency. It is developed and modified by the parental and social interactions to which the child is exposed. Socially significant stimuli are perceived from as early as the second month of infancy, with interaction between infants occurring by about the fourth or fifth month. This develops into closer interactions for the preschool child, with younger children engaging in more physical conflict than older ones, for whom verbal aggression is more important. As the child grows she begins to acquire the values of her peer group, with parental influence subsiding. The self is continually being modified, on a deeper neurological substructure, from birth through childhood, driven initially by parental and then by social interactions. These changes in neural structure are laid down gradually in the brain to determine the nature of the personality and self.

It is relevant to note that manifestation of self-image in children at about two to three years of age is paralleled by an apparently similar development in chimpanzees and orangutans. Preadolescent chimpanzees, for example, were housed individually and each was given a full-length mirror to play with over a period of ten days (Gallup 1979). After an initial two to three days of directing social responses to their mirror images (threatening, vocalizing) as if they were other animals, they began to use self-directed actions such as grooming when in front of the mirror, inspecting parts of their body they could not otherwise see, and removing particles of food from between their teeth. The chimps were then anaesthetized, a patch of indelible red dye was painted above one eyebrow and on the top of the opposite ear, locations unobservable without the use of the mirror. A twentyfold increase of touching the colored patches occurred when the animals were reintroduced to the mirror. A control group with no experience of mirrors showed no particular interest in the red marks on their faces. The first group had apparently developed a self-image during those ten days with the mirror.

The nature and development of the self-image appear to be context dependent. Chimpanzees reared with humans consider themselves humans, explaining the generally poor sexual adjustment that they later show to other chimpanzees. Washoe, a chimpanzee trained to use sign language, called other chimpanzees by sign language "black bugs." Vicki, another human-adapted chimpanzee, placed a picture of her father on a pile of pictures of elephants and horses and placed her own photo with those of humans.

These studies indicate that chimps and orangutans, like children, can develop a self-image to which they respond if exposed to a mirror. We cannot claim that this proves animals who fail the mirror self-recognition test do not have a self-image; they may indeed do so, but their self-image does not seem to be used to deal with otherwise unobservable parts of the body, as with a chimpanzee or an orangutan. Animals that do not get past the stage of responding to the mirror image as if to another animal (and therefore do not recognize themselves) are much less likely to have any self-image.

The Split Self

Our cortical hemispheres are usually joined, but further clues as to the nature of self have arisen from split-brain patients who have had the fibers joining the hemispheres severed to prevent otherwise intractable epileptic seizures. These people have relatively independent thoughts going on in the hemispheres (each is now a separate individual). American scientist Roger Sperry launched a series of tests on split-brain patients in the 1950s and 1960s and concluded in 1966:

Each hemisphere appears to have its own separate and private sensations, its own concepts and its own impulses to act. The evidence suggests that consciousness runs in parallel in both the hemispheres of the split brain person.

These individuals also have independent impulses for action. When the left hand might be making an error, the right hand will reach over to restrain it. In other experiments one hand would write a message on a piece of paper but the other hand constantly tried to stop it. Seeing a film of such patients essentially fighting with themselves is a disturbing experience (Mark 1996).

A great many further observations have been made on lateralization of function in split-brain patients. The important lesson for our present purpose is that self has a strong cortical basis. Neural sites of self must include a very important cortical component that has to be activated. The different functions of the hemispheres are well known—left for logical thinking and language, right for emotional states and artistic expression. The fact that two quite different personalities could arise after separation of the hemispheres is not surprising. If the halves were involved in such different aspects of activity, they would be expected to generate and control quite different responses. This difference is underlined by that occurring between the right and left hemispheres for inhibition of behavior, which has early expression in infancy: the right side is more prone to advance, the left to withdraw.

You could ask at this point, why not a further dissociation of consciousness into left and right? Evidence from split-brain patients strongly supports this further division. I cannot but accept the point, but will not follow it up here. We have enough on our plates as it is, and several excellent books on the subject are available.

Divided Selves

The division of the self may arise not only from surgical intervention but also within an apparently healthy brain. Well-attested cases of multiple personality disorder exist. The condition is defined in the American Psychiatric Association's Diagnostic and Statistical Manual, ed. 3, as follows:

1. The existence within an individual of two or more distinct personalities, each of which is dominant at a particular time.
2. The personality that is dominant at any particular time determines the individual's behavior.
3. Each individual personality is complex and integrated with its own unique patterns and social relationships.

There is always a host personality and several alternative ones, called alters, that usually call themselves by different names and may have different accents, choices in dress, and even different sex from the host. None of the personalities is emotionally mature and rounded, and different ones appear to possess different emotional competences. Thus certain alters appear to be dominant in appropriate social situations such as in making love, being aggressive, dealing with children, and so on. In such situations an alter will completely displace the host or any other alter dominant at that time. The host displays complete amnesia of the experiences of the alter while the latter is in charge. Although general knowledge seems to be shared among all the personalities, personal memories are not. That is why cases of amnesia are sometimes interpreted as arising from multiple personality disorder.

One woman, Mary, in her early thirties, was suffering from depression, confusional states, and lapses of memory (Humphrey and Dennett 1989). She had kept a diary that contained entries in a number of different handwritings. Under hypnosis, Mary changed her personality, and said "I'm Sally. Mary's a wimp. She thinks she knows it all, but I can tell you. . . ."

Over the next sessions of analysis Mary recounted a sad story. From the age of four, her stepfather had taken her into his bed, given her the pet name "Sandra," and continually abused her. On one occasion she said she would tell somebody, but her stepfather hit her and said that both of them would go to prison. Eventually, when the pain, dirt, and disgrace became too much to bear, Mary increasingly dissociated from what he was doing to her. Her psychiatrist speculated that over the following years she was able to develop effectively only by such dissociation, but that "Sandra," who was left with the humiliation and memories of abuse, could not initially do so. To fill in the parts of her experience closed off to Mary, an alter called Sally emerged who was able to please Daddy. Mary's pain and anger gave rise to another alter named Hatey; a further alter enjoyed behaving like a doll, and was called Peggy.

These different alters developed so Mary could cope successfully by calling on the relevant alter as appropriate to the situation. Finally, she could not control them all, and thus began her depression, confusional states, and amnesia. Treatment attempted to fuse these personalities together, and attained some level of success.

In another case, a host, Jonah, had three alters, Sammy, King Young, and Usoffa Abdulla. Jonah was unaware of the alters and was shy, sensitive, and highly conventional. Sammy, who could also apparently coexist in consciousness with his host as well as taking over completely, claimed always to be ready to appear when Jonah needed legal advice or to get out of trouble; he displayed no emotion. King Young took over when Jonah could not find the right words in talking with women in whom he had a sexual interest; he considered himself a ladies' man. Finally, Usoffa became dominant whenever Jonah was in physical danger; he was a cold and belligerent person.

A variety of tests on the different personalities gave almost identical intelligence scales, with exactly the same answers to content questions. Learning was transferred from Jonah to his alters, but the three did not share knowledge. This was shown by each personality in turn learning the associates to a list of ten words, each paired to a response word. The other personalities were then tested on the same list in turn, being asked to respond with the word that best fit the test word. The three alters seemed to know Jonah's word pairs, but when each alter learned his own word pairs, there was little transference to the other alters or to Jonah.

These cases of multiple personality disorder are highly relevant to the nature and modeling of personality.

Autobiographical Memory

This is the form of memory of events in which the "I" is involved. Thus I have good autobiographical memory of the very first scientific conference I ever attended and at which I gave my first scientific paper. It also involved me in a long, again my first, airplane flight, which I also remember well. We all have memories of such events, of the clothes we wore, the food we ate, and the anxieties we experienced. It is possible to divide these autobiographic memories into four classes:

- Single personal memories
- Generic personal memories
- Autobiographical facts
- Self schemata

Single personal memories are of the events in which "I" is involved, such as the ones I mentioned above. Generic personal memories are involved with events such as having lunch last Friday or traveling to work yesterday. They call upon and help build up schemata for personal experience. Autobiographical facts are those about oneself, such as height, weight, and so on. Self schemata arise from single and generic memories as complex knowledge systems.

Let us analyze how personal memory develops to understand multiple personality. Autobiographical memory does not usually begin until about two to four years of age, as testing of adults has shown. The reason for this childhood amnesia may be lack of suitable neural structures. It is also possible that the young child does not have suitable schemata in terms of which the events to be remembered could be embedded. Most children two and one-half years of age can remember events of six months before, but these infantile memories tend to have disappeared by adulthood. Linguistically based schemata develop only at about six years. However, none of these suggestions for childhood amnesia is completely satisfactory.

A more recent suggestion (Nelson 1993) is that a novel event would be usefully kept in a temporary buffer to ascertain if it is the first of a recurrent series of events and should therefore be remembered permanently, or if it is a one-off of no functional significance. Two memory systems would be necessary, one to hold the first event temporarily, the second to hold generic events and allow integration of new events if appropriate. Reinstatement of short-term episodic memories (lasting 6 months or so) would then occur. This would allow weaker episodic memories to be reactivated by means of active response or by linguistic expression. The autobiographical memory system would then be rearranged when linguistic interactions with adults and exposure to adult forms of thought took place. Autobiographical memories of single personal events would be developed first by external discussion with adults, then through internalized speech. Preserved episodic memories would be those to which high social value or self-reference was thereby attached.

Autobiographical memories appear to have a hierarchical structure. They can be divided into those with increasing temporal duration of three types:

- Lifetime periods
- General events
- Specific events

A life-time period could consist, for example, for me of the time I spent as an undergraduate and research student at Cambridge University. A general event could be running in a cross-country race, and a specific event falling in the mud on the Gog-Magog hills near Cambridge on a cold winter day in January 1952. The resulting hierarchical structure appears to be similar to that involved in language structure and manual object combination as described in chapter 10. For this reason it is appropriate to expect that it is supported by similar frontal structures.

A further feature of autobiographical memory was emphasized by Morton (Morton 1991), termed headed records. This accounts, among other things, for the phenomenon of feeling able to recount virtually everything about a person except for his or her name. The model regards memories as the contents of files, each of which is accessed by searching for a "header" or title to the file. It allows for reduction of information being used to set up a description of the memory task, and the description is then used to search in parallel through the headings. A match of a header to a record allows retrieval of the corresponding file. On this account there are two sites of memory, one for the record, the other for the header.

This helps explain the situation when you have completely forgotten an event and only through a special clue—the header—will the memory flood back. A typical example concerns a husband whose wife reminded him of the evening when he had been argumentative at a restaurant. The husband disclaimed all knowledge of the event until she mentioned the thick gravel on the drive leading up to the restaurant. Ah, yes, then he remembered!

The Brain Sites of Self

The features of self presented in this chapter may be summarized by saying that self-image develops at about two to three years of age, that it has important cortical components, and that autobiographical memory is hierarchically arranged in a manner similar to various frontally based schemata. All of these point to a frontally based neural construction of the "I." Other evidence from studying brain lesions hints at frontal and limbic involvement. In this section we consider brain sites for the two features of autobiographical memory: transient buffering of episodic memory and subsequent long-term storage. We will not specifically address generic schemata, since these were discussed in the previous chapter. Instead, we go to the permanent components of autobiographical memory, both as records and headers, and consider sites for transient episodic memory storage, long-term record storage, and long-term header storage (where the header is solely a label required to access the full record).

Well-known limbic regions that are candidates for transient storage are the hippocampus and its adjacent cortex. Absence of these produces permanent amnesia for new memory storage (antegrade amnesia) and for past events, to an extent proportional to the amount of nearby cortex removal (retrograde amnesia). Hence it seems likely that the hippocampus functions as the buffer and nearby cortex as the long-term store. Considerable evidence supports such a conclusion. For example, people who have their hippocampus cut out to damp down otherwise intractable epilepsy caused by damage in that region can learn nothing new.

In the process of choosing the hippocampal system we seem to have found sites for all three components of autobiographical memory. But such an answer is too simple, since it does not do justice to the difference between complete records and solely the headers. Second, it does not give indication as to the overall hierarchical structure involved, and finally, it contains no hint as to the enormous complexity of the limbic system, which is discussed in chapter 13 as part of the emotions. We will try to remedy these three aspects in turn.

Let us agree that the hippocampus can act as a temporary buffer of information. It has suitable internal connectivity for it to act as a recurrent net, allowing incomming activity to persist from all modalities relevant to a given event. Representation of each input activity may then be formed, possibly as a separate set of patterns or as a stored sequence (Rolls 1989; Reiss and Taylor 1992). At this stage all of the information (coded at a suitably high level) has been stored.

The next stage involves the permanent storage of this temporary information as a record and a header. The record appears to be stored in a hierarchical manner, although the header may not be. However, according to the evidence, active search can be performed only on the header.

One neural system relevant to such memorial properties is the loop structure of the medial orbitofrontal (and cingulate) cortex. This can be used to store records in an ACTION network style of processing. It would explain the hierarchical structure of the resulting records as arising from chunking; we saw earlier how similar hierarchies arise in speech and manipulation in frontal lobe. The manner in which a header could be used to access a record would then most naturally be its storage in the hippocampal cortical regions. Activation of a header would activate the corresponding record, allowing access by disinhibition onto the corresponding record. A report could then arise by activating Broca's area and the phonological loop. In other words, the header acts as the beginning element in a sequence stored in the ACTION network of the medial orbitofrontal loop.

Storage of headers alone close to the hippocampus seems to be a good move to reduce storage overheads, since it could well be that space near the hippocampus is at a premium. The model fits the data on mesencephalic amnesia, in which the mediodorsal nucleus of the thalamus is an essential item in storage and recall; lesions in this region are known to cause severe memory loss. At the same time, involvement of the amygdala (which has strong interactions with the ventral striatum and is also part of the relevant ACTION network) allows affective valence to be strongly involved in these representations. It also fits the extended memory abilities of chess players and professional mnemonists.

Evidence is coming from a number of brain imaging experiments for involvement of the cortex around the hippocampus in the development of memories of particular recent events. In one experiment (Binder et al. 1996) subjects had to remember a set of nouns and respond if a word had a particular meaning. In another (Maddock et al. 1997) they listened to names of members of their family, and a third experiment had a similar paradigm (Andreason et al. 1995). The region for laying down autobiographic memories appeared from these results to form quite an extensive network of brain areas in the middle of the brain.

Further brain imaging studies (Tulving et al. 1994a) demonstrated the existence of an even more extensive network involved in memory tasks. A general framework was suggested (Tulving et al. 1994b) in which the left half of the prefrontal region is used in laying down memories and the right side for their retrieval. More posterior parts of these networks are also active. Asymmetry between the left and right sides of the frontal cortex is supported by further brain imaging (Krause et al. 1997). This has allowed determination of strengths of the connections among different parts of the extensive cortical networks involved in encoding and retrieving memories. Much more precise models of episodic memory are becoming available.

Models of the Self

I propose a model of the self based on the facts presented earlier and the nature of the brain sites suggested for the storage of autobiographical memory. Part of the task of this model is to explain certain features of multiple personality disorder. We should also try to encompass ideas of psychoanalysis, which had a strong influence in modern understanding of self. It is important to consider in what manner the Freudian notions of ego, superego, and id, and also repression, are discernible in the model.

The relational consciousness model again seems to be a useful guide toward the self. It reminds us to consider the appropriate long-term (episodic) memory structures and related preprocessing-semantic and working memory pairs. What are the comparable structures for self-consciousness? In answering this it is essential to note that dynamic features of the development of consciousness of self, especially those associated with multiple personality disorder, make this form of consciousness appear to be of a somewhat different character from either the posterior or anterior forms. It depends critically on the interaction with important others, that is, with other people.

Let us start with the episodic memory trace stored temporarily in the hippocampus. That initially has an emotional or salience value attached to it arising from a similar representation in the amygdala, which it is assumed is activated by the hippocampal trace. In multiple personality disorder the strength of the amygdala response may be so high (from a traumatic experience) as to cause strong levels of inhibition along the length of the hippocampus (it is shaped like a seahorse, the meaning of its Latin name). In particular, greatest vulnerability of regions of hippocampus is expected to be between modalities or where multimodular overlap occurs. That would lead to fragmented, single modal traces in short segments of the hippocampus, fitting multiple personality disorder. Abuse at the basis of such a disorder may be remembered separately by the alters, one recalling the light overhead, another the color of the ceiling, another yet the rough feeling of the rope tying the hands or the texture of the sheets, which were all part of the original experience. These separated traces are a basis for the development of separate sets of headers and records along the lines of the previous section, and thereby grow into the separate personalities or alters.

In this approach each personality would correspond to activation of the connected set of records in the medio-orbital frontal cortical ACTION network loop. Inputs would activate headers in the relevant stretch of hippocampal cortex, leading to responses in the associated personality controlled by the set of records connected to the given personality. Switches between personalities would arise by competition on the ventral striatum (the striatal part of the relevant ACTION network), with new input to the latter leading to the emergence of a more appropriate personality in the given context.

How can the sense of self arise? This is usually thought of as self-referral, so there must be some form of comparison of continuing responses to one's self records. That can be achieved by using a comparator on the ventral striatum. Records relevant to a personality would be impressed on the ventral striatum and would act as templates to determine whether or not they give agreement with what is going on there. This agrees closely with the Gray's model (described in chapter 5) of consciousness as a comparator, which uses much of the same neural circuitry as the one proposed here. However, we are here restricting ourselves to "ourselves" and not to the whole of our consciousness.

This model handles the mechanical or "how" aspects of the self and personality. But what of the inner experience of self? Although bizarre, that is seen as disappearing if it is searched for too strongly; the comparison between continuing responses and those predicted by self records has to have incoming activity from the response pattern onto the ventral striatum. Too strong an activation of the records, as could arise in a persistent search for the self, would cause input to the ventral striatum from outside to be so inhibited as to cease, and the experience of self would disappear; only new perceptions would then be able to be experienced. Such is recounted by David Hume, quoted at the beginning of the chapter.

Freudian Psychology

What of Freudian psychology—repression, the ego, the superego, and the id? In his earlier days Freud attempted to construct a neural model of the psyche. We described a possible simple model of repression in the formation of multiple personality disorder. We saw that the repressive mechanism is the arousal of inhibition from the amygdala, itself excited by autonomic, visceral, and hypothalamic brain centers. Thus we site the superego in the medio-orbital frontal cortex (with its comparator ability to keep responses on the straight and narrow). This contains those autobiographical memory structures—records—absorbed from parents and peers during an individual's development, and is the site for projective identification of post-Freudian psychoanalysis.

According to the early Freudian idea, the ego was both a nonreflexive but active form of consciousness. More recent psychoanalytic theory recognizes the ego as more closely involved with active consciousness alone and having a controlling function over the id. This would therefore be sited in the nonmesial ACTION networks of the frontal lobes, as well as in the posterior buffer working memory sites. Finally, the id is suggested as the hypothalamus-autonomic-visceral system, which is the source of drives and has to be controlled by the higher-level cortical functions of the ego and the superego.

An important component of Freudian theory is active repression of libido by the ego. It was in attempting to explain the mechanism of this process that Freud encountered a difficulty that caused him to abandon his project for a scientific psychology. This latter was characterized by his translator as "an extraordinarily ingenious working model of the mind as a piece of neurological machinery" (Richards 1989). The difficulty was giving a physiological explanation of the mechanism used to suppress a hostile memory trace before it entered consciousness. This would have to occur by postulating some form of attentional control system to forewarn and activate the ego, to prevent the unfriendly memory trace being reactivated. But such an attentional system and the resulting suppressive act were precisely the phenomena he was trying to explain in the first place.

In terms of the neural states suggested for the ego, superego and id, is it possible that we can provide a solution to the problem faced by Freud? In fact we have already partly achieved that in the model suggested for multiple personality disorder. In such cases fracturing of the personality is achieved by inhibition from amygdala onto hippocampus and related limbic areas. The negative affect of certain inputs may be damped down by such amygdala output to allow a reduced level of affect to be related to the inputs. The personality most adapted to a given set of inputs is activated (in the orbitomedial frontal loop), with suppression of other personalities by amygdala inhibition onto the ventral striatum. A similar mechanism could be used for a less divided personality, still leading to repression of unpleasant memories that otherwise would become conscious. The amygdala (and the related motivational circuit) is proposed as the attentional suppressor of hostile memory traces that have been stored in hippocampal cortex and the orbitomedial frontal loop, respectively, as headers and records. In this case the component of personality that is activated has no access to the unpleasant memories inhibited by amygdala without conscious activation. Fragmentation of the ACTION-based frontal and active nature of the ego is essential in the repressive process, where passive consciousness plays a lesser role.

We return briefly to the question raised earlier: how much is episodic memory involved in either posterior or anterior consciousness? The evidence presented earlier was ambiguous: it did not distinguish contributions of memories to the two forms of consciousness. We know from brain imaging that autobiographical memory is distributed over a network of modules, some frontal, some more posterior. We expect that the more posteriorly sited components contribute to posterior consciousness and anterior ones to anterior consciousness. The posterior part of autobiographical memory involves more general knowledge used constantly that has reduced emotional significance, such as the names of one's family, one's address, and so on. The frontal part is more emotionally charged, involving knowledge about relations to loved ones. Thus different parts of episodic memory are involved in the two forms of consciousness.

Summary

After an introduction to the nature of self, I described present knowledge about its development in human infants and primates. Further light was cast on it by split-brain patients who, because of surgery, possess two personalities, and people with multiple personality disorder that is probably brought about by childhood trauma. I then explored the nature of autobiographical memory and analyzed sites of brain storage. I developed a neural model of self on the basis of the understanding gained, and briefly related it to multiple personality disorder and to Freudian ideas.

The three basic components of consciousness outlined in the first chapter—passive or posterior, active or anterior, and self—have now been analyzed in terms of the relational consciousness model developed so far. In the next part of the book I first develop a set of principles for relational consciousness that covers these forms of consciousness and at last turn to tackle the hard problem: why is any neural activity conscious? What is the extra value in neural activity that is necessary to produce consciousness?

IV

The Hard Problem of Consciousness

12

Return to Relational Consciousness

Clothed and in his right mind.
—Mark 5:15

Principles of Relational Consciousness

In the previous five chapters I highlighted various features of consciousness, aspects of some of the jumps in the great race, and how they might be got over by suitable neural models. I now put together these various bits and pieces by developing a set of principles for relational consciousness. Earlier models based on consciousness as closely correlated with activity in buffer working memory should be noted as being of relevance. American psychologists Atkinson and Shiffrin stated (Atkinson and Shiffrin 1971; Mandler 1975), "In our thinking we tend to equate the short term store with 'consciousness,' that is the thoughts and information of which we are currently aware can be considered part of the content of short term store."

Such identification of consciousness with short-term or primary memory was made earlier by William James (Baddeley 1986; 1992). The model therefore has a good pedigree.

I now present the main principles of the relational consciousness model of passive consciousness. These are broad enough to encompass all three varieties of consciousness we have recognized so far—passive, active, and self.

Principle 1: For each input code there exists a related pair of preprocessing and working memory modules.

By code I mean the output of several levels of nonconscious analysis acting on primary sensory input in a given modality. For vision the codes are texture, shape, motion, position, and color. Coding can be at the level of so-called primitives, such as for color and motion, or of a high-level alphabet, such as for phonemes or words in sound processing.

Elements of a high-level alphabet arise from preprocessing by successive higher-order feature detectors. These are created by learning the simultaneous presence of increasing numbers of features observed in the environment. In the auditory modality for linguistic input there is processing, as I noted earlier, up to the level of phonemes (and even up to few-syllable and often-encountered words); similar high-level processing is available for music. For touch there is also detection of increasingly complex inputs, with cells being found in higher-order cortex that are responsive only to the simultaneous touching of two adjacent fingers. A similar processing style occurs in vision, with neurons corresponding to increasingly complex object features found at succeedingly higher levels in visual cortex. For shape, for example, low-level neurons code for short edges in pictures of objects, at a higher level for corners and longer edges, and even higher for more complex shapes such as stars and circles. Olfaction is more complex, with no primitives available on which to build higher-order feature detection. The more ancient origin of olfaction is relevant to its having less developed processing.

Experimental support of two kinds exists for this principle. First, psychological evidence points to a broad range (Paulesu et al. 1994; Smith and Jonieds 1995; Salmon et al. 1996; Jeannerod 1995) for different buffer working memory sites in various codes: the phonological store for phonemically coded inputs, visuospatial sketch pads for spatial and shape inputs, and the body metric for somatosensory inputs. Each buffer working memory store holds activity over a limited time, only a few seconds, if it is not refreshed by frontal action. Second, neurological evidence from brain imaging studies indicates the existence of localized cortical visual and auditory working memories. Numerous buffer modules have been discovered, to be expected if both semantic and continued working memory activity is being measured across a number of codes and modalities. Furthermore, these posterior sites are well connected to anterior active working memory sites, extending the principle to apply equally to active and self-consciousness as well as their passive partner.

Principle 2: Competition exists in a given working memory among neural activities representing different interpretations of inputs in the preceding second or so.

I presented support for this principle in an earlier chapter by means of a simplified model of the two modules—semantic memory and buffer modules—as part of the phonological loop. This was used to give a quantitative analysis of the experimental data on subliminal processing of words. Competition arises from lateral inhibitory connections among regions coding for opposed meanings on a given buffer working memory module. Such lateral inhibition does not exist on the semantic module, on which all possible meanings of a given input were activated. That it could arise solely from connections inside a given cortical area was shown earlier.

Various experiments provide other evidence for inhibition inside a given area. One of these is the beautiful demonstration (Salzman and Newsome 1994) of competition in the monkey extrastriate cortex between two inputs for a perceptual decision it makes. One signal arose from the direction of motion of a visual stimulus, the other was introduced by electrically stimulating neurons that encoded a specific direction of motion. The monkeys chose the direction of inputs that was encoded by the largest signal, as in a winner-take-all decision-making process. There was no evidence that decisions relied on any other computation by the neurons encoding directions of motion of visual inputs.

Further, less direct, evidence can be gleaned from the phenomenon of perceptual alternation, such as that in the Necker cube shown in figure 12.1. If it is viewed persistently it will reverse its three-dimensional character every few seconds. Try it! Numerous cases of such alternation are known, and experiments have been performed in which the level of complexity in the ambiguous figures alters the speed of reversal. An analysis by means of two neural modules, one coding for each of the alternative interpretations, and which have self-excitation but coupled inhibition, has also been performed (Masulli and Raini 1989; Raini and Masulli 1990). The model fits in with principle 2 if the two mutually computing modules are regarded as part of Baddeley's visuospatial sketch pad (the

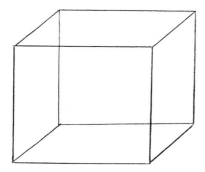

Figure 12.1
Necker cube, for which times between alternations in interpretation appear to be a low-dimensional attractor. This can be modeled by a competitive neural network.

site of the visual working memory). When the active working memory components of a given system are more active than the posterior one (as in the n-back experiment for n larger than one), passive consciousness is replaced by its active or self companion as the main component of consciousness; the principle still applies.

Principle 3: Competition is run among activities on different working memories, with the winner gaining access to consciousness.

I developed this principle in chapter 7 and added further support for it in chapter 8 in terms of the important results of Libet and colleagues. Additional support comes from experiments on intrusive thoughts by Baddeley (Baddeley 1993). Understanding and controlling these is important for depressed patients, whose thoughts are often of their own inadequacy and form one of their major complaints.

The two types of such stimulus-independent thoughts are sequential and coherent, and those of a more fragmented type. A subject sits silently in a quiet room. At random he is asked what his thoughts consist of. Results of this experiment for several subjects led to the discovery that just over three-fourths of the time they did have intrusive thoughts, of which roughly three-fourths involved coherent sequential thoughts and the other one-fourth much more fragmented ones. Performing distracting tasks, such as listening to and repeating a five-digit sequence presented at the rate of one a second, led to considerable reduction of the coherent

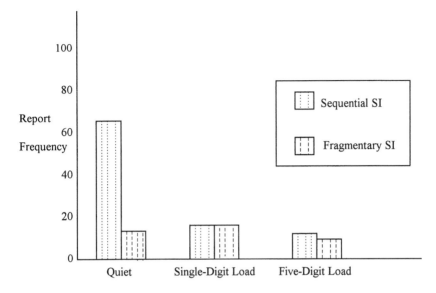

Figure 12.2
The influence of memory load on the frequency of report of fragmentary and coherent stimulus-independent thoughts. (Adapted from Baddeley 1993)

intrusive thoughts (to the level of the fragmented thoughts), but little change in the level of the production of fragmentary thoughts themselves (figure 12.2). In addition, suppression of stimulus-independent thoughts was more or less independent of the modality in which distractor tasks were involved, with about the same level of reduction brought about by a visual tracking task as by an auditory distractor.

An additional experiment on intrusive thoughts is of geat relevance. The subjects who were repeating five digits were divided into two groups: those who reported being aware of the digits during the task, and those who were unaware. Aware subjects had intrusive thoughts in less than 10 percent of instances in which they were asked. On the other hand, subjects who performed the task without being aware of the digits said that they had stimulus-independent thoughts just over half of the time.

This underlines the crucial role played by awareness of digits in considerably reducing the level of intrusive thoughts. Once consciousness of the digits occurred, such thoughts were reduced six-fold compared with when no other task was performed or when the digit repetition was automatic.

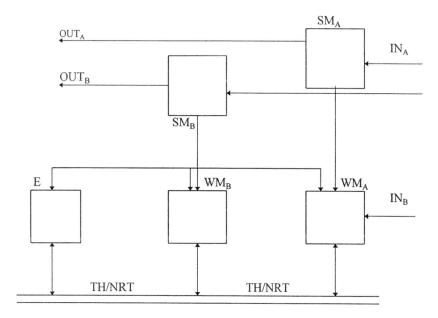

Figure 12.3
A competitive relational model of the results on stimulus-independent thoughts.

In both cases no conscious processing was going on other than awareness of intrusive thoughts.

A simple model to support the generation of such thoughts consists of two preprocessing-semantic memory-buffer working memory pairs, each coupled to an episodic memory store and to the thalamus-NRT-cortex system for global competition. One of the pairs codes for words, the other for digits (figure 12.3).

I suggest that intrusive thoughts are most likely produced uncontrollably from the episodic memory system based on past unpleasant memories and on low self-value. They could be generated due to loss of an internal control system able to inhibit them. Healthy subjects' control circuits would function properly and they would not be plagued by self-denigratory thoughts.

Intrusive thoughts enter consciousness when input entering the preprocessing memories of figure 12.3 (one for words, the other for digits) is reduced and internally generated fragments or sequences (expected to be verbal) from the episodic memory gain control of the modes on the buffer module for words. The level of intrusive thoughts is reduced when one of the working memories has won the suggested competition (by principle 3), as in the case of awareness of the digits in the distractor task corresponding to its working memory winning. This causes reduction of activity in the competing buffer module for intrusive thoughts. Such reduction will not occur when the digits are processed automatically, as in the case of input to the preprocessing module for digits giving output without arousing awareness. This explanation is completely consistent with experimental results.

Principle 4: Feedback from episodic memory is involved in competition among different preprocessing semantic memory-buffer working memory pairs or the associated lower-level and higher-level regions in anterior working memory.

This principle is part of the basic hypothesis: relations are set up using past memories including episodic memories. What I have not justified by the more detailed discussions and simulations presented earlier is the claim that episodic memory is involved in posterior consciousness. Support for principle 4 comes from analysis of intrusive thoughts discussed above (see figure 12.3). In chapter 6 I described various reported individual experiences and more controlled psychological experiments as qualitative support for this principle. An even more dramatic result indicating the influence of past experience on present awareness (Roediger and McDermott 1995) involved creation of false memories, in which previously experienced material was used to cause subjects to respond falsely to related material to which they had not been exposed as if they had been. It can be seen as involving active filling in of missing elements while remembering, in contrast to automatic or rote reproduction of material from memory. Such false memories have led to tragic (and completely refutable) charges, by relatively young but not completely balanced adults of childhood abuse. It is therefore important to discover how easily they are created.

In the experiment, subjects heard, and then recalled, lists of words related to another word, which was not itself heard, such as *table, set, legs, seat, soft, desk, arm, sofa, wood, cushion, rest,* and *stool,* all related to *chair.* A recognition list, consisting of some items that had been studied and some that had not, was later used to test subjects' recall abilities.

The experiment was performed as follows. The list was read aloud and subjects were immediately tested for free recall; they were later tested with the recognition list. The most important finding, for our purposes, was that in nearly half of the tests the related word that had not been presented was recalled at the first test. This is to be compared with a much smaller error in recall of other English words, so that subjects were not guessing wildly as to what they had previously studied. On the later test with the recognition list the subjects were "sure" that the critical nonstudied items had been on the originally presented lists over half of the time.

The explanation given by the experimenters is that during study, nonconscious or conscious activation of semantically related words occurs. This leads to false recognition from the residual activation and even to false remembrance of the critical but not-presented word having been on the list when tested later with the recognition list.

Consider the phenomenological experience of subjects while they were being tested, and in particular how they came to think they had actually seen a word on the list when it definitely had not been there. This could be due to conscious recollection of newly created episodic memory. Let us look at the figures coming from the experiment to see if this could have happened.

The critical item had a higher chance of being remembered if it had been produced on the immediate free recall test compared with no such production (by 20 percent). So the critical nonstudied word had a 20 percent chance of being produced at free recall in an implicit manner, it becoming consciously reported. The memory of that report was then laid down in episodic memory for later use during a recognition test as a basis for remembering. This interpretation of both conscious and implicit incorrect recollections is in direct support of principles 3 and 4, since the earlier activities of associated words, either in the semantic or episodic memory modules of figure 12.3, were used to modify the response and thereby the conscious experience of the subjects during testing on the later recognition lists. Moreover, this interpretation of conscious remembering is in support of principle 4 through the involvement of episodic memory that has only recently been created (at free recall). It also supports the next principle.

Principle 5: Upgrading of episodic memories occurs from the output of the winning working memory.

This underlines the manner in which episodic and working memories have excitatory feedback interaction. Temporary storage of the output of the winning site in the hippocampal region must occur, and allows us to extend principle 5 further.

Principle 6: The output of the winning working memory is stored in the hippocampal region.

We have left unspecified the manner of the temporary storage of the output of the winning site. It is most likely through some form of alteration to the connection strengths rather than just as a long-duration neural activity (as in working memory sites); the details of such storage are experimentally unclear.

I have now presented the main principles of the relational consciousness model of both the passive or posterior and active or self aspects of consciousness, and discussed support for them. Figure 12.4 incorporates them. Now that the principles have been set up for the model let us turn to the question of reportability, supposed by some to be a crucial aspect of consciousness.

Reportability

We can explore various features of the detailed nature of the reportability of consciousness. The relational consciousness model leads to two remarks on this question.

First, what is reportable is the content of the winning working memory, determined by the related preprocessing memories as well as episodic memories that have been most heavily used to gain ascendancy of the winning working memory module. Such feedback involves very recent episodic memories, such as in the case of the experiments in false memory creation.

Second, the reporting process is achieved by activating articulation for the associated winning working memory so that its content is broadcast to other working memory sites. Ultimately, response can be given in any modality. However, transmission of material for conscious report

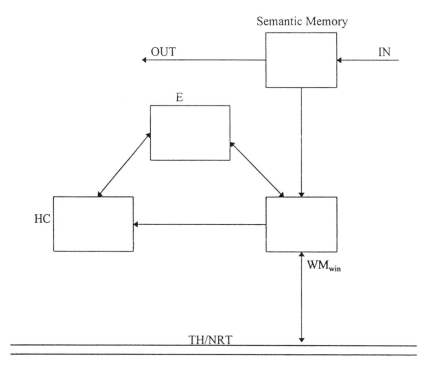

Figure 12.4
Flow chart incorporating main principles of the relational consciousness model (see text for details).

between working memories is certainly not error free, as experimental results of Marcel (1993) aptly demonstrated.

These experiments show us how noisy or low-level inputs are reported quite differently by different modalities. The resulting separation of knowledge from awareness is known to occur in blindsight, as mentioned earlier. That similar effects occur in healthy persons was demonstrated by Marcel with ten subjects who had to guess the presence or absence of a dim light.

The main tasks involved sets of trials, for which a light was on for only half of the time, in which subjects were required to respond in three different ways if they felt that a light had come on: by blinking with the right eye, by pressing the button beneath the right forefinger, and by saying "yes." When the subjects were urged to report a conscious sensation of the light as fast as possible but as accurately as possible, results showed a simultaneous dissociation. For example, on the same trial there might be a "yes" reply with one type of response, but not with another. Success rates in a later set of trials were 77.5 percent, 67.5 percent, and 57.5 percent, respectively, significantly different.

The model suggests the need to broadcast the output of the winning working memory site, in this case the visuospatial sketch pad, to other working memory sites. For example, when input is made to the phonological loop, owing to noise in transmission, errors in responses will occur. However, the only phenomenal experience will be that of the winning working memory.

The time of reportability is dependent on the development of a model of response; it can roughly be identified with that of the output of the winning site. It is interesting to note that the highest level of accuracy (and the lowest level of false alarms) in the experiment of Marcel was that of the eye blink response. The relationship between the visuospatial sketch pad (the working memory for spatial vision) and eye movement is closer than any other. It was suggested that the visuo-spatial sketchpad is refreshed by such movements. So Marcel's results support the thesis that the visuospatial sketch pad is the winning working memory, and that motor and verbal response wait on its initial report. This also agrees with reaction times for the response, for which the speeded reaction times in the three modalities were about 310 to 320, 570 to 580, and 830 to 900 msec, respectively. Thus the data support the next postulate.

Principle 7: Report arises in different modalities from the output of the winning working memory module.

A prediction of the relational consciousness model is that the error rates and reaction times in the above experiment should be changed according to the modality in which the signal was sent. If it was auditory, there should be the highest success rate and shortest reaction time for verbal response; a testable prediction, but yet to be done.

Summary

Seven principles of the emergence of consciousness, forming the full relational consciousness model, were developed from the competitive relational mind model by incorporating results of earlier chapters.

But we are still faced with the explanatory gap between neural activity and phenomenal experience. In the next chapter I consider possible sites of this emergence, leading to a simple two-stage model. In chapter 14 I present a way in which the gap could be bridged by means of a more detailed approach to modeling the sites of buffer working memory. I probe the nature of these modules by asking how they can achieve their power to hold neural activity for so long. The answer will lead us to take a much closer look at the explanatory gap.

13

Where the Raw Feels Come From

Burningly it came on me all at once,
This is the place! those two hills on the right.
—Robert Browning

The methods of science proceed by giving ever closer scrutiny to a phenomenon, so that ultimately it gives up its secrets to the patient probers. So must it be with consciousness: we must be prepared to look at it in all its guises till finally it gives way before our curiosity. To do that we must know where to look. If we look in the wrong place we will have no chance to gain useful knowledge. But how can we know where to look?

I have noted several times that we do not know very much about where consciousness arises. I claimed in previous chapters that it arises in various of the sites of working memory, as suggested by several psychologists and brain scientists. But is it true? What is the evidence? I must now try to describe how much (slim) evidence exists for this idea and discuss more generally the problems we meet in mounting a full and careful search for the sites of emergence of the various components of consciousness. We indeed know from the effects of lesions that different consciousnesses—phenomenal, active, and self—emerge from different sites. One component can be lost completely without the other, which could not occur unless different sites were available in which relevant experience was created. However, we do not have exact locations. So I try in this chapter to explain what is presently known about the sites of consciousnesses and how we might to tease them out.

Table 13.1
PET results on posterior cortical site of buffer working memory

Task	Brain area	Nature of task
Spatial	Left BA 40 (posterior parietal)[a]	Object shape discrimination
	Right BA 40/19 (occipito-parietal)[b]	Object shape discrimination
	Right BA 19 (occipital)[b]	Orientation discrimination
Object	Left BA 40 (posterior parietal)[a]	Object discrimination
Object	Left BA 37 (inferotemporal)[a]	Same
Phonemes/Words	Left BA 40 (posterior parietal)[c]	Word disambiguation

[a]Smith et al. (1995).
[b]Dupont et al. (1995).
[c]Paulesu et al. (1993).

Sites of Buffer Working Memory

In the relational framework I presented earlier I stated that consciousness initially arises in the relevant sites of buffer working memory in a given modality. These sites are composed of modules with activity persisting over seconds. Competition among different interpretations of inputs, such as might arise in ambiguous visual inputs or when different inputs are presented separately to the two eyes, are able to run their course thanks to this extended activity. Such prolonged activity also allows a suitable level of context to be included in the processing. For seven or so objects, one arriving on the site every 300 msec or so, to be able to be held to give context to a given input (as observed psychologically) requires an effective decay time of about 2 seconds; this fits together nicely with the measured decay time in the buffer sites.

Brain imaging tells us where these buffer memories are sited. For instance, PET results (Dupont et al. 1993; Smith et al. 1995; Paulesu et al. 1993; Salmon et al. 1996) on the positions of these sites (summarized in table 13.1) justify their identification with working memory sites introduced on a psychological basis (Baddeley 1986). We will look at these results more closely.

The PET studies of Smith (Smith et al. 1995) showed with a number of different experimental paradigms that spatial and object short-term memory are in different sites in the cortex. In one experiment the positions of a collection of dots shone on a screen for a second had to be compared with the position of a small circle shone on the screen 3 seconds later. This was contrasted with the memory for a set of geometrical objects whose shapes had to be held in short-term memory during 3 seconds before being compared with a further object shone on the screen. Suitable control tasks were used that involved passive processing at the earlier stages. The resulting PET activity was then subtracted from the results of short-term memory trials to remove these passive processing effects.

The other PET study of spatial working memory by Dupont and colleagues (Dupont et al. 1993) considered a discrimination made by the subject between a set of ruled parallel lines shone on a screen and one at a different orientation shone 350 msec later. The most active region (after removal of suitable control activity) was in the right superior occipital area. This is suggested to contain "the additional computation involving the short-term memory and matching required by the temporal same-difference task." We should note the difference in the areas involved in such processing for different attributes or codes; they are not all on top of each other in some supersite in the brain.

We have good evidence for the existence of the phonological store in area 40 of the left cerebral hemisphere; this fits in well with psychological evidence on working memory in word processing described in chapter 9. Table 13.1 also supports the concept of separate working memories in the visual codes for spatial position and for object shape. The general nature of each of these and their possible interrelationships are discussed next.

Awareness in Vision

We can understand how visual awareness emerges along the same lines as that for the conscious awareness of words discussed in chapter 9. There we analyzed Marcel's paradigm in which the speed of decisions as to whether or not a letter string was a word was influenced (speeded up or slowed down) by the previous word having been experienced subliminally or consciously or not experienced at all. In vision the analogous situation to making a decision about the meaning of a polysemous word is deciding between percepts for ambiguous visual scenes.

When different scenes are presented separately to the two eyes (by being shone onto the lenses of suitably designed glasses worn by the subjects) binocular rivalry occurs in which the eyes switch between the percepts. Rivalrous concepts for motion, for example, emerge when two sets of parallel lines moving in opposite directions are presented simultaneously, one to each eye. The subject successively perceives oppositely moving lines. For example, if your right eye were shown an upward movement and the left eye a downward one, the motion you would perceive would alternate between up and down every few seconds.

The similarity of principle expected to be present between interpreting visual inputs and assigning meanings to words is clear: each should involve a stage of preprocessing up to the level of all of the possible interpretations before consciousness of a single percept can emerge by some decision being made between them on a later neural module.

When measuring the activity of single nerve cells in monkeys when they are experiencing binocular rivalry, neurons in the visual area of the temporal lobe, denoted MT (middle temporal), are seen to prefer one direction of motion of the object to the other and respond differently when the percept changes from one of those directions to the other. However, as the experimenters reported, "Half of these units responded to the preferred direction of the cell, and the other half responded when the preferred direction of motion was present in the suppressed eye." They concluded that further processing must be required at a later stage to achieve emergence of the rivalrous percepts of motion. No majority of cells gave the same signal as that corresponding to the percept of the direction of motion actually experienced by the monkey. This is the visual analogue of the semantic level of processing in Marcel's experiment, when both meanings of the word palm were active at semantic level.

A similar result was determined for orientation perception, which Dupont (Dupont et al. 1993) observed in PET studies in humans as having a possible working memory site in visual area 19 in the occipital lobe. Measurements from single nerve cell in the visual areas denoted V1, V2,

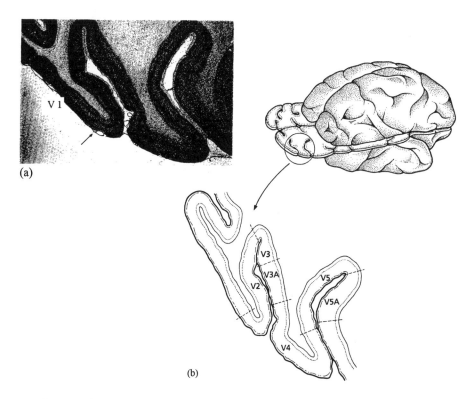

Figure 13.1
(a) Detailed structure of the primary visual area V1 in the macaque monkey, shown by a horizontal section taken through the back of the brain. (b) Visual areas V2, V3, V4, and V5 involved in subsequent processing of visual input. (Reprinted with permission from Zeki 1993)

and V4 (in the occipital lobe at the back of the brain; figure 13.1) were made in monkeys (Leopold and Logothetis 1996) experiencing binocular rivalry for perpendicularly oriented lines presented to the separate eyes. Results for area V4 showed, beyond the existence of an increased number of cells whose activity was modulated by the percept switch compared with those in the areas V1 and V2, that "the majority of cells in all areas continue to respond to their preferred stimulus even when it is perceptually suppressed," as reported by the experimenters.

But how and where can one determine which of the percepts the monkey is aware? From the result quoted earlier, visual area MT plays the same role in motion detection as that played in word processing by the semantic area; all possible interpretations of the visual input (in this case up or down) are encoded by this activity. A similar result holds for the emergence of the percept of orientation: V1, V2, and V4 are all parts of semantic modules and do not directly create consciousness.

Because input is ambiguous, the ambiguity must be removed for a single percept to emerge into consciousness. Therefore another visual cortical area must exist where either the up or down neurons are in the majority and, through competition, can generate the unambiguous percept. Few neurons in this area should be active when their preferred direction is perceptually suppressed. This area is the visual motion equivalent of the phonological store (in area 40) for words. Such a site may also be near the phonological store and have longer effective decay times than cells in V4 or MT. It must also support the required competition between inputs so as to produce a single percept at any one time.

Continuing work by Logothetis and co-workers (Sheinberg and Logothetis 1997) tracked down higher cortical areas where indeed, a majority of nerve cells increased their firing rate significantly when their preferred stimulus was perceived under the binocular rivalry paradigm for objects. The authors wrote,

the areas reported here may represent a stage of processing beyond the resolution of ambiguities, where neural activity reflects the integration of constructed visual percepts into those subsystems responsible for object recognition and visually guided action.

Thus phenomenal consciousness for objects arises in these higher areas as part of the binding process across the various visual codes, which were constructed at the lower semantic, ambiguous level in V1, V2, and V4.

The conjecture of competition being at the basis of the decision as to the percept becoming conscious is supported by results of an experiment designed to analyze the processing in the motion-sensitive area MT of simultaneous, naturally presented stimuli and direct electrode stimulation of a local region of encoding a specific direction of motion (Salzman and Newsome 1994). As mentioned in chapter 14, monkeys were required to make a choice (among eight possible alternatives) between alternative directions of two stimuli, one a set of moving spots of light, the other internally created by electrical stimulation (like Libet's experiment with touch of chapter 8, but now for vision). The monkeys used a winner-take-all strategy to make their decisions between the two directions being activated in their brains according to the resulting direction of motion they were experiencing. The monkeys' choices were not biased to directions intermediate between the signals. Instead the animals chose in favor of the direction coded by the neurons responding most strongly: a competitive process was clearly present. The site of competition at the basis of the decision was not detected by this experiment; it is again conjectured to be some form of working memory with effectively long decay times for the neurons and suitably strong lateral inhibition to support a winner-take-all strategy between opposing possibilities. Other earlier activities support or hinder, according to their excitatory or inhibitory relationship to it, the latest activities in the competition.

Important results emerged when using fMRI techniques on the motion aftereffect (Tootell et al. 1995). This effect occurs when a subject's visual processing neurons sensitive to motion slow down their response (termed adaptation). The aftereffect is experienced after about 20 seconds or so of exposure to moving visual images; when this ceases, a stationary object appears to move in the opposite direction. For example, if one looks steadily at a waterfall for about 30 seconds and then looks at the rock next to the fall, it looks as if the rock is moving upward; that is why the aftereffect is sometimes called the waterfall effect.

In the motion-sensitive area MT the time course of the decay of the activity observed by fMRI is about the same as that for decay of the perceptual experience of the motion aftereffect as reported by subjects (lasting about 9 seconds). However, there were also other regions of transient activity. In one of these the measured brain activity was more transient than the psychophysical duration of the aftereffect, whereas that in another was about 3 seconds longer.

Noninvasive results on siting the emergence of object and face awareness were obtained by MEG and fMRI. Several different networks of localized regions of cortex are involved in supporting consciousness in specific codes or modalities. Which of the modules in a given network are necessary and sufficient for the emergence of consciousness is unknown. Because of the number of different cortical sites both for vision and other modalities, we expect visual awareness to split up into separate parts under abnormal conditions. If a particular region is lost, that part of awareness supported by the region will also disappear.

Support for this dissociation has come from two sources. One is analysis of a blindsight patient, GY (Weiskrantz et al. 1995), who possessed two forms of discrimination of a moving spot in his blindfield (the area in which he was not aware of the visual form of an object). His task was to choose (by guessing, if necessary) in which of two successive intervals of time an image illuminated on a screen in front of him had occurred, or in a single interval choose to which of two alternatives of horizontal or vertical motion the single stimulus belonged. It turned out GY had a clear-cut dissociation between two forms of experience in either task condition. The first experience was for low speeds of the moving image and corresponded to true blindsight (knowledge without awareness); the other arose for higher speeds of the image and had the form of "contentless awareness," in which GY could not say what the image looked like very clearly but was aware of where it was.

We can explain this important dissociation, in particular the experience by GY of contentless awareness, in terms of the model of the emergence of awareness discussed above. GY's contentless awareness occurred when there was no activation of working memory sites in the ventral "what" processing stream concerned with content going down the temporal lobe. But there was activation of a working memory in the "where" dorsal stream for spatial position going up to the parietal lobe. These experimenters (Weiskrantz et al. 1995) noted that signals of retinal origin can reach later visual cortical areas in humans in the absence of cortical area V1. It appears from the analysis of monkey deficits and experiments described above that such sites would be at or higher than the motion processing area MT (for monkeys) of V5 (for humans).

The second source of experimental support for dissociation of visual awareness is from the creation of blindsight in normal observers (Kolb and Braun 1995). Visual inputs experienced by subjects involved dots moving in opposite directions or short bars with orthogonal orientations presented to different eyes. A small patch was chosen so that the direction of movement of the dots or the orientation of the bars was perpendicular to that over the rest of the visual scene. The local patch was unavailable to awareness for each subject, but its presence or absence could still be discriminated against at a normal level. The natural explanation of such normal blindsight is in terms of cancellation between opposing orientations or movement directions that is input to higher areas. Cancellation caused by the inputs prevents a strong input being sent to the perceptual decision area, but does allow response; again knowledge without awareness.

In a beautiful experiment performed by a group at Harvard (He et al. 1996), adaptation to oriented lines (so they cannot be seen as easily) still occurred even if the lines could not be detected as a result of being crowded by other lines nearby. The crowding effect was different if the lines were above the horizon compared with below it. This indicated that consciousness was not constructed in V1, the first part of the cortex devoted to vision, since that is symmetrically activated by inputs from above or below the horizon.

Finally, a personal dissociation of visual awareness happens to me when I drive for a long distance on highways. If I know the route well, most of the way I relax into a "where" mode of awareness: I do not take notice of the details of other vehicles but have a general picture of where all the vehicles are in my vicinity, even up to ten or so at a time. Only at certain places do I snap out of this trancelike, or more aptly contentless, state, such as at an international border—French guards are very annoyed if you do not have your passport to wave at them. I find this contentless state so necessary for effective long-distance driving that I recommend it be taught to advanced drivers; it would also make an interesting brain imaging study with the use of a driving simulator.

The experimental results reported here give strong support to the two-stage model of consciousness, with no awareness of activity in modules at stage 1 but phenomenal consciousness emerging in stage 2:

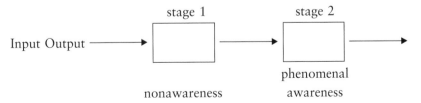

Dissociations of Awareness: The Three-Stage Model

Progress is being made thanks to conditions that allow us to detect different regions in the brain, some of which are being used at the preprocessing level, some at the level of passive awareness, and others at active consciousness. Under subliminal or unattended conditions it is expected that activity will be observable only in preprocessing modules; with passive awareness further modules should be observed as being active. Finally, under attended conditions, even further modules (those for active consciousness) should be detectable. This extends the two-stage model to that of three stages that is illustrated in figure 13.2.

This idea was tested using data measured while subjects heard a sequence of syllables and had flickering lights shone into goggles they were wearing, while images were taken of their brains by an fMRI machine. They were given three commands: ignore auditorily presented syllables, but attend to the flickering light (inattention), listen passively to the syllables (passive), and discriminate among the syllables (attention) (Taylor et al. 1998). An average of the results for fifteen subjects is shown in figure 13.3. It is clear that additional regions are indeed activated as the conditions involved increasing levels of awareness of the syllables and less distraction from the flickering light. Passive awareness occurred especially in the expected auditory areas, while there was strong frontal activation when attentional processing was occurring. So neural sites for the emergence of awareness dissociate into those involved with passive awareness or unfocused attention, and those concerned with focusing that attention onto a specific object or sound. Evidence from the experiment reported above further supports the simpler two-stage model for vision.

Summary

I developed a qualitative form of the earlier simple model of the emergence of consciousness of words to help explain the emergence of awareness in various visual experiments, such as on rivalry in visual processing or motion aftereffect, both at a single cell and a more global cortical

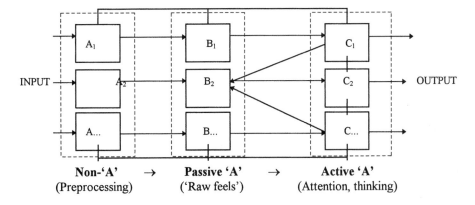

Figure 13.2
The structure of the three-stage model for awareness, in which the cortex is decomposed into three sorts of modules. First, those labeled Non-'A', for which there is no direct awareness of the corresponding activity, are identified with brain areas in which preprocessing is occurring, such as in early visual cortex, as well as lower-level processing in other areas. Second, those labeled Passive 'A', for which there is direct awareness when experience occurs in a passive mode of sensory processing, are placed in the posterior "slave" working memory sites. The third and highest level, Active 'A' modules, are able to support both thinking and attentional control. This latter can in particular be focused back onto the passive and preprocessing areas. The third stage is mainly sited in frontal cortex.

module level. Initial answers to questions about the model were given to help flesh it out and in particular relate it to further aspects of phenomenal awareness as arise in automatic processing such as driving and in imagery.

Possible sites for the emergence of phenomenal consciousness were noted for words and for vision, both for spatial aspects and object concepts. These early sites were the buffer working memory posterior sites. However, I could not prove that consciousness actually arose there. The experiment on hearing, involving different levels of attention and corresponding awareness, shows that awareness does have its place of emergence in posterior cortex. As in experiments on imagery, the sites of this emergence are relatively similar to sites of buffer working memory in-

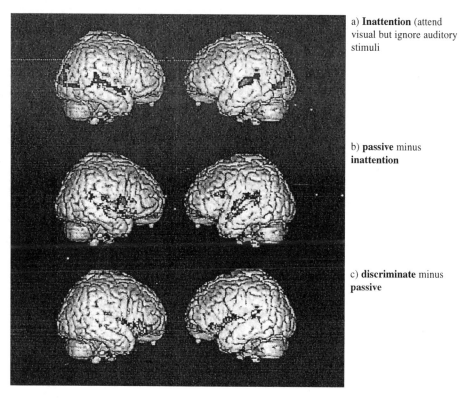

a) **Inattention** (attend visual but ignore auditory stimuli

b) **passive** minus **inattention**

c) **discriminate** minus **passive**

Figure 13.3
Surface-projected schematic representation of mean activated areas of cortex (a) during inattention to an auditorily presented stream of syllables due to attention to a visual signal presented to both eyes. (b) The additional cortical area brought on stream when subjects passively listen to the syllables (no visual distractor). (c) Additional cortical area when attention is focused on the syllables. (Reprinted with permission from Taylor et al, 1998)

volved in other modalities: posterior parietal and temporal as well as occipitoparietal sites. So we are beginning to track consciousness down, but we have a long way to go before we can really say we know exactly where it emerges in each modality. To help in the search we need some sort of theory to guide us. Otherwise we are in danger of falling into the same trap of the man who lost his keys in the dark and was searching for them under a street light; when asked why he was looking there instead of closer to where he had actually lost them he replied, "I can see better here." We next consider the "how" of consciousness; that is the hardest problem of all.

14

How Does Consciousness Emerge?

To find the mind's construction.
—William Shakespeare

The mind is so subtly constructed its full design eludes us. But so far we have picked up a number of clues from beautiful and audacious experiments to probe this subtlety. One of the most important is that consciousness requires a suitable length of time to emerge from the neural activity of the brain. Here I develop a simple model to help us understand this temporal aspect of the emergence of awareness and lead us to suggest where possible sites for such temporality could occur. Properties of the resulting neural activity in this model are compared with those claimed to be introspected for qualia. We finally arrive at the dreaded explanatory gap—the highest jump in the great race. I briefly glance over this jump from the neurobiological side to see if anything on the other side looks remotely like what we might expect.

In this discussion I use the word consciousness to mean phenomenal awareness, which involves the raw feels of conscious experience. These are claimed by some philosophers to have the properties that they call "perspectival, transparent and present" (Metzinger 1995) (whose meaning I explain later). It is these features of consciousness that are currently being singled out by some as being the most difficult to probe and model scientifically. Even more difficult to understand is the property of being "intrinsic," claimed to be possessed by qualia. This denies any relational characteristics for them—our whole relational mind approach appears to be completely stymied by that.

However, the nature of the phenomenal aspect of consciousness is hotly debated among philosophers of mind. As noted earlier, Dennett eliminated it completely (Dennett 1988), writing "so when we look one last time at our original characterization of qualia, as ineffable, intense, private, directly apprehensible properties of experience, we find that there is nothing to fill the bill. In their place are relatively or practically ineffable public properties we can refer to indirectly via reference to our private property detectors—private only in the sense of idiosyncratic." If we accept Dennett's arguments, the puzzling character of qualia dissolves completely. Yet both Thomas Nagel (Nagel 1974) and John Searle (Searle 1992) do not accept such dismissal of qualia. Searle, for example, accepts something "ontologically subjective" about consciousness, and Nagel claims that first-person characteristics of consciousness simply are different from the third-person features. We also do not take such a dismissive approach to raw feels. The hurdle on the track cannot be made to crumble away so easily that we could just step over it onto a course that has been leveled flat. So we still have to face up to very hard problems.

I will not say much here about the perspectival character—that sense of "being" or a perspective on experience—supposed to be part of phenomenal consciousness, because to have a perspective requires a sense of self. This arises from more complex neural structures than are involved in early processing in posterior cortex, as seen from loss of some crucial features of self caused by lesions of the middle parts of the frontal lobes, but without a loss of low-level consciousness. Those with such brain damage become poor at social relationships and planning, and find personal relationships difficult. The perspectival character of raw feels is supported neuroanatomically by different neural regions than those that create the qualia themselves. Such separation must occur in animals that have consciousness but lack self-consciousness or self-recognition.

The notion of transparency of the raw feels, the next item on our list, is that "we look through them" (Metzinger 1995) at the world. From the same aspect, raw feels are almost always fully interpreted; that is, they are immediately meaningful. The ability to sense that I am directly in contact with my own phenomenal consciousness indicates that such consciousness must involve little processing internally; it is a modification of activity without much obvious transformation of the final inputs once they have achieved consciousness. This is understood to apply only to the phenomenal component of consciousness, without the perspectival factor. In any case the perspectival character is added by contributions from self, and so can be explored by extending the ideas in chapter 11; in so doing we do not expect to meet any additional hard problems.

At the same time the raw feels are paradoxically infinitely distant. It was suggested by German philosopher Thomas Metzinger that (Metzinger 1995) "they do not convey information that they are indeed data structures." This is not to be interpreted as saying that qualia do not convey information, but that they completely hide how they achieved their present status, so they seem indeed to be at infinity. They cannot be probed further from inside the system. This feature arises when a rather sharp and irreversible processing step is involved in the ultimate emergence of consciousness. A lot of to-ing and fro-ing happen to inputs to the brain before they emerge into phenomenal awareness with closed loops of neural activity converging to all sorts of final activity. Yet the final step into consciousness appears to be short, sharp, and final. It does not seem possible to go back and linger over the manner in which such emergence occurred. It is this aspect of consciousness to which we return at the end of the chapter to see if the mechanisms brought forward for the final emergence of phenomenal awareness have the characteristics of transparency and infinite distance I described briefly above.

The character of presence in raw feels, involving the sense of the "now" of conscious experience, is part of the subjective present. The experience of time as part of consciousness has been probed by experiments such as those of Libet (Libet et al. 1964) and discussed by many from a more general viewpoint (Ruhnau 1995).[1]

It appears that the subjective present varies according to the state of the subject, but a period of at least 200 to 500 msecs is required for the consciousness of an input to develop. This supports the thesis put forward at the beginning of this section, and in earlier chapters, that consciousness requires time to develop, so specialized structures, the sites of buffer working memory, have been developed by evolutionary pressures to allow for this delicate and subtle process.

We explore the subtle ways that time is intermixed in the emergence of consciousness from various angles in the following sections.

Activity Bubbles in the Cortex

How can we understand the strange properties of special cortical regions, with lifetimes of activity that are over 100 times longer than activity on neurons (when isolated) that compose them! We would expect some sort of cooperative phenomenon to be at work here. This was suggested as arising from amplification of input to cortex so as to sharpen the sensitivity of the cortical cells to features of various sorts.

The principle behind this amplification was explored some twenty years ago by Japanese scientist Shun-Ichi Amari (Amari 1977) in terms of the formation of bubbles of activity in local cortical regions owing to the recurrence or feedback of neural activity. Once a neuron has been activated by an input, it feeds back activity to itself and its neighbors so as to keep them all active. The bubbles are triggered by a small input, so function as an amplifier of that input. To keep them going, excitatory feedback has to occur from one neuron to its near neighbors; to prevent the bubble from spreading out and dissipating itself across the whole of the cortex there also has to be longer-range inhibition. Such effects can be appropriately spread across the cortical sheet by assuming a "Mexican hat" shape of the dependence of the connection strengths between two cortical neurons with the distance between them (figure 14.1). From the figure nearby neurons will experience excitation from the central neuron, while more distant ones will be inhibited by its activity sent to them by the Mexican hat structure of the lateral connections. A simulation of the emergence of one of these bubbles is shown in figure 14.2.

In the original model the bubbles persisted until disturbed by later competing input. It is more natural to assume that single cells slow down (or adapt) their response either because of a buildup of internal inhibitory effects or by direct inhibition from local circuit neurons (Douglas and Martin 1991). The bubbles die away after a certain length of time.

This recurrence of neural activity in corticocortical circuits helps us understand the slower decay of the activity on working memory neurons as follows. Analyses of the detailed architecture of cortex indicate that higher regions (Barbas and Pandya 1991) have an increased density of cells in the upper layers; in particular, this is clearly indicated for frontal cortex, with areas 8, 9, and 46 having highest density of cells in these

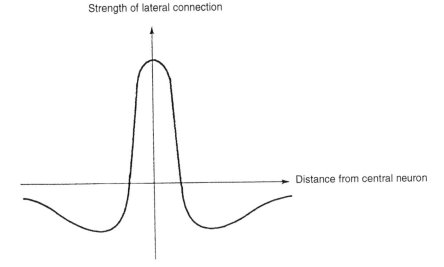

Strength of lateral connection

Distance from central neuron

Figure 14.1
Shape of the lateral connection weight function w(|x − x'|) between two points
x and x' on the cortical surface. The height of the function denotes the value of
w and the horizontal axis denotes the value of the variable |x − x'|. Note the
similarity of the shape of the curve to that of a Mexican hat, hence the name for
this lateral form of connection.

layers. Similar results are known for the multimodal associative regions
of parietal and temporal lobe (Mesulam 1981). It is in these latter regions
that the working memories of table 13.1 and the frontal regions observed
by noninvasive methods are mostly situated.

   Cortical cells mainly have input that arrives from other, especially
nearby, cortical cells. This recurrent excitation helps to keep activity on
the cell recycling, and so leads to a longer lifetime of activity on the cell.
The resulting longer decay time is largest when the local feedback connection strength is maximum (owing to the largest amount of recycling of
this activity). This is the case in areas with many cells, so many connections feeding to each other. The longest recycling persistence is expected
to occur in areas with highest cell density (Ben-Yashai et al. 1995; Somers
et al. 1995; a detailed model of the effect is in Taylor 1997).

   The lifetime of the bubbles of activity produced in cortex by input is
therefore longest for areas of cortex that have highest density of cells in

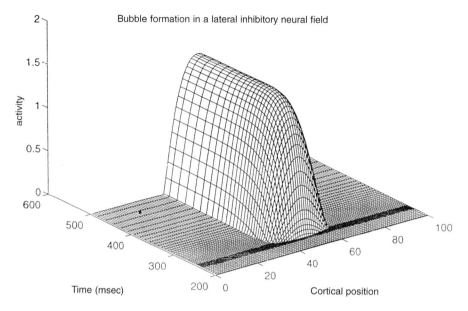

Figure 14.2
Bubble formation on the cortical surface from the effect of the lateral connection weight function of figure 14.1. There is a small input at the cortical position 50; the bubble grows rapidly to its maximum in about 300 msec.

the upper layers. Those are the multimodal areas in the occipitotemporoparietal, inferotemporal, and frontal cortices. They contain the sites of working memories as determined by the PET studies that were summarized in table 13.1.

The increase of effective decay times is evident as we ascend the processing hierarchy from primary to associative auditory cortex. This was discovered by measuring changes in neural activity when subjects were exposed to trains of tones or flashes of light. The researchers (Lu, Williamson, and Kaufman 1992) stated, "The present study provides evidence that decay of the activation trace in each cortical area can be characterized empirically by a single lifetime for the class of stimuli employed." They gave values for the decay times in primary and secondary auditory cortex ranging over 1.5 to 3 seconds and 3.5 to 5 seconds, respectively, for four subjects. A more recent study in two subjects gave a map of the decay times in different places over the cortical surfaces of the subjects. These times ranged from tenths of a second to up to nearly 30 seconds, an enormous range; the largest values were in the multimodal areas. They also had subtle differences between them. Imagine having the time-decay map of your whole brain—what a picture to contemplate about yourself!

From these features we can identify working memory sites in various modalities with those areas of posterior cortex identifiable with the highest density of cells in the upper layers. Some experimental support for this conjecture is available.

Because different sites of emergence of consciousness exist for different codes and modalities, such awareness will dissociate into its different components for motion, color, and shape. Evidence of this was considered in chapter 13. What is so special about these sites?

To begin to answer that, let us consider the crucial sites where phenomenal consciousness emerges in cortex. What about the suggestion that frontal lobes are required for emergence of primary awareness (Crick and Koch 1995)? The frontal memory system has neural activities persisting for 30 or more seconds, so would appear to be a very good candidate. However, patients with little frontal cortex lose the ability to hold neural activity over such long time periods, yet do not lose phenomenal consciousness. Frontal cortex cannot be a critical site for the emergence of qualia; the posterior sites identified earlier as those of buffer working memory are still the best bet.

We must now turn to consider why a multilayered cortex, which we mammals, together with mollusks (e.g., octopi) and arthropods (e.g., spiders) possess is important in the process of creating consciousness. Analysis of connectivity between cells in cortex showed that, "local excitatory connections are much more likely to provide significant intracortical amplification of signals in layer 2/3 than in layer 5 of rat visual cortex" (Nicoll and Blakemore 1993). This supports an earlier proposal that the higher the density of cells in the upper cortical layers, the longer the time of persistence of locally recurrent activity. The lower layers are different since they have few recurrent connections and are unable to support such persistence of activity.

This suggests that the lower layers of cortical cells are driven by longer-lasting bubbles of activity in the upper layers. Since the lower layers provide output to thalamic nuclei and other cortical areas, they are to be regarded as output nodes sending signals of the activity in the upper layers to those other sites. Such an output system shields the bubbles in the upper layers from too much interference.[2]

Outputs from the lower layers of cortex to the thalamus lead to more global competition among different working memories run, say, by a net of inhibitory neurons such as the NRT (Taylor 1992; Alavi and Taylor 1993; Taylor and Alavi 1995; Baars and Newman 1993, 1994), to help explain the long time taken to create consciousness artificially, as in the experiments of Libet discussed in chapter 8.[3] In this way the activity over cortex is dumped onto the NRT network by outputs from the lower cortical layer cells. More rapidly changing cortical activity, from other than working memory sites, gives a lower average level of activity injected into the NRT compared with the more slowly changing working memory activity. The posterior cortical competition on the thalamus-NRT-cortex system ends up being between the averaged activity on the working memory sites. This relates back to and expands the model of global competition developed in chapters 7 and 8.

In all it is seen that whereas a complete answer is far from being given regarding the necessity and sufficiency of multilayered cortex for consciousness, some hints are available as to what various of the layers do to help create it:

1. The upper layers create bubbles to extend the life of input activity and sharpen the spatial sensitivity, ultimately creating the first bubbles of phenomenal awareness in buffer working memory sites.

2. The lower layers are involved with sending activity down to the thalamus for the thalamus-NRT-cortex competition for global awareness.[4]

3. The middle layer is needed for access to each area by others (lower in the hierarchy of areas) or by sensory input.

The Emergence of Qualia

What about the deeper question of how the properties of phenomenal experience can be seen to arise from the specific process of neuronal computation described in this chapter? In particular, how can the properties

Table 14.1
Comparison of properties of qualia with those of bubbles on working memory

Qualia		Bubbles on working memory
Presence	Persistence	Persistence
	Latency	Latency in creation
	Seamlessness	Rapid destruction of one bubble and emergence of another
Transparency	Can look through them	Smooth broadcasting to each other
	Fully interpreted	Bubbles produced only at highest coding level
Ineffable	Infinitely distant	One-way creation of bubbles
	Intrinsic	Bubbles produced at highest level, with no strong feedback to lower levels
Uniqueness		Only one winning bubble
Binding of object features to make object concepts		Correlation between different codes at different levels

of transparency, ineffability, and presence described in the first section be seen to occur? This is indeed the crucial question raised by Shakespeare: "To find the mind's construction." These properties for qualia, summarizing those discussed in the introductory section, are presented in table 14.1. We will consider them each in turn.

The first is presence, and includes the sense of the subjective present. The involvement of self is not part of our discussion here, but the temporal component of phenomenal awareness is. This has three characteristics, as shown in table 14.1: persistency, latency, and seamlessness.

Persistency is the temporal extension of phenomenal experience; it is an important component of the sense of the subjective now.[5] It is an intrinsic part of the neural process of winning a competition, the opposite side of the coin to latency (the delay of the onset of consciousness after input occurs). Until another winner arises the earlier one persists as number one. In the competitive model, latency is the time required for a competition to be won on a working memory site. With the property we call seamlessness, the transition from one content of awareness to another happens rapidly enough to provide a sense of the experienced continuity in awareness.

Both latency and seamlessness were probed by Libet in various experiments (Libet 1964, 1994). He showed that about 500 msec is necessary to cause the artificial arousal of consciousness by direct electrical stimulation of somatosensory cortex. He also told me privately that the change-over process of consciousness, as reported by patients, was brief, occurring in less than a tenth of the time it took for the total process of changeover. This and other observed features of the dependency of latency on stimulation parameters were obtained from a neural simulation of the thalamus-NRT-cortex system by Alavi and me (Alavi and Taylor 1993) and described in chapters 7 and 8. Seamlessness arises in the competitive model; once nearly won, competition is concluded rapidly.

Various features of the persistence of consciousness were studied by German psychologist Ernst Poeppel (Poeppel 1997) who discovered a general pattern for the way that time is intertwined with behavior. We all employ two particular times as we move about and perform our daily acts: 30 msec and 3 seconds. The first is about the shortest time we can discriminate between two clicks or other brief stimuli. The second is a common time arising as part of sequences of actions. People of all cultures use roughly 3 seconds to chunk their actions; video sequences show that this is the normal time quantum for action sequences such as moving about in a kitchen, a cafe, or a crowded street. Poems are usually written with lines that take about 3 seconds to read or speak.

Consider, for example, these lines from a sonnet by Shakespeare, each of which lasts about 3 seconds:

> Shall I compare thee to a summer's day?
> Thou art more lovely and more temperate,
> Rough winds do shake the darling buds of May,
> And summer's lease hath all too short a date.

This feature is valid across many languages. It also occurs in music: the opening theme from Beethoven's Fifth Symphony lasts about 3 seconds, as does the Dutchman's theme from Wagner's *Flying Dutchman*. Some believe that modern composers who change the nature of their music so that it does not use this basic temporal language lose considerably in their aesthetic effect. The listener has to learn a whole new language of musical timing and structure to be able to appreciate the music at a similar level to that of earlier music.

This second time packet of 3 seconds is close to our old friend the decay time of activity on the buffer working memory. This is a very natural identification. We would expect these buffers in our brains to be used constantly in our daily lives to coordinate our actions; so they seem to be. They can buffer about 2 to 3 seconds of activity and allow it to be most effectively chunked into automatic action sequences or allow meaning to be extracted.

The shorter time packet—30 msec—is also of some interest, being close to the 25 msec it takes for each wave of a 40-Hz cycle to last. This also fits with the fact that 40-Hz synchronization occurs in the brain during many daily acts. This is also observed in other animals. When your cat next looks at a mouse, there will be (or should be, if your cat is any good as a mouser) a lot of 40-Hz activity in the brain of your little pet. You may not be thinking of that if the mouse is actually inside your house—you may well have other thoughts going through your own brain! But at least you should realize, when the mouse has been removed, that your cat is in a good state to be maximally effective if the 40 Hz is synchronizing all the relevant parts of its brain so it can pounce at the most opportune moment. Don't denigrate that 40 Hz!

Let us move on to the next notion of transparency—that qualia can be "looked through" without seeing any inner workings. This can arise from a strongly connected system of buffer and frontal working memories; for it must be easy to transfer correlated information, especially to the frontal lobes, once a winner has occurred. Such transfer would also carry with it correlated preconscious material across different codes, since good connections exist between modules at the same level of complexity, defined earlier in terms of either transience of activity or cell density in the upper layers 2/3.

In conclusion, transparency is achieved by the crucial well-connectedness of the set of buffer regions, including those in the frontal lobes, thus giving a transparent feel to the activity.

Qualia also have a fully interpreted character, mentioned in the introduction as part of transparency. Such a property arises from the fact that buffer working memory sites are at the highest level of the posterior processing hierarchy. All the coding and interpretation, in informational terms, has been achieved when the competition has been won and incompatibilities ironed out. Indeed such competition is the final step in the interpretation process, achieved in the model presented here, as part of awareness being reached.

The third property of qualia shown in table 14.1 is ineffability, that qualia are impossible to probe and get behind, they are atomic or intrinsic. This is well mirrored in the one-way character of the appearance of bubbles on buffer sites posited in our model. The manner in which imagery is created by activation of nonconscious areas of cortex (to fill out the details of the input) does not contradict this interpretation since these earlier areas were activated to create the longest-lasting bubbles in buffer working memory sites. This persistence is one of the necessary conditions of consciousness not possessed by much shorter-lasting activity in the lower cortical areas.

Another important meaning of ineffability is that of being indescribable, and relates to their intrinsic and atomic character. Words were initially developed to relate to objective features of the world. It is only by very hard work that a novelist can effectively portray the inner phenomenal experience of his characters, and even then only superficially. However, other aspects such as privacy and self intrude, making such writing difficult.

Ineffability can also arise from the way qualia emerge onto the global arena of consciousness (the well-connected set of sites of buffer working memory) without a trace of their origin being available to these sites. That is due to the lack of feedback able to recreate earlier activity (without attention in imagery) from long-lasting activity in later areas.

In conclusion, all of the characteristics of qualia suggested by Metzinger (except the self aspects of perspectivalness) are mirrored in the properties of activity emerging onto the well-coupled buffer working memory system mainly in posterior cortex. This gives support to the suggestion that the model is indeed one for the emergence of phenomenal awareness; in particular it helps toward answering the "what is it like to be an X?" question for animals with no sense of self.

Local versus Distributed Emergence of Consciousness?

Before we become too cocky over the suggested view we think we have of the other side of the explanatory gap, let us take note of some criticisms of what that view really is like. First, an alternative model can be proposed for the emergence of consciousness. This involves it being sited in many more cortical areas than those at the highest level, with highest density of cells and most persistent activity in the upper layers. On this new model even more transient activity could enter awareness; it was suggested by experimenters whose work was mentioned in the earlier section on visual awareness.

This distributed consciousness approach goes back to the doctrine that a neuron's receptive field—those inputs that turn it on—describes the percept caused by its excitation (Barlow 1972). By this doctrine the separate neurons in an early area of visual cortex create the percepts of their receptive fields. A neuron in the early cortical visual areas V2 or MT responding to the motion of a particular part of the visual field gives rise to the percept of motion in the recipient.

This doctrine is being generalized by experimenters whose work was described above to take account of more distributed regions of activity. In earlier experiments on visual awareness in rivalrous and other situations it was suggested that the percept, for example, of motion or of orientation, was achieved by a combination of activities from all of the different visual areas involved in the processing. In other words, there was no specific place where the awareness of the percept emerged. Instead, such phenomenal awareness was suggested as being a feature of the overall activity of the coupled areas; as such it is a throwback to the one-stage model.

That is in contrast to the relational consciousness model, in which consciousness emerges only at, or immediately after, the winning node had arisen in a competitive process (in the case of ambiguous inputs). This is in spite of numerous areas coding for attributes that have not yet, according to the model, reached conscious awareness.

How can a distinction be made between these two possibilities? One line of argument is to use the features of qualia noted in table 14.1. Strong analogies have been drawn between these properties and those of emerging activity in the two-stage model; it does not seem so straight-forward to develop similar arguments for the one-stage model. Transparency, for example, is not present in activity in this model since incompatibilities remain in interpretations of data on the lower areas, as is clear from measurements in the experiments reported. This is not activity at the highest level, since it has not been fully interpreted. Consciousness of these lower-level activities would arise, in contradiction to our experience, in the one-stage model. Nor is ineffability clear, since it would be possible to discover through introspection some of the earlier processing activity if it were directly involved in awareness.

There is also experimental evidence against a one-stage model for words. Word activity is encoded up to a semantic level without entering consciousness, as the subliminal activation of incompatible meanings of the word palm, demonstrated by Marcel, shows only too convincingly. This backs up other experimental evidence cited in chapter 9. If the same principles are in operation in other modalities for the emergence of awareness, the one-stage model is not correct.

We can differentiate between the models by extending the experiment for competition on a monkey's decisions as to the direction of motion of visual inputs competing with externally applied electrical stimulation, by discovering a region in which a strong correlation is seen between the decision and the encoding of active neurons. A similar situation would arise in the binocular rivalry experiments of Leopold and Logothetis, in which the site for encoding the decision as to upward or downward direction of perceived motion was encoded by the activity of a preponderance of suitably sensitive cells. In the case of object recognition we reported work showing that in a suitably high visual area such sensitivity is present; the two-stage model has been validated for objects. Further support for the two-stage model is given by the very long decay times that occurred in relation to the motion aftereffect in a human cortical area higher than MT. In the model presented here that area would be an appropriate candidate for the emergence of awareness of this effect.

The following specific predictions follow from the two-stage model we have developed:

1. Localized buffer sites of continued activity (for a few seconds) for competitive processing.

2. Lateral inhibition to support competition between inconsistent coding; more specifically effective in localized buffer sites.

3. Strong local recurrent corticocortical excitation to support effective long-time constants.

4. Highest density of cells in layers 2/3 to achieve sufficiently large corticocortical recurrence.

5. Good involvement of layer 5/6 neurons in inter-modal competiton run at the thalamocortical level.

6. Working memory as the site where activity is coded for a perceptual decision, in a localized manner, with competition occurring between incompatible interpretations; specific changes of neural activity should be seen.

A number of localized sites of temporally extended activity should be detectable during visual processing in various codes. Moreover the highest decay times should occur in sites that have a correlation with awareness. We must observe these sites by brain imaging instruments so that the localization and time courses are accessible. The overall processing model indicates that the greatest competitive processes should occur in these sites to gain phenomenal awareness. It is important to pursue the experimental program to find the position and detailed dynamics of these sites.

A Spanner in the Works: Inattentional Amnesia?

A possible spanner could be thrown into the bubble machinery of relational consciousness and grind it to a halt. This involves attention, something we introduced as part of the highest or third stage of consciousness in chapter 13 (see figure 13.2). One aspect of it, the attentional blink (Duncan et al. 1994, 1997), is highly relevant to our view of the explanatory gap and arises as follows.

Suppose you are sitting in front of a screen onto which is projected a rapid stream of pictures. These may be numbers, letters, or words, or just lots of xs. Your task is to detect particular phrases or short words, such as cog and tag. If the stimuli change too rapidly, you will find it difficult to detect the consecutive appearance of, say, tag then cog, within about 400 msec of each other. You are effectively "blind" after attending to and processing one target for that length of time until you have resources available to turn to the next stimulus. This blindness is tested by asking you, a second or so later, "Did you see tag and cog"? You will answer yes to tag but not often yes to cog. This is an interesting phenomenon in its own right, but the catch for us is as to the level of awareness you have of cog: were you aware of it but forgot it before you could respond, so suffered from what has been termed *inattentional amnesia*, or were you truly blind to it since your attention was occupied elsewhere in a state of inattentional blindness? We just do not know at this juncture.

A study showed that during the period of apparent blindness, during the blink itself, words are processed to the level of meaning (Duncan et al. 1994, 1997). This was proved by the fact that a special brain wave signature, called the N400 since it is a brain wave of negative electricity 400 msec after the stimulus has appeared, signals that a person has heard a semantic discrepancy. For example, subjects just heard the sentence, "The man put on a pair of buckets" instead of the expected, "The man put on a pair of trousers." Using the N400 tag, subjects had to attempt to detect the discrepant word, such as bucket in this example, during their attentional blink. They were not aware of the discrepant word but they did show the tell-tale N400 signal. Thus they processed the meaning of the word to appreciate its incorrect inclusion in the sentence.

How could the relational consciousness model face up to the fact of the attentional blink, and in particular, decide between inattentional amnesia and inattentional blindness? Results processing words up to the level of meaning as part of the phenomenon are consistent with the model. It does not seem to be possible to push the model to choose between the possibilities of blindness and amnesia without further clues. A faint clue is that the N400 used to detect the high level of processing of stimulus during the blink did not become reduced during the crucial duration of the blink. Interference is greatest in being aware of the second stimulus when it is about 300 msec after the first. Yet the N400 did not grow smaller during that crucial period, as expected if the lower level of awareness (assuming inattentional blindness) arose since the second input could not gain the buffer working memory since the first one was already ensconced and repelled boarders efficiently. But the N400 continued willy-nilly, as they say, so that could not be the explanation (according to the model). In fact the N400 result and the model predict that there must have been a fleeting awareness but it was lost by the time response was made. How that prediction can be tested is not clear, but careful thought may allow us to devise a subtle enough experimental paradigm to discover which it is—blindness or amnesia. The model predicts amnesia. This fits with the earlier suggestion that attention is necessary to remember conscious activity. Without attention, what emerges into awareness is forgotten. If indeed blindness exists, certain dynamics of the model will have to be changed. In any case the bubble approach to consciousness is not affected, so the other side of the hard jump is still as accessible as before.

Return to 40 Hz

There is another critical point on which to deflate bubbles for consciousness. This goes back to the old 40-Hz model of consciousness that had been somewhat discarded by its progenitors, as we recounted in chapter 4, but is still fighting a strong battle for its relevance to early processing in a number of modalities. Increasing experimental evidence supports 40 Hz being present in a lot of early visual and auditory processing (Singer and Gray 1995; Fries et al. 1996; Roeflsema et al. 1997). The case of your cat and its 40-Hz view of the mouse was mentioned. But what happens to bubbles? Can they also oscillate at 40 Hz? Do experimental results show the presence of such oscillating bubbles? And if they do not, should the existence of bubbles be severely questioned? We do not know the answers to these questions. Decay time maps of the two subjects mentioned earlier, if taken at face value, indicate the presence of some form of continued neural activity throughout the cortex after it has heard a tone or seen a light. But the form of that continued neural signal is not clear: it could be a bubble in the form I described earlier, or it could be one oscillating at 40 Hz. We have no data to tell us which is valid (if either).

Yet all is not lost, and in fact very little is by this new paradigm. Either type of bubble would still allow us a similar picture of the other side of the explanatory gap, although with different temporal behavior. However, either would lead to a similar explanation of qualia to that already given. I previously suggested a bridge over the gap between the activity of single neurons and the emergence of raw feels by means of approximating the cortex by a continuous sheet of neurons and observing that it can then support bubbles of semiautonomous activity. Now we have looked at the temporal aspect of the same problem: how consciousness can emerge from the combination of trains of single spikes emitted by nerve cells. The detailed mechanism for this is still not filled in, going from single spikes to consciousness, but it may involve 40 Hz continued activity, as hinted by the latest data. (Singer and Gray 1995; Fries et al. 1996; Roeflsema et al. 1997). However, the result of this combination of neural activities across a module and across cortex must be such as to lead to support of buffer working memory sites and to competitive processing, and so to relational consciousness principles. We can therefore proceed with the model, recognizing that many open questions remain about its detailed implementation, not least at the single neuron level. Given that confidence, we must turn to some of the other problems that we have neglected—those concerned with the nature of the broad range of states of consciousness over all our experience.

Summary

I enriched the two-stage model of the emergence of awareness by more detailed use of the creation of activity, termed bubbles, in cortical sites and by analysis of how the lifetime of these bubbles were determined by cell density in upper cortical layers. Sites with highest cell density were predicted as being sites of buffer working memory, and therefore those of the emergence of phenomenal consciousness.

Initial answers to various questions about the model were given to help flesh it out and in particular relate it to further aspects of phenomenal awareness as arise in automatic processing such as driving and in imagery. The model was also compared with a more distributed one for the emergence of consciousness, in which awareness arose conjointly in a number of regions at different levels in the processing hierarchy. Apart from evidence against a distributed model from data on subliminal processing of words, experimental support in vision for the localized model was also noted there.

The various properties of qualia, in particular ineffability, transparency, and presence, were delineated and observed as being similar to properties of bubbles of activity in the working memory sites as part of the local two-stage model for emergence of consciousness. This comparison gave strong support to the two-stage model, whereas identification could not be as effectively achieved for the global one-stage one; transparency and ineffability did not seem to arise naturally from it. This may be taken as support for the local against the global model. I made a set of predictions that could test various features of the local model.

Finally some caveats were expressed. Questions were raised about inattentional amnesia versus inattentional blindness and the 40-Hz phenomenon, indicating that the other side of the explanatory gap is still far from clear.

We have reached the end of part IV, with its emphasis (as also in parts II and III) on the three components of waking consciousness in the normal state. We now move to part V to consider the much broader range of conscious experiences in the variety of states we can find ourselves in our lives: in sleep and dreams, in altered states of consciousness, in the seven ages of man, and people with brain damage and disease. This will allow a better test to be made of the explanatory powers of the relational consciousness framework.

V

Aspects of Relational Consciousness

15

The Varieties of Consciousness

The multiplicity of agreeable consciousnesses.
—Samuel Johnson

Consciousness comes in many guises—in infancy and old age, under drugs or hypnosis, in sleep, in a high emotional state, and with loss of crucial parts of the brain. However, we have yet made no attempt to apply the relational consciousness model to these varieties. In this chapter we attempt such an extension; not only will the total model of consciousness be thereby tested more fully as to its validity, but at the same time further insights might be obtained.

To start with, the change of consciousness from an awake state to one of sleep is familiar to us all, but remarkable nonetheless. We glide into an almost completely unconscious state that is interspersed with cycles of a bizarre form of conscious experience in which we appear to have no control. The experience can be terrifying if the dream is in fact a nightmare. How does this form of consciousness, if it can be called that, fit into the model of consciousness presented so far? Where is the relational structure? There are numerous forms of dream experience, from slow logical thinking in deep sleep to remembered dreams. Can that difference be explicable in terms of the model?

Besides sleep, alterations of consciousness are brought about by external intervention or by internal damage to the brain. Thus lesions caused by stroke or illness, or by surgical operations for intractable epilepsy or tumors, can lead to deficits in conscious awareness that are sometimes disabling and bizarre. Patients may experience neglect in which they do not have awareness of one side of their visual field, or one side of their body. What is the source of such lack of conscious awareness of parts of their body that they vehemently disown them? In the opposite phenomenon, subjects who have lost a limb still experience pain in it. This phantom pain has been known to disappear, but what is the cause when it is present?

The opposite type of phenomenon occurs when early visual cortex is lost. This leads to blindness, but the person is still able to guess that lights are being shone in the otherwise blind field. This power is what has been called blindsight (Weiskrantz 1986) in which knowledge is present without visual awareness. Is that explicable in terms of the model of consciousness?

A broad range of changes in ability or personality occur as a result of damage to limbic or frontal regions. In the process we may detect little reduction in general intelligence as determined by a standard intelligence test, yet the person may experience a catastrophic reduction of the ability to handle real-world situations, especially when decisions have to be made. On the other hand, someone can suffer a frontal lesion, say due to a stroke, leading to a marked change in personality. How does the model of consciousness explain such cases?

Beyond these medical cases are drug-induced experiences of consciousness that have been claimed by some to lead to an altered reality, but for numbers of drug users resulted only in a damaged and reduced one. Extensions of consciousness also arise from meditation and hypnosis, which may have some affinity to those caused by drugs yet differ in terms of both the interpretation and possible brain sites involved. How are they to be fit into the proposed framework?

Myriad cases of mental ill health occur, with patients suffering from schizophrenia, autism Parkinson's disease, Alzheimer's disease, and various forms of psychoses and neuroses. Is it possible to fit this catalogue of illnesses into the emergent mind framework?

Besides the range of such disorders in which consciousness is modified and sometimes bent out of all recognition, some people are afflicted with a dissociation of consciousness and personality. Multiple personality disorder was described earlier, so we need not return to it here. A similar phenomenon, but apparently under better control, is hypnosis. Here personality is dissociated apparently into a more passive part, with a more active monitor kept out of direct control. Hypnosis seems to indicate that the posterior part of consciousness can be separated from the anterior, active part. The details of this seem clearly to be relevant to the present model building and analysis.

Another alteration of consciousness arises in the case of pain. What is pain? It can completely fill awareness in extreme cases yet, through surgical intervention, can be experienced but not felt. A lot still must be understood about pain, but its incorporation into relational consciousness is important.

Emotion is a major component of all our experiences. How does it fit into our model of consciousness? Is there, after all, a separate center in the cortex for emotional consciousness?

Finally, the model might be said to be trivially falsifiable because a baby has no memory, but it is surely conscious! A resolution of this apparent paradox is presented as part of a discussion of the manner in which the model has implications for the development of consciousness through Shakespeare's seven ages of man.

Sleep and Dreams

Differences exist between the two states of sleep—slow-wave sleep (SWS) and rapid-eye-movement (REM) sleep—based on differences in EEG records from scalp and eye muscles. In SWS there are slow oscillations in the EEG recordings but no eye movements, whereas in REM sleep there is high-frequency EEG activity, and rapid eye movements are recorded from eye muscles. A person who is in one of these states usually has a characteristic style of thought, movement, and sensation:

• In SWS, thought, if experienced, is logical and perseverative and contains representations of current concerns; movement is episodic and involuntary; and sensation is dull or absent.

• In REM sleep, thought is illogical, bizarre, and emotionally charged; movement is commanded but inhibited; and sensation is vivid and internally generated (as we all know from our dreams).

These differences indicate that different brain sites are at play in the two forms of sleep (Hobson and McCarley 1977). In REM sleep there is considerable posterior cortical and some frontal cortical and limbic activation (supporting the experiences of vivid sensation) with a certain degree of emotional content. In contrast, SWS involves little posterior cortical activation but considerable frontal and self-consciousness activity to support the processes of logical thought, current concerns, and episodic memory.

I am afraid disagreement is rife on the origin of dreams and of other aspects of sleep.[1] I will attempt to relate the phenomena being discovered in sleep laboratories to the relational consciousness model, but avoid this lack of consensus by working at a general level.

I earlier suggested that passive consciousness was supported by a set of pairs of buffer working memory and preprocessing-semantic memory modules in the posterior cortex, with added involvement of posteriorly sited components of episodic memory. The coupled buffer working memory and preprocessing-semantic memory pairs are active in REM sleep, as shown by evidence I just gave. Thus a level of passive conscious experience will be an important concomitant of the experience in the REM sleep process. Little frontal activation will occur except for the frontal eye fields; little of the anterior and self-conscious components will be added to the posterior conscious experience. Episodic memory is reduced in REM sleep, so experiencing in REM sleep is a weakened form of posterior consciousness with a reduced contribution from episodic memory, and little ability to send items of experience onto frontal sites of active memory to support reasoning processes. That agrees with the general experience of dreamers. A crucial prediction of the model is that during REM sleep some buffer sites must have considerable activity, which is correlated with that in the frontal eye fields.[2]

We may understand SWS sleep by relational consciousness in terms of various features discovered in other mammals; for example, in the rat during SWS the hippocampus is highly active (McNaughton and Wilson 1995). There is also the logical and perseverative character of SWS experience I mentioned above. Together, these results indicate that both frontal and limbic activation will occur so that anterior and self consciousness will be present. However, the posterior component will be reduced. The experiments I noted above indicate that in SWS an update of episodic memory occurs, as by hippocampus feeding its buffered memories to nearby cortex. Such frontal and hippocampal activity is necessary for updating to take place.

The converse of episodic memory development in SWS is that in REM sleep preprocessing-semantic memories are updated. This is supported by experimental data on the reduction of skill memory in subjects who were wakened when going into REM sleep so that this component of sleep was considerably shortened. Such semantic updating is consistent with the greater posterior cortical activation supposed to occur in REM sleep, and which is required to augment preprocessing-semantic memories. It is to be expected that companion working memories would be updated at the same time.

We must now consider possible activation of the overall global control structures involved in bringing order and unity to different components of consciousness in sleep. These were proposed as the NRT and the basal ganglia in chapters 7 and 10. The former is not able to act as an effective network to support long-range inhibition during sleep, since then neurons of NRT cannot respond in an effective information-transmitting manner. Instead they give out bursts of activity that, in association with similar bursts of thalamic neuron output, prevent any input signal from getting to the cortex (Steriade, Jones, and Llinás 1990). This explains the bizarre character of the REM and the SWS experience. Both depend on external input to posterior cortex to give the normal content of awareness, and that will now be missing.

An interesting implication of the experience of some form of consciousness in sleep is that working memory activity to achieve that form of consciousness is not supported by associated activity in the thalamus and NRT. Since some form of awareness is present in REM sleep, the thalamus and its NRT component are not required for this form of consciousness. It would seem that this form of awareness is composed solely of disjointed bits of raw feels, together with some limbic components. It also gives support to the claim that consciousness is a cortically based phenomenon; what unity it has in dreams must be achieved by the effect of inhibitory nerve cells in cortex playing the strong-arm game.

Thinking and reasoning are possible in SWS, indicating that the frontal system, including the basal ganglia and mediodorsal thalamus, are in a satisfactory information-processing mode. That is a further prediction of the relational consciousness model. We also expect associated hippocampal activity, which should be observable as part of the medial orbitobasal loop action for the presence of self consciousness.

We can now see how the SWS and REM sleep components of consciousness are constructed from different combinations of brain structures that support waking consciousness. The experiences are quite different, but the neural supports are the same in total but used in different sets of combinations.

Deficits and Their Effects on Consciousness

A range of effects on consciousness is brought about by loss of specific parts of the brain, particularly of restricted regions of the cortex. The loss occurs in a variety of ways as noted and can produce either very specific deficits in awareness or a broader one that has effects on a range of abilities (Shallice 1988). It is my purpose here to consider how relational consciousness can accommodate changes in awareness brought about by these modifications to the brain.

The general manner in which these alterations can be understood is shown if figure 15.1 showing a pair of modules for the preprocessing-semantic and working memory for a given code. Input enters this part of the system at the preprocessing module and is fed to the buffer working memory as part of the model of posterior consciousness (developed in chapter 9 and discussed more fully in chapters 12 and 13). Output comes from both the preprocessing and working memory modules, the former being at a preconscious level, the latter involved in competition to attain consciousness with other sites of working memory through the NRT system, as suggested in chapters 7 and 8.

Episodic memory is involved in overall competition by feedback of appropriate memories to the buffer working memory module (and to other working memories). The working memory for self is also part of the medial orbitofrontal loop (not shown in figure 15.1).

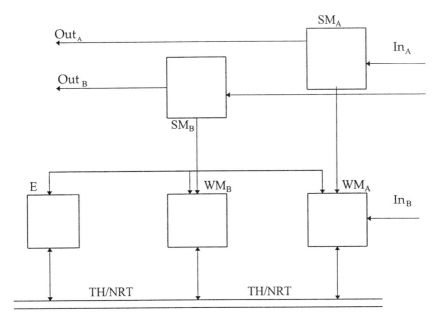

Figure 15.1
Overall processing style of the relational consciousness model: inputs IN_A and IN_B enter their appropriate semantic memory regions on cortex, which either send (low) activity for automatic response or have it further processed on the relevant working memory buffer sites; there is a competition between these sites (run by NRT-thalamic connections as well as by suitably inhibitory intercortical connections), with additional feedback contribution from episodic memory sites.

I will use this model as a framework from which to understand deficits in awareness that arise from brain damage. It would be possible to go through all of these deficits one by one and relate them to the model. I will not be so thorough, but discuss the broader general principles indicated by the overall processing style of figure 15.1.

Inputs to the preprocessing module can be reduced or lost, as would occur if primary sensory cortex is damaged or destroyed. That happens, for example, in the case of blindsight, when a subject loses visual cortex from one half of the brain. While apparently blind, as far as visual awareness of objects is concerned, the person has knowledge of what is in the visual field when asked to make a guess as to where, say, a spot of light might be. The person can respond with a success rate well above chance.

In some cases two levels of such knowledge appear to be at work. One is that of pure guess, where there is no conscious knowledge at all; the other involves a more definite experience, as of a wave pattern or other such visual effect that helps the subject to respond effectively.

We can explain the nonaware form of knowledge of a blindsighted subject as arising from a direct connection from the retina to later visual cortex (bypassing the primary cortex). It is known that a sparse visual pathway exists that is thought to survive early visual cortical damage (Prigatano and Schachter 1993). The question is how it is possible to have knowledge without visual awareness when the actual cortical inputs are of a form in which full processing is not able to be performed due to lack of primary cortex.

Visual input does indeed go to the preprocessing module, but is not strong enough (since it is only a sparse direct input from the retina to extrastriate cortex, bypassing the striate cortex) to achieve a suitable activation on the buffer site so as to bring the input into conscious awareness. But the preprocessed output can be used to activate responses, as it would do in the case of an automatic response. In this case the degraded input still allows knowledge to be obtained from it. Such knowledge can also have a contribution from subcortical circuits. A higher degree of activation, say, through a spot of light moving fast enough, can produce some level of conscious awareness, although it cannot have much content since the signal still would not be strong enough to activate circuits related to the buffer module involved in object recognition. This explains the second form of low-level consciousness, but with little detail available.

Another instance of knowledge without awareness is loss of ability to recognize faces. Subjects with this disability were tested with various faces that they would have recognized before the defect. It was found that they had autonomic system changes (e.g., in skin resistance) indicating that they actually recognized the faces even though they had no conscious awareness of them.

We can explain the preservation of nonconscious knowledge in these people in a similar manner to that of blindsight. Input cannot activate a suitable buffer module, even though the preprocessing module has had activation, so conscious awareness is lacking although an automatic re-sponse is possible. In this case brain stem circuitry is activated to develop an autonomic response; however, output from the preprocessing module or connectivity between it and the buffer site is still insufficient to achieve conscious awareness of the face and resulting reportability.

Other important effects on consciousness occur with loss of temporal lobes, especially the hippocampus. A patient in whom a surgeon removed both medial temporal lobes had very severe recent memory loss; he be-haved as though he had no memory of earlier times. As Shallice reported, "Thus a patient will show no recognition of having met someone if that person leaves the room and then returns after an interval of just one or two minutes." Such a patient (who has to be institutionalized due to the severity of memory loss) shows no deficit in short-term memory or drop in intelligence. The person's conscious experience involves posterior and anterior consciousness, together with a frozen level of self-awareness, stemming from the time of surgery. He will look in a mirror and not recognize himself as being so many years older, but complain that he should look as he did just before the operation.

Clearly the posterior component of consciousness is reduced for these patients in that recent episodes will not be buffered, so memory of events in previous minutes or earlier is completely lost. The battle for conscious-ness will be helped only by components of episodic memory laid down and still accessible before the operation. Such patients can also acquire skill memory, such as motor skills and mirror image writing; whether that extends to increasing their preprocessing-semantic memory is unclear.

Some people lose buffer working memory systems. One subject was asked to memorize words in a language unknown to her. Compared with her ability to memorize new words in her own language, she could not do so in the new language. This woman had a very short span of working memory, which was suggested as being correlated with memory loss; she had no other deficits, especially in word processing in her native language. So she had obviously been able to compensate for the loss of her phono-logical store, but could not do so under certain situations, such as in processing completely unknown foreign words, and hold them in her buffer long enough to lay them down in longer-term buffer memory. She did not have the necessary brain apparatus—a working memory—to hold the foreign words.

From relational consciousness we expect no conscious experience of new words of a foreign language to enter the deficient phonological store. Compensation by way of setting up alternative arrangements for holding such inputs in the subject's natural language (e.g., in active working memory of frontal lobe) would avoid deficits in normal experience. The report did not state whether or not the subject was conscious of the new words; the relational consciousness model would indicate that in fact she was not. A similar modification of the brain used for consciousness was discovered in a patient mentioned earlier in whom brain imaging found that he used parts of his frontal lobe when he was "aware" of moving spots before his eyes.

Further deficits of awareness arise in cases of neglect, involving lack of response, say, to objects in the right visual field, although the subject is not blind to any region of vision. Numerous kinds of neglect exist, although all seem to involve inability to foucs attention on the appropriate region of the visual or other sensory field.

In the context of relational consciousness it is possible to explain neglect in terms of loss of one of the components of the posterior attentional system, which uses the NRT system (discussed in chapter 7) to achieve amplification of inputs, and winning a competition between objects in the sensory field by means of NRT lateral inhibition. The difficulty experienced in the case of neglect is that an object in the neglected field has no support in the competition for attention and conscious awareness owing to loss of parts of the system. The relevant cortical region for neglect is the parietal lobe, which has strong connections to the pulvinar nucleus of the thalamus. This can also be damaged in some patients who possess slightly different features for sensitivity to cues and speed of reaction times compared with patients with parietal damage.

In some cases a patient with hemineglect (usually of objects on the left side) will improve to such an extent that the original inability to detect stimuli on the opposite side to the lesion disappears. However, if stimuli are presented to both hemispheres at once the patient will neglect the one opposite the damaged hemisphere. That can be explained by the fact that the stimulus on the side that had always been attended to is still able to dominate in the competition for awareness with the stimulus on the opposite side, very likely because of persistent damage. Such competition is an intrinsic part of the relational consciousness model, as I explained earlier.

Lack of awareness of the deficit can take a variety of forms (Prigatano and Schacter 1993). It may rise from repression of knowledge of the deficit, or from indifference to it. Alternatively, it may be caused by an underlying organic brain loss related to the deficit or to an injury. It may occur in cases of neglect in vision or touch, or from damage to the frontal lobes when amnesia occurs. All of these cases go under the label of anosognosia, a deficit of awareness of damage to whatever mode of processing where the person suffered a loss.

We can regard anosognosia as arising from loss of the relevant circuits (or their inputs or outputs) for self in the frontal lobe system, discussed in chapter 11. I suggested this involved the medial orbitobasal frontal cortex, with particular use of the loop circuitry of the ACTION network type to allow for comparison and self-schema generation. Loss of this system due to destruction or damage of the internal module or connection, or damage to input from a suitable posterior processing unit, will cause deficit in self-knowledge. Without the ability to compare the present level of effectiveness of a posterior processing module with its efficiency in the past, no information would be available to make decisions as to the breakdown of the posterior system. Anosognosia would then ensue, which could take a number of different forms according to which particular part of the relevant circuits was damaged or destroyed and the extent of that damage.

It is consistent with this hypothesis that the frontal lobe is recognized as the crucial site of brain damage leading to deficits in self-awareness and self-monitoring; Stuss (Stuss 1993) writes:

First, damage to frontal lobe or at least to frontal functions results in a general deficit in self-awareness and not a focal disturbance of awareness such as neglect. . . . Disorders of awareness after frontal lobe damage are different at least in part from disorders secondary to lesions in posterior or basal brain regions.

Many other deficits are brought about by frontal damage, such as in planning, thinking, and social interaction, with a corresponding lack in consciousness. However, subjects with frontal brain damage do not appear to have loss of conscious awareness per se; it is in the higher functions supported by the frontal lobe that these processing deficits show up. This supports the supposition that the posterior component is the basic entry to consciousness, and that its anterior partner uses such inputs as a springboard to develop more powerful coping and planning responses to achieve desired goals.

Drugs and Mental Health

In modern society many people experiment on themselves in attempts to remove the pressures of their lives or to enhance their experience of their surroundings. The manner in which drugs affect the brain, and thereby conscious experience, is much more diffuse than deficits produced by localized brain lesions. A broader range of changes in experience is therefore to be expected.

An important feature of psychoactive drugs is that they generally function as modulators of the fast-acting chemical neurotransmitters acting at synaptic gaps between nerve cells. Many of these chemicals are already present in the brain and their modes of action are being increasingly understood, among them acetylcholine and the biogenic amines dopamine, norepinephrine, and serotonin.

The brain has three dopamine circuits, one from the hypothalamus to the pituitary, one from the midbrain projecting to the motor-related part of the basal ganglia, and one also from the midbrain projecting to the limbic system and frontal cortex. The functions of the second dopamine circuit are known to be crucial for satisfactory functioning of the frontal loops through the basal ganglia. Loss or deficit in dopamine production, as occurs for unknown reasons in most cases of Parkinson's disease and in some cases of substance abuse, leads to loss of various frontal functions discussed in chapter 10. The loss may be reduced by giving the patient a precursor of dopamine such as L-dopa, or by grafting fetal tissue, which is a source of dopamine.

The third dopamine circuit has been implicated in schizophrenia, in which the patient loses contact with reality. A schizophrenic may have false beliefs that she is being persecuted, and often has hallucinations such as hearing voices.

Careful analysis shows that antipsychotic drugs such as chlorpromazine or haloperidol achieve their effect by binding to dopamine receptors better than dopamine does itself, but do not activate cells to the same extent. It was suggested that schizophrenics may have an excess of dopamine receptors in the brain. Distortions of consciousness occur in schizophrenia that may be caused by overactivation or underactivation of the third dopamine (and the serotonin) system. This is crucially involved in the sleep-wake cycle but is also related to lysergic acid diethylamide (LSD), one of the most powerful psychoactive drugs, and to depression, in which thought processes are normal but involve strong feelings of unworthiness.

Many individuals who have no mental health problems take drugs to increase the level of dopamine and similar neurotransmitters. As expected, such agents bring about a feeling of elation by increased effectiveness of the processing in the brain. A similar change of experience can be caused by the action of other drugs that reduce the efficiency of fast transmitter action.

If responses of neurons in the cortex are modified so that some regions have overactivity and others have less activity than normal, any theory of consciousness based on brain support will lead to a change in conscious experience. If specific sites of buffer working and preprocessing-semantic memory are targeted (being major sites of posterior consciousness) the relational consciousness model will lead us to expect further modifications of consciousness that could not be attributed to distortions of earlier processing by associative cortex. In particular, if targeting of sites in the limbic system is excessive, as occurs with drugs that enhance the amount of dopamine, the result is increased emotional experience and possibly heightened sexuality. Depression, on the other hand, could be due to modification of the motivational circuitry where emotions cross the gateway to bring about actions; there is increasing evidence for such an explanation.

We should note again the suggestion that some drugs, such as heroin and amphetamine, are rewarding because they increase the interest value of all inputs, even those that are familiar from experience. Under drugged conditions emotional relational memory seem to take center stage and be somewhat in control of normal consciousness. In such states the emotional component of consciousness may well have moved from the sidelines into the center stage of consciousness. A further feature of the drug experience bears directly on relational consciousness. Visual experiences under drug influence have often been reported as spiral or similar shapes before the eyes, and cartoons of characters under drugs are often shown as having spirals on their eyeballs. The fact that such visual content could naturally arise I explained earlier in terms of waves of activity being created on the visual cortical sheet (Ermentrout and Cowan 1979). This is due to stronger connections made there between cortical neurons by the drugs. The actual visual experience is that of spirals, which could be understood as shapes that have to be focused on the eyes for them to create a plane wave of excitation on the cortex.

That still leaves out a reason for the experience of spirals. The mental image actually experienced is what would have to be focused on the eyes (spirals), not what actually occurs in the cortex (plane waves). How is it possible to apply the relational consciousness model to explain why the conscious experience is of a spiral? The deep question as to why things look as they do—a spiral looks like a spiral, for example—is at the basis of the model. The external world of appearances has been built up by transforming raw input into activity in the higher levels of cortex to allow for effective responses. The appearances themselves in our brains involve various forms of semantic memory activations, including a range of action-perception sequences. For spirals these would consist of your finger tracing around a physical form of the spiral, your eye following around the details of its shape, and so on. The experience of the actual spiral shape would require activation of later regions, besides early visual cortex, containing memories of such processes. Activation of visual cortex either directly and internally, as in the drug experience, or externally, as when viewing a spiral, should lead to activation of the same later cortical regions and so to the same experience—that of viewing a spiral.

Hypnosis

Hypnosis involves subjects submitting themselves voluntarily to acquiesce to the wishes of the hypnotist. Subjects reduce their monitoring of external reality, and suffer memory loss for recent experiences. Criticism of contradictions in appearances are reduced, apparently by repression of remembrance of the way reality normally proceeds. Thus Hilgard (Hilgard 1977) noted:

The broken watch item in one of our scales may be cited. Here the hypnotized subject is told that when he opens his eyes he will see a broken watch, with the long minute hand operating, but the shorter hand missing. When some subjects open their eyes the working watch is seen as a broken one, but the meaning of that fact is ignored because of the failure of memory; when asked to tell the time the subject tells it as if the two hands were overlapping, reading the time as if the hour hand were beneath the minute hands. He has not lost all memory, for he has interpreted the present in terms of an instruction from the past and retains information from the past about how to read time. However, the critical controls that memory ordinarily provides are missing, as he is influenced solely by the present set of stimuli as he perceives them.

Under hypnosis the subject not only has less use of memory as an arbiter of what reality should be like, but also has dissociation of personality. A subject can be made to experience pain, say, by having her hand thrust into a pail of ice for a few minutes and being told by the hypnotist, "you will feel no pain." When asked if she feels pain, she will say no, but when asked if anyone "in there" feels pain the answer will be yes. This hidden observer, who does indeed take note of all the experiences, is present as a silent monitor of the proceedings even though the subject cannot report them herself.

Hypnosis has considerable similarity to multiple personality disorder. At least two levels of reportage are involved, one at the surface level by the subject who obeys the commands of the hypnotist, the other from a hidden observer deeper inside the subject's self structure who experiences and remembers all that is occurring. It is as if the hidden observer were an alter, as in multiple personality disorder.

We can use the relational consciousness model to regard hypnosis as a dissociation between posterior consciousness and its anterior and self partners. The subject expresses lack of control as well as a lack of drive.

Under hypnosis, when asked to go to the end of a room, the subject will say "if you really wish" but tends to sit and stay relaxed and silent if not pressed further. The dissociation of posterior consciousness from its partners is seen explicitly in these cases: dissociation of a person's self into a pliable personality and a hidden observer. The pliable personality is cut off from episodic memory laid down during hypnosis; the hidden observer, however, is not normally accessible to report, which can be due to the fact that its memories are not available in the normal state. This is similar to the amnesia shown by the "boss" in the experience of alters in persons with multiple personality disorder.

To summarize, hypnosis is of relevance to relational consciousness since it provides a clear dissociation between the two main posterior and anterior parts of consciousness. The complexity of the resulting experience, in terms of the hidden observer, of reduced reality monitoring, and of resulting amnesia, indicates the complex structuring of the interaction among all components of consciousness. Further elucidation by means of noninvasive measurements on the brain while subjects are under hypnosis would be a way to develop a better understanding of this complexity.

Pain

We all experience pain yet it is still not completely understood. Its close link to injury leads one to expect that it is always and only the result of damage to the body. But that is not so. Bodily injury will normally result in pain, but pain may not occur until minutes or even hours after the injury takes place. Moreover, pain can occur with no observable bodily damage, as in the case of lower back pain, from which many people suffer. Some individuals are born without the ability to feel pain. Various neural sites important for the experience of pain can be identified, such as the intralaminar nuclei of the thalamus (which are described later on p. 317). The nature of the origin of pain is considered more fully here.

In cases of so-called episodic analgesia, pain is not experienced until some time after an accident. During wars, soldiers who have been severely wounded often deny being in pain or say that they have so little that they do not require medication. Most of the men in a study of traumatic amputations after the Yom Kippur war spoke of their initial injury as painless, and called the initial sensation a "bang," "thump," or "blow." Many felt no pain until numbers of hours later. At least a third of patients admitted to the emergency clinic of a big hospital reported no pain until minutes or hours after injury, which may have involved, among other things, amputated fingers or fractured bones.

There are strong cultural determinants in the experience of pain; for example, in East Africa people undergo trepanation, in which the scalp and underlying muscles are cut to expose a large area of the skull that is scraped by the *daktari* as the patient sits calmly, without flinching or expressing any sign of pain. Indeed some stoically hold a pan under their chin to catch the dripping blood. The operation is accepted by the culture as a means of relief for chronic pain.

Pain has several thresholds: that of sensation when tingling or warmth is first reported; of the perception itself with commencement of the pain experience; of tolerance when physical withdrawal of the stimulated region occurs; and encouraged tolerance with higher tolerance after encouragement from others. Most people have about the same sensation threshold independent of culture or race. This effect of culture is strongest on tolerance levels, which reflect different ethnic attitudes to pain. It is also possible to alter thresholds by concentration and meditation.

Some years ago I was invited to consult regarding a man who had an entry in the *Guinness Book of Records* for walking barefoot on the world's hottest fire. He stood at the edge of a pit that had an even fire burning on it at 1500 degrees. He was able to walk across it in about 12 seconds, having stood in silent meditation for half an hour beforehand. His feet suffered considerable burns; in answer to my question as to how he was able to stand the pain he said that such burns often happened as part of his fire walking, but they did not bother him. Here was somebody who had indeed put his high pain threshold, possibly raised further by concentration, to effective use.

The sensation of pain is decidedly a conscious one; it is very difficult to ignore, so how does the relational consciousness model explain it? It would not seem likely that consciousness of pain arises solely from comparison of continuing input with memories of similar experiences.

Yet that pain has an important memory component is indicated by the strong cultural factor in thresholds. Memory involvement is accepted by Melzack and Wall (1988), who commented on the difficulty of supporting the claim that pain is a primary sensation subserved by a direct communication from skin receptors to a pain center: "Activities in the central nervous system, such as memories of earlier cultural experience, may intervene between stimulus and sensation and invalidate any simple psychophysical law." They went on:

> The evidence that pain is influenced by cultural factors suggests that early experience influences adult behaviour related to pain. It is commonly accepted that children are affected by the attitudes of their parents toward pain. . . . There is reason to believe, on the basis of everyday observations, that attitudes toward pain acquired early in life are carried on into adulthood.

Melzack and Wall described several experiments in animals in which rearing in an isolated environment led to failure to notice normally unpleasant stimuli. This was also shown by Pavlov as part of his conditioning experiments. Dogs received food just after being shocked electrically on one of their paws; after several such occasions the dogs would salivate and wag their tail after the shock to the paw, but a shock to a different paw caused them to react violently. The conclusion of this was, "The meaning of the stimulus acquired during earlier conditioning modulates the sensory input in any unconscious manner and alters perception and response." This is relational consciousness applied to pain: experience gives content to the pain experience.

From our point of view the thesis is that the experience of pain is achieved as part of awareness in a relational manner. It is given its painful connotations only by the activation of earlier memories of response patterns to painful stimuli. If a child hears a great many negative comments about pain expressed by adults, especially its parents, the child will develop into one with low pain thresholds; if the child receives no such fearful input, pain threshold will likely be much higher.

The deep question remains as to whether there is more to pain than the evocation and intermingling of past events with present input—the foundation of relational consciousness; in that case the newborn would be expected to suffer no pain, which sounds extreme and contrary to many peoples' expectations. Yet, according to a standard text on human development:

Newborn infants apparently have little sensitivity to pain, and there is doubt as to their ability to sense it at all. . . . At birth there is no clear evidence of pain, although Lipsitt and Levy observed toe reflexes and withdrawal of the foot from electrodermal stimulation. (Munn and Carmichael 1974)

Such a grounding of all experience on the reflex arc was discussed earlier as a part of the developmental process. The consequence of accepting the above quotation is that the newborn has to build its experience of pain de novo. If this is true, the experience of pain is after all relational.

However, we should not forget possible experiences before birth. Considerable debate surrounds the ethics of performing operations on the fetus in the womb (discussed briefly in chapter 2) due to increased indicators of fetal stress. It is not clear that this corresponds to consciously experience of pain, especially since the level of consciousness the fetus possesses cannot be high (Hepper and Shajidullah 1994). We consider that problem more fully later in the chapter. In the meantime, it is expected that the fetus develops a primitive form of pain memories in the womb. It may use these when it begins to have its first glimmer of conscious experience (toward or just after birth), as the relational consciousness model would suggest.

Imagery

Imagery, picturing in the mind's eye, is usually regarded as part of normal consciousness. Yet our usual experiences of sensory inputs are of external objects, as opposed to hallucinations (where no external object causes the experience) or images of objects that have no possible existence (such as a unicorn). A separate process can be going on in the mind when images are formed. As part of a complete discussion of the nature of mental experience from the viewpoint of the relational consciousness model we must see how imagery fits in.

Numerous controversies surround the nature of imagery. One of the most recent is as to whether or not images are different from verbal thoughts. Noninvasive instruments, deficits brought about by brain lesions, and single cell recordings in monkeys have been used to determine the neural substrate of imagery and helped to resolve the controversy on the side of the nonverbal interpretation. Experiments with EEG and PET were conducted when subjects performed imagery in a range of tasks. From the results we can conclude that passive imagery involves similar posterior cortical sites (other than primary sensory receiving areas) to those involved in input processing of the same structures. Active imagery, involving the rotation of imagined shapes, was considered in chapter 10 as being a component of frontal activity and supported by the ACTION network. The actual shapes being rotated would be created by activity in the posterior sites.

That images involve activation of those associative cortical areas involved in their preconscious input processing supports the claim that they have a visual nature and are not propositional. As noted by Farah:

The existence of common neural substrates for imagery and perception demonstrates rather directly that imagery is a function of the visual system and . . . carries the further implication that images also have this format. (Farah et al. 1988)

The conscious experience of the passive image therefore arises in a similar manner and in the same sites as a visual input. Consciousness occurs in the sites of relevant working memory. The active image has a further anterior cortical rehearsal process able to keep the posterior representation in mind.

Emotions

The emotions make life worth living, but can also make it hell. Lovers strive for ecstasy in their union, the artist for perfection in a painting. The poet tries to arouse emotions in readers: "The suggestion, by the imagination, of noble grounds for the noble emotions," as critic John Ruskin wrote. These emotions can give a sense of satisfaction and fullness to life. Yet in excess they are capable of causing people to break into murderous rages and even become killers. I start by briefly describing the understanding that exists of these important threads running through our conscious existence and how they meld into the passive and active components of consciousness. Normally, emotions provide a general color to all we do—bright if we are feeling happy, dark if we are sad or depressed. Doesn't that show that they are really a part of the background furniture of the mind, and don't present much of a jump in the great race? But not so fast—emotions can totally take over a person's behavior. So the emotional jumps are higher than we thought!

It is becoming accepted (Izard 1993) that emotions have three components. The first is a neural substrate in the brain in which particular neural processes are involved, as in tumors in the limbic system. People so afflicted can lose control and try to kill those who normally are nearest and dearest to them. Specific neural pathways and neural modules, such as the limbic system, acting as the most crucial substrates of the emotions, can be traced in the brain. Certain chemicals involved in communication between nerve cells (neurotransmitters) are also implicated as more generally controlling mood and affecting the efficiency of information processing. These changes are known by many from drug experiences.

A second component that most researchers include in emotion is associated motor activity. Particular expressive movements or action tendencies may be taken to help define emotion. One of these was noted by the poet Matthew Arnold when he wrote, "the heart less bounding at emotion new." Precise objective methods, including direct observational psychophysiological techniques, help identify such movements, including facial expression, head and eye movements, posture, and muscle action potentials. Most of us intuitively know these signals, but now they can be objectively measured. Watch your nonverbal signals if a scientist is watching you!

A universally accepted component is the emotional conscious experience itself. No agreement has been reached on the form this takes but, in general, it can be identified as motivation to prepare for or take action, to bias perception, or just to feel. A person who has acquired language is able to report on the emotional conscious experience. Language, however, is an imprecise medium with which to express emotions, especially deeply felt ones, in spite of the strivings of artists and poets over the centuries. Shakespeare's love sonnets come close.

In summary, emotions are made up of a neural substrate, associated motor activity, and a conscious component. One of the most famous models of the emotions was that of William James. He proposed that the perception of bodily changes brought about by responses to a stimulus gives rise to the emotional feeling about the stimulus. Bodily changes precede emotions, not the more commonsense theory that the order is reversed. Moreover he suggested that the quality of an emotional state could be altered from undesirable to desirable, for example if "we . . . assiduously . . . go through the outward movements of those contrary dispositions which we wish to cultivate." (This has been extended by further studies [Duclos et al. 1989].) More recent research supports the thesis that emotion includes a motor component or similar activity in the nervous system, so James was not as wrong as some suggested.

Activation of certain underlying neural structures can cause emotional states. Much work has been done in connection with electric brain stimulation on humans for diagnostic and therapeutic purposes (Redmond 1985; WhyBrow, Akiskal, and McKinney 1984) and also in animals such as cats. In particular, (Hess 1957) anger or rage states in cats are elicited by electrical stimulation of the hypothalamus through implanted electrodes in freely moving animals.

A remarkable demonstration of this was achieved by the neurosurgeon Jose Delgado (Delgado 1969). He placed an electrode, controlled by a radio transmitter from a distance, inside the aggression center of a bull. As the animal charged at him in the arena he calmly clicked on the current into his transmitter and stopped the bull in its tracks. A beautiful demonstration of the power of electricity over mind—and remember Libet's patients with their consciousness turned on or off at the press of a switch.

This understanding of the neural networks controlling emotions was extended by Papez (Papez 1937), who proposed a special circuit in the brain, now called the Papez circuit (figure 15.2) composed of

mamillary body → anterior thalamus → cingulate cortex → hippocampus → mamillary body.

Papez noted that it was through the circulation of activity, initially at subcortical levels but arriving at cortex in the loop, that conscious emotional experience arose. The Papez circuit was later extended to include

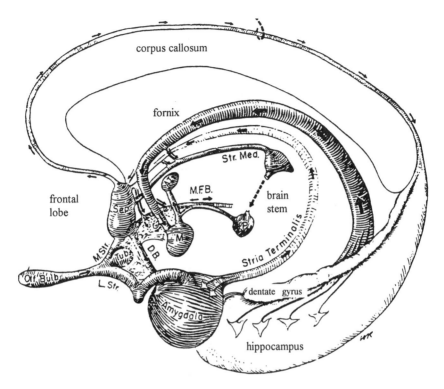

Figure 15.2
A general picture of the limbic connections in the brain, emphasizing the Papez circuit. (Reprinted with permission from Smithys 1970)

other structures, such as the amygdala (so called because of its almondlike shape at the end of the hippocampus), the tip of the temporal lobe, the hypothalamus, and the orbitofrontal cortex. These and other nearby regions of cortex, the parahippocampal gyrus, are all part of the limbic system.

But all this goes on at a nonconscious level, so I can hear you, anxious to get on to the real problem, ask, how does emotion rise into consciousness? An important component is significance or appraisal. Thus ". . . a grasp of personal significance of what is happening in an adaptational encounter is necessary for an emotion to occur" (Lazarus 1991). A somewhat similar approach is taken by Frijda and Moffat (Frijda and Moffat 1993): "Emotions can be considered the output of a subsystem for safeguarding and satisfying the individuals' concerns, that is the individuals major goals and preferred states in the world. The emotion system detects the relevance of events, with regard to these concerns. . . . Because events at any one time may be relevant to any individual concerns, detected concern relevance is transmitted to the remainder of the system by means of a centralized, general, and pervasive signal, namely affect, or the awareness of pleasure or pain."

It is natural for such a general signal of concerns to be transmitted through the consciousness system. In the relational consciousness model this is proposed as a system of coupled working memory modules in the cortex that report to each other the items of relevance for further processing. What better for the continued and more effective survival of the system than to inject into it a general signal of concern, be it of achievement or failure or general appraisal? Concern is broadcast to the cortex by means of a general and pervasive signal of affect. This signal is transmitted, in the case of pain, for example, by a neural system such as the intralaminar nucleus of the thalamus, which spreads throughout the cortex and whose destruction causes a general coma of the unfortunate individual concerned. Awareness of pleasure or pain was further proposed as "one of the defining characteristics of what we mean by emotion" (Le Doux 1992).

Emotions play a strong role in interrupting activity. In humans, they appear to have a number of ways in which they bring about control. They can interrupt activity or cause that activity to deteriorate. They may also preempt cognitive mechanisms so as to lead to single-mindedness and irrational actions. This is related to the precedence achieved over attention and planning connected to the most emotionally salient concerns. Macbeth's fascination with the imagined dagger ("is this a dagger that I see before me, the handle toward my hand—come, let me clutch thee") just before murdering Duncan is an example of this inner working of concerns against each other before his first desperate act on the road of no return.

Emotions cause control shifts between automatic sequences of response actions by means of the generalized affect signal of emotion spread over the cortex, which also uses various neurotransmitters (norepinephrine, serotonin, dopamine) and neuromodulatory systems of neurons in specialized brain regions.

Emotions and concern are the most urgent and powerful mechanisms for behavior control. They may even lead to complete replacement of a current, less emotionally demanding goal. Control precedence itself depends on a number of factors such as a roughly hierarchically ordered set of concerns (without food and drink you will die) and an estimate of expected reward or penalty (how easy will it be for you to get that food?).

Let me summarize. The emotions must be considered a crucial part of any system for control of action. This involves signals at both nonconscious and conscious levels. Both activities undergo interaction with various forms of cortical knowledge.

Finally, let me use the relational consciousness approach to obtain an answer to the question regarding the manner of conscious emotional experience. In particular, can it arise as a truly independent component of consciousness in the way in which it is claimed that passive, active, and self consciousness do? Should we also introduce a separate emotional consciousness and accept a fourfold division of consciousness?

The source of consciousness in our model is interaction among various sites of buffer working memory, all fed by their associated and preprocessing-semantic memories and competing against each other. Buffer working memory sites have bubbles of activity created with properties similar to those posited for raw feels. The competition between buffer working memories is supported by evocation of suitable episodic memories. Are similar sites of buffer working memory dedicated to the emotions?

The most appropriate cortical site so far considered to fit the bill of such a working memory is the anterior cingulate cortex, although an important limbic circuitry contribution also comes from the most anterior part of the temporal lobe. Epileptic seizures of these two cortical regions lead to emotional experiences. However, those could have been caused by activity fed to the limbic system and then distributed about the cortex. Activation of the anterior cingulate is known to lead more generally to active responses, although there is also a mediation of the experience of pain in this region.

General analysis of the temporal lobe seems to assign to it a primary memory function as a memory buffer (a working memory) rather than as the site of an independent emotional consciousness. The cingulate cortex is heavily involved with motivational modulation of conscious experience and making decisions, but not directly with emotional experience itself.

To recapitulate on the emergence of the emotions, much unconscious machinery whirrs along in the limbic system. Thus values of inputs are stored and reactivated in the amygdala, and content memories are developed in the posterior cingulate. Comparisons are developed in the hippocampus or its nearby regions of cortex and goals, and drives may be stored and used in the anterior cingulate and the orbitofrontal cortex, with current values of inputs stored in the latter. Signals are sent out from the cingulate to both the posterior and anterior cortices through the motivational circuit, gated by a putative dopamine signal containing salience, for further action. This is the center of the will. But where is naked emotional consciousness in all of these signals? The classical philosophers always separated will, intellect, and emotion, but we cannot so easily separate them in the brain.

It appears from this description that the most important features of affective signals developed by the limbic circuitry are nonconscious ones. They can emerge into consciousness only when they arrive at suitable sites. Other than in the temporal lobe, orbitofrontal, or cingulate cortex, no suitable set of working memory structures is available for the creation of naked conscious emotion. But these regions are involved in other tasks; deficits and disease (e.g., tumor) have never indicated loss of emotional experience from damage to them. They are involved in memory and control action, but emotional modification seems to arise especially from more widespread activations emanating from the limbic system.

In any case it appears that there is more value for the emotions solely to color cognitive consciousness than for there to be a separate emotional experience, as the latter would have to be melded with other components of consciousness. Although we cannot discount that a separate emotional consciousness site does exist, evidence from the apparent lack of good candidate working memory circuits solely for emotions leads us to the conclusion that in all likelihood no separate emotional consciousness exists, and at a conscious level, emotions are parasitic on passive, active, and self consciousness. They exist on the fringes of consciousness and only indirectly can they come to the center of the stage.

The Seven Ages of Man

The final item to be discussed through the relational consciousness model, as part of the general approach to the varieties of consciousness, is the development of consciousness through the seven ages of man. As I indicated above, a newborn infant has little or no conscious awareness of pain. Is that also true for other forms of experience? Is it further the case that consciousness grows as suitable memory and other structures develop and, in general, begins to decline in old age and senility? These seem to be strong conclusions, but relational consciousness would naturally lead to them.

Considerable controversy arises as to the answers to these questions. A reviewer of one of my papers on the model stated, in opposition to the theory, "A newborn baby, most people would agree, is a conscious being and yet he/she will initially be unable to relate to any 'somewhat similar past activity.'" This is an important objection to the emergent mind model, so I will answer it by carefully considering the facts.

It is clear that the newborn infant has a good repertoire of abilities that were helped by the fetal environment. It is not tabula rasa, but has had some experience to which it adapted. Yet the description of the states of a newborn infant in a text on child psychology (Hetherington and Parke 1993) indicates that the infant is limited in its initial abilities. A classification is given of infant states as regular sleep, irregular sleep, drowsiness, alert inactivity, waking activity, and crying. None of these states seems to be able to support the level of consciousness that is relevant to the quotation from the reviewer except that of alert inactivity. In that state, Hetherington and Parke write, "His eyes are open and have a bright and shining quality; he can pursue moving objects and make conjugate eye movements in the horizontal and vertical plane; he is relatively inactive; his face is relaxed and he does not grimace." Is the newborn conscious in this state? If not, then when is consciousness supposed to occur?

These questions are posited on the supposition that consciousness is an all-or-none experience. However, the thesis of relational consciousness indicates that *the level of conscious experience is determined by the level of past memories* of the various sorts outlined so far. The level of consciousness will continuously increase from a very low level (provided by fetal experience) as the newborn begins to acquire such memories.

Consciousness is not all or none, but emerges from suitable brain structures and associated activities. Such a process of development was outlined as part of the study by Piaget and child developmentalists. Development is gradual, proceeding in different faculties at different rates, as determined by the growth and maturation of neural tissue and the assimilation and accommodation of the infant's experience to its environment. That progress continues for the whole of life, with decay of brain tissue and concomitant loss of memories leading to continued reduction of consciousness as death approaches.

However, we are running ahead of ourselves. Let us return to the newborn infant. We still have to determine whether it has consciousness in the alert inactive state. In particular we can also ask what it experiences during the large proportion of the time it spends in REM sleep, which is about eight hours per day. Does it dream, and if so, what about? Of course the infant is not able to answer, so we cannot know. However, it was suggested earlier that REM sleep is important for the development of semantic memories; is that what it is achieving as part of REM activity?

An alternative theory is that the function of REM sleep in the infant is to stimulate higher brain regions for development. This may be the reason for the large proportion of its sleep spent in REM, compared with only 10 percent or so in the adult. But we can question why any REM sleep occurs in the adult if its only function is to achieve autostimulation of the brain. In later adulthood considerable external stimulation occurs, so further autostimulation may not be necessary. In that case it may be that part of the function of REM sleep is to build semantic memories, the other part (which disappears in the older child and adult) being for autostimulation.

If the newborn is building its semantic memories ab initio (but based on reflex responses), it will have no consciousness of novel objects to which it is responding in its environment. It is only when a set of early brain structures is able to encode objects that consciousness can be said to begin. Even then it is at a low level since the code will be very primitive, in comparison with the one- or two-year-old who has developed a large repertoire of responses to its surroundings. We see the importance of early experience, especially of a social form (contact with the mother or mother substitute), from animals raised alone. They seem to have no conscious experience of pain, since they appear to have no comprehension of noxious stimuli.

Yet the newborn follows moving objects and makes conjugate eye movements. Are these not indications of conscious processing, I hear you sensibly ask? Not necessarily, since they appear to be only reflex responses that are, nevertheless, soon used to build up more complex responses along the lines outlined in the earlier chapters. Consciousness thereby grows in proportion to the range of responses and the associated semantic and episodic memories of past experiences that inputs can excite to fill it out. It is interesting to note that childhood amnesia indicates the child will not have much use for these very early infant memories in later conscious experience.

The conclusion is that the claim that the newborn is conscious does not have much support. The level of consciousness that does exist is only very low and, it is suggested, arises from prenatal experience that is known to exist and be relevant to later responses.

The relational consciousness model both survives the problems about the emergence of consciousness and leads to a new way of looking at infancy. For the infant mind is developing in direct proportion to the level of its memorial experiences and memories, and strongly supports an enriched environment.

At the other end of the spectrum, similar strong support exists for attempting to keep an enriched environment in old age. There is no doubt that poor intellectual stimulation at a later age will not help people keep their mental faculties in good shape; as brain cells die and memory degenerates, consciousness decreases. As a text on aging noted, "This view is supported by the work of Schultz, Kaye, and Hoyer, who found that individuals who continued to use their cognitive abilities on regular basis into their older years were much less likely to show a decline in intelligence" (Brodzinsky, Gormley, and Ambron 1986).

We can even begin to quantify the amount of consciousness that any person has at any time, although this is heavily dependent on the level of intellectual stimulation experienced, which clearly is highly variable from one person to another. We can define the level of consciousness as the average daily number of past memories, both preprocessing-semantic and episodic, evoked in a person over a day. We expect it to increase up to middle age and reach a plateau, and ultimately begin to decline. Preprocessing-semantic and episodic evoked memories have different levels, so that two measures of consciousness may have to be introduced, one for each type.

We expect these two measures of consciousness to change at different rates over the life span. But a further dissociation of consciousness is indicated: the slow, progressive decline in intellectual abilities from the fifth decade onward, observed in studies of aging subjects, appears to be mainly in the areas of perceptual integration ability, memory, and inductive reasoning (general areas of fluid intelligence) as well as in areas of psychosomatic skills and speed of response. Social knowledge seems to be little affected by the aging process. This further dissociation in abilities corresponds to a split of consciousness along lines discussed earlier. Self consciousness persists well to the end, but the anterior nonself component decreases, as might the posterior part (although, from the facts stated above, not as strongly). More careful studies must be carried out to correlate in detail degeneration of neural modules with reduction of faculties. Observation of its emergence in correlation with the growth of these modules, as also its correlated disappearance with the degeneration of neural modules, will allow its more detailed structure to be understood.

Summary

There is a wide range of varieties of consciousness, some of which were analyzed here by means of the ralational consciousness model. These were states of sleep (slow-wave, dreaming), a range of deficits (lack of awareness of deficit, neglect, blindsight), drug-induced hallucinations, hypnotic trance, pain, imagery, emotions, and changing levels of consciousness that each of us travels through as we are born, grow up, and move into old age. The possibility of such a large variety was explained in a general manner by relational consciousness; in particular, the nature of the change of consciousness with age was correlated to the changing memory and active processing powers, initially growing and decreasing as the brain decays.

I explained all of the forms of consciousness by means of the relational consciousness model, thus allowing the beginnings of a better understanding of their nature. But the model may not survive the scrutiny of philosophers, who have spent millennia attempting to understand the mind. Confrontation of some of the most recent ideas in the philosophy of mind must be achieved before our model can be said to have stood up to some of its most important critics. That is considered in the next chapter.

16
Philosophical Questions

Thou wert my guide, philosopher and friend.
—Alexander Pope

The mind-body problem has been the province of philosophers over the millennia. However, the subject is now also being considered more generally by scientists in a broad range of relevant fields. Earlier I presented a list of the constituency to whom the relational consciousness model must be addressed. That list has so far been encompassed only partially; the most important group not yet addressed is the philosophers, original and deep thinkers on the problem. Philosophical thinking, and especially that on the mind-body problem, changed over the centuries as progress was made and relevant scientific facts were discovered. However, some philosophers, here called negativists, claim that such scientific facts are irrelevant. Mind, they claim, is and always will be a hard problem. It possesses intrinsic features that make it impossible ever to reduce it to mere matter. Other philosophers, pessimists, claim that such a reduction is possible but very difficult, and that we are light years away from such a solution. Finally, eliminativists state that there is in any case no problem regarding consciousness; they reduce it rather trivially by denying it features that their colleagues claim are impossible to understand physically.

The continuum of philosophical positions thus consists of two extremes and a middle: pessimists, eliminativists, and negativists. These positions have many subtle nuances, and people occupy one or other of them for quite different reasons compared with others of the same faith. We will not try to consider all of the possible positions, but dwell only on particular instances of the three groups who raise what appear to be especially crucial questions for the model presented here.

The purpose of our final exercise is threefold:

1. To discover, for philosophical problems presently regarded as the center of interest for the mind-body problem, the manner of the solutions that relational consciousness provides.
2. To determine the nature of modifications that must be made to the model to solve still unsolved philosophical problems.
3. To make further clarifications to the model as necessary by considering these philosophical positions.

Several possibilities might occur as a result of this exercise:

1. The relational consciousness model solves all of the major problems.
2. The model solves some of the major problems but needs some inessential or essential modifications to solve the remainder.
3. The model cannot solve some of these problems without such radical revision as essentially to nullify it.

The Pessimists: What Is It Like to Be?

American philosopher Thomas Nagel (Nagel 1974) expressed a pessimistic view of understanding consciousness in his famous paper "What is it like to be a bat?" He raised the point that it will never be possible to determine what it is like to be a bat or any other species. To echo Nagel (1974), "every subjective phenomenon is essentially connected with a single point of view and it seems inevitable that an objective, physical theory will abandon that point of view."

How can the relational consciousness model approach this supposedly scientifically impossible inner point of view? As Nagel stated it more precisely, the problem is, "I find the hypothesis that a certain brain state should necessarily have a certain subjective character incomprehensible without further explanation."

To answer this question, I will describe the possible nature of such a point of view from within the model to see how far its singleness can be arrived at.

To start with I take the point of view of the sentient being X to mean the detailed content of conscious awareness of X. This detail, according to the model, is composed of the working and/or active memory activities that have just won the consciousness competition. To that is to be added all the feedback and parallel activated preprocessing-semantic and episodic (autobiographic and value) memory activities related to the input. Moreover, parallel activities in the other, preprocessing, working, and active memories may be involved in symbolic or linguistic report (as in the case of the phonological loop in humans). In higher states or states of reflective awareness activities in the other components of consciousness will be incorporated with the posterior component, as I described earlier. But most especially I think the point of view is determined by preprocessing-semantic and episodic memories related to input in the appropriate working and/or active memory. We can explore this view of the subjective character of experience in more detail by considering their contributions separately.

The preprocessing-semantic memory content of consciousness has general culture- and species-specific characteristics; for example, words of the natural language in which the person was brought up, as well as words of other languages learned during schooling or as part of general life experiences. For animals such as dogs, similar encoding of the few words with which they are familiar occurs, although no corresponding phonological loop may be present to give conscious experience to words, but only direct output to spatial working memories allowing the conscious experience of such words to acquire a visual form. Similarly, other modalities have culture-specific preprocessing memories, such as for shapes in the visuospatial sketch pad described in chapter 13. We expect more person-specific encodings in the preprocessing-semantic memories, such as dialects or particular shapes, although these are usually shared with others in a local area; the preprocessing-semantic encodings have a degree of objectivity associated with them.

An important aspect remains that we have yet to explore. Nagel indicated that the point of view of X being searched for is critically tied to the concepts possessed by X and evoked by the inputs that cause that point of view. I emphasized earlier the preprocessing-semantic memory as giving a major part of the point of view; the more detailed nature of the concepts encoded thereby was not stressed. According to Nagel, the nature of the concepts developed and used by a species is the main entry to the inner point of view. The nature of preprocessing-semantic memory requires more analysis.

The preprocessing-semantic memory developed by X is based on the sets of sensorimotor responses it uses in experiencing the object that evoked the concept in the first place (to which linguistic encoding may be added for species having such skills). From this approach we can objectively analyze the neural activity excited by a particular object and describe those sensorimotor acts that are involved with it (where semantics is here equated with relevant virtual actions). We can then, by a suitable stretch of the imagination (assuming the species X is not too distant from our own musculature), begin to imagine what it would be like to be an X experiencing the object in question.

In the case of the bat, the central features of action sequences are the manner in which it avoided obstacles, how it related to others of its own kind, and how it hunted and devoured its prey. The actions it takes in these cases are guided by radar returns, a coupled set of returns and actions taken for the different sorts of object. Even if no actions were taken, the virtual actions, coded by means of threshold modifications in structures similar to the human basal ganglia, would provide neural activity that gives to the input a semantic structure appropriate to the bat. There need not be direct experience of these virtual actions, but the latter would give constraints on responses to the objects, which are proposed as corresponding to the inner feel that is part of Nagel's quest.

It is through episodic (autobiographic) memory content that an additional inner or subjective point of view arises. I described the manner in which that is constructed in the brain in chapter 11. I claimed that personal coloring added to consciousness, the subjective feel of the experience, is given by relational consciousness by the parallel activation and feedback of memories associated with present input. Particular people, buildings, or, more generally, sight, smells, tactile feelings, and sounds from relevant past events are excited (usually subliminally) and help guide the competition for the creation of consciousness of present input. The restricted range of these episodic memories indicates the filtered content of neural activity of the winner of this competition. The level of relevance and significance of these past experiences to continuing activity is not absolute but depends on mood and emotion. Such stored memories are energized both by inputs and basic drives, and guide corticothalamic activity in a top-down manner from limbic structures (Taylor 1995b).

Most crucially, episodic memory is a private diary of an individual's experiences and responses to them. It is so private that it would be difficult to discern its meaning, since it is expressed in a coding that is not easily accessible to an outsider. The engraved traces in the diary are trained connection weights, developed by using unsupervised and reinforcement training algorithms. Knowledge of the values of these weights is not necessarily enough to know all that the inner point of view would receive for its specification. Mood and the resulting neuromodulation of the relevant nerve cells by various chemicals are an essential boundary condition, as are contextual inputs involved in the experience. What is required to recreate the conscious experience of sentient being X for any one period is not only the internal record of the connection weights of memory, but also a possibly imperfect record of mood and place.

To analyze further, two features have been conflated in the problems raised by Nagel, point of view and the innerness or subjectivity of the experience. The first was considered above in terms of a sensorimotor schemata or virtual actions approach to preprocessing-semantic memory. The second is related to the introspectability of the experience. That exists only provided special neural structures are present, which are very likely absent in the bat.

Introspection and sense of self are part of the function of the anterior and self components of consciousness. These, I claimed in chapter 11, develop as a mechanism to compare continuing responses to present inputs and situations with those that were taken in the past and laid down in autobiographic memory; it corresponds to the comparison "I responded like this in the past" or "I did it differently then." The "I" consists of the set of all autobiographic memories developed up to now. Such memories serve the important function of being a repository of response patterns and their outcomes (as successful or not). Updating this memory corresponds to keeping the self up to date.

Neural apparatus for this self process is given by the ACTION net (chapter 10) coupled with autobiographic memory (chapter 11).

The continuing response is held on the active memory network of an ACTION loop and compared with previous self memories in some suitable neural structure such as the basal ganglia (in the ACTION net) and coupled to the hippocampus (Gray 1995). It is by holding activity and its comparison with self memories that the subjective sense of consciousness arises. We note that this comes back to a particular case of relational consciousness in which memories being related to are those of the self.

Finally, the answer to the question as to what makes neural activity conscious is, as given by the model:

1. Holding input on a suitable buffer to allow for its further processing (which is termed evocation and intermingling in the model, and is achieved by the creation of bubbles of activity)

2. Activation by input of suitable memory representations from similar past activity (evocation)

3. Intermingling of those representations with the buffered input to remove ambiguity, reduce information throughput, and perform possible transformations on the buffered activity

This answer was analyzed at considerable length throughout the book; here we finally see how it can answer the two conflated points raised by Nagel.

The Pessimists: Consciousness and the Computational Approach

One pessimist is John Searle (Searle 1994), who states, "Given our present explanatory apparatus, it is not at all obvious how, within that apparatus, we can account for the causal character of the relation between neuron firings and conscious states." Searle is particularly well known for his Chinese room argument against the computational approach to the mind, which equates the latter to a program on a suitable computer. As he noted (1980):

There is a simple demonstration that the computational model of consciousness is not sufficient for consciousness. . . . Its point is that Computation is defined syntactically. It is defined in terms of the manipulation of symbols. But the syntax by itself can never be sufficient for the sort of contents that characteristically go with conscious thoughts. Just having zeros and ones by themselves is insufficient to guarantee mental content, conscious or unconscious. This argument is sometimes called "the Chinese room argument" because I originally illustrated the point with the example of the person who goes through the computational steps for answering questions in Chinese but does not thereby acquire any understanding of Chinese.

I think we all accept, as Searle's Chinese room forcefully requires us to, that syntax by itself is insufficient to give the content to consciousness and in particular, to give it intentionality. The relational consciousness model solves this philosophical problem. An answer to the question of how semantics is learned was proposed in chapter 10, which equated it to the creation (through suitable neural architecture and learning rules) of perception-action sequences chunked at an ever higher level. These chunked sequences were activated by features of objects and led to the notion of semantics as virtual actions. Moreover, the approach is supported by observation of the initial identity and later closeness of the developing brain structures for manual object combination and word combination in the child's frontal lobe. Intentionality is thereby included at a deep level in the very notion of object and its manipulations.

Now here comes the rub. What if a computer program were to be written that contained as its objects sets of neurons and their interactions through nerve impulses, as would a program based on the simplified equations that are used to model the living nerve cells of the brain? the model neurons could be quite complex, being described by thousands of variables detailing their three-demensional shape and response characteristics. If this program were run to mimic the outline of relational consciousness or any other models described in chapter 5, could conscious experience, in principle, be created in the resulting program?

The answer is that, with sufficiently complex simulation of the brain, constructed to incorporate principles that are thought to create conscious experience and run *in real time,* with bubbles of consciousness *appearing as well,* it should be regarded as a putative candidate for possessing the experience of consciousness. If the brain is assumed to create consciousness, so is running its own simulation of the situation, provided it has a real-time feel about it. Why can we not attempt a close enough approximation to that simulation so as to have a conscious program?

We can use as an escape clause the fact that the neurons and their connections are not complex enough in the simulation suggested to represent the real brain. But let me remind you of the universal approximation theorem of artificial neural networks, stated earlier: given enough very simple neurons, they can compose a network that will implement the computation of any function. In other words, no loss of computational power is caused by the use of simple neurons, provided one has a large enough supply of them. Thus there seems to be no let-out. One has to accept a conscious experience of the computer system, albeit one that may be very different from our own. It would experience a very different flow of time.

The computer simulation would have to proceed by developing an emergent mind and be trained in a suitable interactive environment, as is a baby, to develop its own semantics on the basis of an assumed set of reflexes already present. Such an approach was outlined in earlier chapters and is clearly part of our model, being the stage of creating the coupled semantic working memory components of the total model. To achieve this there would also have to be a frontal type of system to be able to chunk the action sequences. Initially it would not be necessary to build the self component, since that would correspond to a self conscious system, which is of a higher order of computational hardness compared with the simpler solely conscious system. However, in principle, there is no reason why such a program cannot be written.

Negativists: What Is Mind? Never Matter

Important philosophers consider that mind will never be reduced to matter. According to them, something further is required to explain consciousness apart from workings of brain neurons. One of the leaders of this approach is David Chalmers, whose division of problems of explaining consciousness into hard and easy was described in chapter 3 (Chalmers 1996a). I will repeat my remarks briefly here. The division I mentioned can be seen as arising from the following situation. First, some problems assume that conscious experience has arisen and the difficulty solving them lies in modeling suitable systems in the brain to achieve even higher-level processing. These systems would support attention, thinking, planning, feeling, and so on. Such problems are considered easy with respect to the basic problem of explaining consciousness.

Second, hard problems of consciousness are reduced basically to bridging the gap between mind and matter. They try to solve the problem as to why a specified activity in matter could lead to consciousness of any sort. The main hard problem is thus, what are the sufficient conditions for consciousness?

Chalmers claims that none exist and that it is impossible to obtain phenomenal conscious experience from insensate matter. Such experience can be obtained only by regarding it as an entity independent of matter. This is what Chalmers does with appeal to an "information space" supposedly separate from the material world.

He posits an explanatory gap between performance of functions underlying consciousness (the easy ones) and the experience of consciousness; this gap is difficult to cross. The difficulty he raises is that consciousness performs no clear corresponding function whose modeling would explain it.

However, the claim that the explanatory gap is impossible to bridge was challenged in chapter 14. The basic properties of raw feels, of ineffability, intrinsicality, transparency, and privacy, appear to arise in the formation of bubbles of neural activity created in the specialized sites of working memory in posterior cortex as they struggle to win the competition for emergence into consciousness. If successful, they glide around as if out of the control of solid earth. They are the bubbles of consciousness. Such semiautonomous neural activity is available to upload onto the frontal sites of active memory that were observed to function along the lines of the global workspace of Baars, ready for later use and higher-order processing. This occurrence of increasingly complex levels of processing being associated with ever higher levels of conscious content is also part of many cognitive models of consciousness. These later stages of increasing complexity Chalmers consigned to the easy problems. They cannot be totally neglected in giving content to raw feels so as to allow them to be more effectively used to achieve effective action.

Yet the emergence of bubbles of activity on working memory sites that is posited here is the key to the creation of phenomenal experience. I claim the explanatory gap has tentatively been bridged through analysis of this process of emergence. The function being performed in the process is allowing input to be held over for a sufficient time for competition and combination between inputs to be completed. This allows for the best interpretation of possibly ambiguous inputs, which can then enter the global workspace.

This process entails consciousness, albeit at a very preliminary raw feel level, and was shown by the analysis of chapter 14. The features of raw feels are present in the resulting activity. However, the detailed mechanisms and their interplay have to be explored at a much greater depth in the future.

The claim made here is that a new feature is entering the neural arena. It is the possibility of splitting or bifurcating neural activity in particular special parts of the multilayered cortex. The resulting activity is essentially free standing, to a large extent independent of input. This leads to a degree of autonomy and apparent freedom from input that fits well with the inner experience itself. Consciousness is a skater gliding so smoothly over the ice that the motion is miraculous.

Eliminativists: There Ain't No Such Thing as Qualia

The philosophers cited so far have been at pains to accept a problem about the mind-body interaction, and they have responded to it with various levels of pessimism or negativism. However, a different approach is to state that no problem exists, and follow that up by the even stronger claim that this is so because one or more difficult features of consciousness—intentionality, introspectability, inner content, or qualia—are simply absent. Therefore they present no problem. Other philosophers of a different persuasion, and certainly most ordinary folks, are just plain wrong about the character of their inner experience. One of the most famous of the eliminativists taking this strong line is Dennett, who in 1991 wrote about qualia

My claim, then, is not just that the various technical or theoretical concepts of qualia are vague or equivocal, but that the source concept, the "pre-theoretical" notion of which the former are presumed to be refinements, is so thoroughly confused that, even if we undertook to salvage some "lowest common denominator" from the theoreticians' proposals, any acceptable version would have to be so radically unlike the ill-formed notions that are commonly appealed to that it would be tactically obtuse—not to say Pickwickian—to cling to the term. Far better, tactically, to declare that there simply are no qualia at all.

An explanation of the characteristics of qualia given in chapter 14 as part of relational consciousness disagrees with Dennett's position. Apparently his annihilation of qualia developed from his disbelief that they can be atomic, nonrelational, ineffable, incomparable, and incorrigibly accessible from the first-person point of view. In particular, Dennett's worry about the corrigibility of memories of past qualia led him to destroy them entirely. Yet that does not seem to mesh with one's own continuing conscious experience. There are indeed raw feels, although as indicated in previous chapters, complete experience of them may develop over a period of time and involves a set of past memories of a contextual form about similar past experiences; they are not incorrigible, nor are they intrinsic and atomic. But they nearly are all those dreadful things, and that is why we have the corresponding feel about the raw feels.

The nature of the qualia experience arises naturally from the relational consciousness model. At no time has an attempt been made to bring in any of the detested features of qualia from the outside as primitive elements. Yet it was indicated in earlier chapters, and especially in chapter 14, that some folk experience properties of qualia do arise from this approach: inner privateness, and belief in their reality and in their nonrelational, primitive or atomic, and ineffable character.

Eliminativists: Destroy Folk Psychology!

Besides the problem of the explanatory gap, an approach that is much closer to that espoused here is reduction of psychology to neurophysiology and neural computation. It was championed in particular by the distinguished husband and wife team of American philosophers Patricia and Paul Churchland. Over several decades they made important contributions both to the discussion of the philosophy of mind and brain and the philosophy of science, arising out of problems related to the reduction mentioned above: if psychology is reduced to neurophysiology how much of the former will be preserved? In particular, how will the concepts of folk psychology, such as the commonsense notions about beliefs and desires and the manner in which they give a basis for a theory of human behavior (Churchland 1986), be mapped onto underlying neurophysiological processes? The insight that such psychological concepts provide a background theory for understanding much of human behavior proved important, and from folk psychology developed a more precise scientific psychology.

The position taken by the Churchlands is well expressed as eliminative materialism in the sense that

Folk psychology suffers explanatory failures on an epic scale . . . it has been stagnant for at least 25 centuries . . . its categories appear (so far) to be incommensurable with or orthogonal to the categories of the human background physical science whose long-term claim to explain human behaviour seems undeniable. Any theory which meets this description must be allowed to be a serious candidate for outright elimination. (Churchland 1997)

Furthermore, once neuroscience is more effective, our internal states and activities, they claim, will be able to be reformulated in terms, for example, of our neuropharmacological states and neural activity in specialized anatomical areas. The Churchlands attempt the process of reduction by means of principles extracted from simple neural computational models of motor control and visual processing. These principles are associated with the manner in which the brain gives a response to an input that is a prototype vector (Paul Churchland) or has a suitable dynamic behavior in response to inputs (Patricia Churchland).

It would appear from the quotation above that the problem of consciousness will soon be effectively eliminated by the complete destruction of folk psychology at the hands of advanced neuroscience. However, Paul Churchland made a recent disclaimer to this rather natural interpretation of the eliminative position. In particular, he stated:

So when one suggests that the category of "consciousness" may be fragmenting (PS Churchland 1983) and that it may be replaced by a different set of categories, people may assume that we are denying there is any phenomenon there to be explained. This is just a mistake. Of course there exist phenomena to be explained. We are in no doubt that there is a nontrivial difference between being asleep and being awake, between being in a coma and being fully functional, between being aware of a stimulus and not being aware of it.

The conclusion of this is that considerable agreement can be seen between the program of the Churchlands and the basic aim of the program set out in this book. My attempt to bridge the gap between folk psychology and neuroscience uses concepts of folk psychology as they are and does not try to destroy them. Instead, I attempt to explain the manner in which they may be supported by brain activity in terms of the broad principles of neural networks and neuroscientific knowledge. In particular, the manner in which psychological processes can be decomposed into component subprocesses was discussed toward the end of chapter 14. I showed how the functions carried out by these component subprocesses could be modeled, at least in principle, by known neural network systems. In this way it might be expected that folk psychology becomes more effective through its support at a (neural network) micro level. That appears to be in agreement with the present position of the Churchlands.

Summary

In this chapter relational consciousness was brought face to face with some of the major philosophical problems raised by modern thinkers on the mind-body problem. The main ideas were divided into the three classes of pessimistic, negative, and eliminative. In the first category was Nagel, who raised the difficulty of ever being able to explain what it is like to be a bat. This was answered in terms of developing the details of subjectivity and of semantic and conceptual notions to fill in subjective and point of view aspects.

Searle and his Chinese room were answered by a discussion of the manner in which semantics is to be included in the emergent mind model. This led to the question of the nature of the consciousness that might be experienced by a computer simulating the model. It was concluded that, provided this was achieved in real time and led to bubbles of neural activity, it was a putative candidate for possession of such experience.

In the second class was Chalmers's description of the hard problem of experience, which is why it is necessary at all to have inner experience associated with brain activity. This was analyzed and shown not to lead to the no-go theorem that consciousness could never be given a neural explanation. Instead of the more problematic dualist model suggested by Chalmers, analysis of chapter 14 was shown to allow the beginnings of an explanation of how the inner experience of raw feels must occur from activity in special parts of a six-layered cortex through the creation of bubbles of neural activity. These bubbles have an independent mode of existence compatible with the nature of raw feels.

Dennett's multiple drafts model of consciousness was considered in terms of the eliminativists viewpoint. The claim as to the need for the elimination of qualia owing to their possession of incompatible and incomprehensible properties was not seen to be fully justified. Bubbles of relational consciousness are capable of producing aspects of phenomenal experience possessing the surface properties of qualia.

Finally, I considered the eliminativist position of the Churchlands in relation to the model. The very latest position of the Churchlands has close similarity with my position.

In conclusion, relational consciousness faced up to some of the major modern problems of the philosophy of mind and is still viable without any drastic changes. We should note that it must be subjected to even more important and scientific tests that are crucial to determine its continued existence. The nature of these tests was stated in various places in the text. They wait on the further development of noninvasive measurements at the fast time scale of tens of milliseconds, which is relevant to the development of consciousness and in particular the running of the competition between the different working memories described in chapter 9 and 13 as basic to the emergence of posterior consciousness. It will be in terms of scientific tests that relational consciousness persists, is modified, or ultimately fails.

17

A Scientific Model of the Mind?

The perfect presence of mind.

—Henry James

In this book I have given a reasonably detailed model of the mind, termed relational consciousness, based on the relational mind thesis that I suggested more than 25 years ago. I explored, developed, and used it to explain the main features of the complexity of consciousness. Part I set out various basic criteria for consciousness, followed in part II by a description of the general nature of the brain, its observation, and its modeling. Part III was devoted to a detailed exploration and expansion of the model for passive, active, and self consciousness. In part IV, principles were developed for relational consciousness and a glimpse was taken across the explanatory gap. Finally, part V dealt with the manner in which the developed model could help explain further varieties of consciousness—in sleep and dreams, caused by brain injury or drugs, under hypnosis or in pain, through imagery, in emotional states, and as a person grows from infancy to old age. Answers to outstanding philosophical questions about mind and body were given in the previous chapter from the standpoint of relational consciousness.

In all of this discussion experimental data were drawn from both psychology and the brain sciences of neuroanatomy, neurophysiology, and neurochemistry. It was also based on scientific methodology; as such, the model should be both refutable, if recalcitrant data become available, and expandable, if new experiments are performed that allow the model to be developed further and made precise.

This chapter attempts to summarize the scientific status of the model and specifies a set of experiments that are of importance for its continued existence and further development. These should be able to determine if and when the model is finally accepted. The necessary experiments are scattered throughout the book, either explicitly or implicitly. It is fitting to gather them here at the conclusion. Furthermore, what the model may contribute as being of most value to the future of research is a set of predictions of brain activity associated with varieties of consciousness. It also provides a framework from which to look at the global program carried out by brain and mind as part of intermingled conscious and un-conscious processing, and of intertwined active, passive, self, and emotional components.

This chapter starts with the take-home message, which naturally leads to a general definition of consciousness; this is shown to be consistent with the relational consciousness model. It continues with a list of predictions of greatest importance and concludes with comments on some social relevances of the model.

The Take-Home Message

The idea of relational consciousness was outlined in chapter 6, in which the main thesis was that consciousness arises through evocation of past memories and their intermingling with present input. However, it was realized that this thesis had to be fleshed out considerably, especially since consciousness arises from preconscious activity, and the latter process is critical for the emergence of conscious activity. After detailed development in chapters 7 to 11, the manner in which this emergence might occur was presented in terms of the principles of chapter 12.

These principles specified some features that consciousness should possess, and in particular the relational structure contained in the semantic-buffer working memory pairs of encodings and the use of episodic memory activation by encoded input. Chapter 12 gave considerable evidence to support those features of consciousness. There was also the competitive feature to allow the emergence of the unique, most highly valued, concepts into the arena of the working memories for general report by any of them and to generate the approximate properties of the raw feels in chapter 14.

In addition to the principles of chapter 12 were those developed as part of applying relational consciousness to frontal and self-aware activity. This in particular involved recognition of the great motor loop and its four companions in the frontal lobe as carrying out several crucial functions, such as active memory, comparison and attention, temporal sequence encoding (chunking), the resulting formation of semantics of objects encountered in the environment, and transforming activity on other active memories. The overall sites in the brain for creating the various components are given in table 17.1.

The take-home message of all this is that the parts of consciousness arise through competitive processes in a relational framework in such a manner as to suggest a tentative solution to the hard problem, the source of the emergence of qualia or the raw feels of phenomenal experience.

A Definition of Consciousness?

How does relational consciousness allow us to develop a general definition of consciousness? I promised that at the beginning of the book; the time for me to produce it has now arrived.

We must accept that consciousness is complex, with one extreme form of it being passive and input driven and the other active and response driven. We might also claim there is a third form that is internally driven, when one is in a state of planning or more general thinking, or when emotionally aroused. The strongly cognitive state may also be regarded as one that is action driven, since thought is most basically used to solve problems where resolution demands some action or other. The most general form of problem solving is determining a path through a cognitive space to attain a suitable goal position. We conclude that the cognitive internal states are all concerned with action in one form or another.

So far it is difficult to reconcile these two extremes of active versus passive. The active form of consciousness is frontally based, the passive posteriorly. One apparently involves spatial pattern analysis, the other changes of inputs or outputs over time. We can bring the two together in terms of time. Consider the definition:

Table 17.1
Brain regions supporting various components of consciousness

Consciousness component	Brain area supporting relevant competition	Brain area supporting relational processing	Brain area supporting
Posterior	TH, NRT, cortex complex	Semantic, episodic memories	Posterior working memories
Active	Frontal cortex, dorsal basal ganglia	Same	Heteromodal (frontal) anterior active memory
Self	Medialorbitobasal frontal cortex	Hippocampal gyrus	Cingulate and related prefrontal cortex
Emotional	Ventral basal ganglia, intralaminar nucleus of thalamus	Amygdala	Whole cortex

Consciousness arises in using traces of the past in a semiautonomous manner to clarify what comes afterward in achieving the goals of the system.

This involves three key words: clarify, afterward, and semiautonomous. The first requires a process that singles out parts of the environment, for example, those that tend to occur together, and builds internal representations of them to use them in the process of clarification. The second involves either the present or the more distant future. Thus both passive (more immediate) and active (more temporally distant) aspects seem to be parts of consciousness defined in this manner.

The third describes a manner of neural processing, special to a multilayer cortex, in which preprocessed activity ceases to be slavishly attached to the input producing it but glides off onto the ice rink to perform its gyrations miraculously released from the ties that previously shackled it. This process becomes freed from input by means of bubbles of activity in the upper layers of the cortex; the emergence of these bubbles was suggested in chapter 14 as giving a solution to the hard problem.

Let us explore the first two aspects further. Clarification can be achieved by some form of template matching to relate representations of the past to those currently observed in the environment. It is natural to consider using some form of competition between past representation and new input to detect any such match. This was developed in posterior cortex as part of the model and also in the frontal lobe by means of ACTION networks there. Various forms of such competition are related to the possible varieties of memory, in particular, memories of skills versus those of specific events. The former were considered as encoded in schemata associated with the frontal lobes (more specifically with the basal ganglia), and the latter were in both preprocessing-semantic memory and episodic memory sites.

Afterward denotes any time after the preceding second or so. It could consist of the next few seconds or any time over the life of an animal. These are considerably different time spans and would be expected to require different forms of processing and memory. The division of time in this manner agrees with the divisions of consciousness we gave earlier into the passive and active forms.

Passive consciousness has activity for no more than about a second or two, as evinced by the working memory model of Baddeley described in chapter 9. This range of time into the future evokes consciousness as a part of the continuing processing of input and evoked memory states over that time scale. Passive consciousness is for short-term future guidance, using a second or two of input to clarify interpretations of those inputs by removing ambiguities. It was suggested that consciousness arises in the process of ambiguity removal.

The active form of consciousness was analyzed most fully in part III. It has the uses noted in the previous section, involving passive consciousness as a component to tap into knowledge bases relevant to planning. In this manner it is possible to use memories of the long distant past to help clarify the future. Once the ability to use images of the past evolves, there need be no barrier (modulo/neuronal computing power) as to how far ahead one might attempt to view the future. These powers also enable goals to be formulated that are based on past memories of drive reduction and reinforcement.

Tests and Predictions

We can consider the range of tests of the relational consciousness idea as determining the features of competitive processing and relational processing. Each was discussed with relevance to the posterior, active, emotional, and self components of consciousness (although emotions lie only in the fringe), and supported by the neural structures listed and discussed in parts II and III (figure 17.1). From the modes of action of the TH-NRT-C complex discussed in chapter 7, the coupled preprocessing and working memories in chapter 9, and the ACTION network in chapters 10 and 11, we can make predictions about a host of detailed correlations expected to be observed among activities in different regions (spatial correlations) and at different times (temporal correlations) when a subject is in a particular conscious state. Specific predictions of these various sorts of activity are as follows:

1. Passive consciousness
   a. Spatial and temporal correlations on winning and losing semantic and working memory modules of specific forms (modality and input dependent)

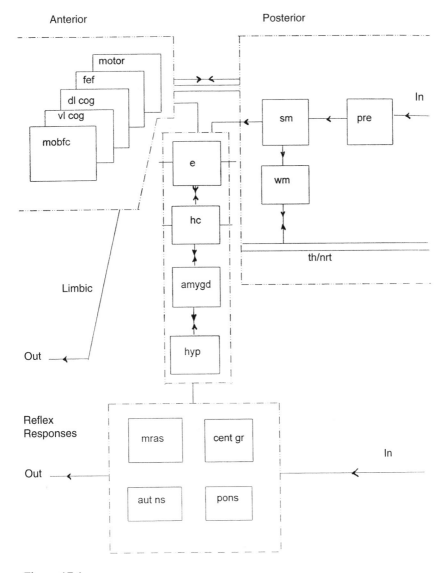

Figure 17.1
General wiring diagram for the brain, with four regions delineated for automatic
(reflex), posterior conscious, anterior conscious, and emotionally dominated (limbic) conscious processing. sm, semantic memory; wm, working memory; e, episodic memory; hc, hippocampus; mobfc, medialorbitobasal frontal cortex; vl and
dlcog, vetral and dorsal ACTION loops; fef, frontal eye field ACTION loop; hyp,
hypothalamus; amygd, amygdala; aut ns, autonomic nervous system; mras, midbrain reticular activating system.

   b. Ditto across NRT, thalamic, and cortical SM/WM regions
   c. Ditto in episodic memory and WM regions
   d. Increased hippocampal activity correlated with WM win activity
   e. Similar correlations as above in SWS and REM sleep
   f. An exogenous reset wave on NRT in externally directed attention
   g. Switching correlated activites between two-semantic working memory sites in dual attention tasks
   h. Continued activity traces (over several seconds) in various specialized cortical posterior buffer working memory sites (located in the same places as observed by PET measurements as noted in the text)
2. Active consciousness
   a. Correlated spatial and temporal activities among appropriate prefrontal cortical, basal ganglia, and thalamic sites during active processing
   b. Correlated activities from frontal to posterior semantic-working memory sites in attentional search tasks
   c. Feedback to semantic-working memory sites in imaging tasks
   d. Correlated activities in appropriate ACTION network regions in schema generation or learning or in semantic processing
3. Self consciousness
   a. Correlated activities in parts of the MOBFC
   b. Ditto in hippocampal cortex, especially during headed memory records searching
4. Emotions
   a. Correlated activities in the cortex stemming from diffuse emotional output from intralaminar thalamic nuclei and limbic circuitry
   b. Correlated activity in the cortex and MOBFC driven by the amygdala
   c. Diffuse cortical activation during high emotional arousal

As seen, many tests must be carried out. Some of the correlations may not last longer than several hundred milliseconds, so it would be especially necessary to use MEG, with its short time scale and subcortical sensitivity, as the method. This would be in collaboration with EEG, PET, and fMRI.

In all of these tests the subject's concomitant psychological state must be monitored. The general form of this state is given under the four headings of passive, active, self consciousness, and emotions. In some states several of the four components will be intertwined, but we would expect the resulting activity to be a rough combination of the activities under the separate headings. Far more complexity will be obvious in such jointly activated cases than when a sole component occurs. Moreover the details of the correlations, across either space or time, will have to be calculated by simulations of realistic models of the appropriate regions. These have yet to be done, but will become feasible as ever more powerful computational facilities are available.

Animal and Infant Consciousness

We still have some loose ends to clear up that may be puzzling you. For example, if all it takes to have consciousness is a multilayered cortex, are arthropods and mollusks (which also have such a neuropil) also not conscious? In addition, if the relational consciousness model is correct, why can we not determine when a fetus (or infant) develops consciousness, and even develop a test for each one separately that would allow surgery to be performed with more assurance of not causing consciously experienced pain. As to the latter question, I look forward to the time when such is possible, but the race for consciousness has still to be completed and the final winner judged before such an important development will be possible (or at least dependable).

The first question takes us back to animal consciousness in general, and also to machine consciousness, since to answer it we need to know what the parts of a model add to provide the total conscious experience. Let me restate the crucial features of the brain that our model requires and go on to what is lost if one feature is missing. The checklist for consciousness supported by the brain is:

1. A suitable set of memory structures
   a. Of buffer form
   b. Of permanent form
2. A processing hierarchy
3. Suitably long-lasting bubbles of activity at the highest coding level of the hierarchy

4. A competitive system to produce a winner among all the activities on the buffer memories at any one time

Absence of any one of these reduces possible conscious experience the animal can have in a quite definite manner. That the residue of experience is still consciousness is a moot point. For example, if there are no bubbles at all because of too little recurrence or too much inhibition in association with it, there is no conscious now. It is therefore debatable if phenomenal experience exists. We can go through the other features on the list and see how powerful a model is in giving externally verifiable criteria as to the nature of inner experience.

A Blueprint for the Mind

We are now in the position of designing a master blueprint for the brain of a conscious animal. Figure 17.1 is designed on the basis of the model presented in this book. It will be necessary to modify and expand it and the neural networks that fit into the parts of the modules as developments occur in brain science and information processing. The present accelerating pace in these fields should allow neural network models to achieve increasingly higher levels of consciousness. However, the principle underlying such consciousness is that it will emerge, and not automatically result, only from the combination of neural networks. In other words, it will not just immediately spring into action when the connection of modular networks is active. It will have to emerge by a process of training, as does a child.

Such developments have numerous societal implications. These come under the headings of animal consciousness, mental health treatments, education, and intelligent industrial machines (machine consciousness). Animal consciousness should become more accepted and a certain level of legal rights be extended to those animals, such as the great apes, that are thought to have a sense of self. They should be regarded as having a level of responsibility similar to that of a child, and, like a child, should be legally guaranteed freedom from pain, torture, and premature death, and have a level of personal freedom appropriate to their level of responsibility.

Modeling the human brain, including aspects of consciousness, will lead through controlled experiments on the model to greater understanding of mental disorders such as autism, schizophrenia, and many others. Experiments on circuit modification caused both by neural and biochemical alterations will allow probing of the causative factors at work in a broad range of mental deficits. With better understanding it will be possible to create better treatment.

A program to build a truly intelligent machine, endowed with reasoning powers close to our own, will be driven and financed by the demands of industry. Service and heavy industry and the financial and business worlds are increasingly using neural network and similar adaptive systems to solve difficult problems with no formal rules, but many pressing problems remain unsolved. Several research groups are trying to create truly intelligent machines using neural network techniques. This will doubtless intensify until such machines are built.

One final question that leaves food for thought is this. If conscious machines are built, what legal safeguards will they possess? Furthermore, what safeguards must be put in place to prevent them from becoming too intelligent for the safety of humanity? These questions have been much discussed in science fiction literature. It would seem that they will have to be answered in terms of science fact in the next century.

The Race for Consciousness

The race for consciousness has started in earnest. Even as this book was being written it speeded up. Various research groups have been formed in different parts of the world, United Kingdom, Germany, Japan, and United States, to name the main players, to pursue consciousness and the concomitant question of obtaining better understanding of the human brain in all of its complexity. Philosophers are being brought in as partners in these enterprises to help clarify the nature of the phenomena associated with conscious experience.

A possible entry for this race in this book has been outlined. The main ideas and models were presented in chapters 5 and 6: the global workspace of Baars and related cognitive science models developed earlier, the recurrence theme of Edelman, the relational mind model I first presented in 1973, the notion of thalamocortical resonance, and suggestions of Crick and other neural network researchers about the manner in which attractors and persistent activity is crucially involved in consciousness. These were fused together, along with an analysis of consciousness that decomposed it into several component parts (passive, active, self, and others not made so explicit), to provide a general model that I call relational consciousness. I extended this by analyzing in more detail how the needed temporality of buffer working memory sites could arise, and found an interesting feature that they could possess. This involved the notion of bubbles of cortical activity, which I suggested as being at the root of a solution to the hard problem of the emergence of qualia by the generation of semiautonomous neural activity.

It would appear that the relational consciousness idea presented as an entry into the great race has several features in its favor:

1. A well-established scientific basis (biological neural networks) for the model

2. A reasonably complete approach to varieties and complexities of consciousness

3. Agreement with some important experimental data on the emergence of consciousness in various modes

4. The possibility of developing the theory further by suitable experimental tests

5. A mathematical framework (dynamic systems theory applied to neural networks) to be used to develop many more predictions and understanding of human experience

Work on the model has only just begun. As Winston Churchill said: "This is not the end, nor is it the beginning of the end. It is the end of the beginning."

Notes

Chapter 2

1. Considerable developments have also occurred in terms of the analysis of early visual processing by means of the use of information theory. See Linsker (1988) and Atick and Li (1994) for recent results.

2. Baars's book is a seminal work on consciousness from the cognitive science point of view.

Chapter 4

1. A fifth lobe, the insula, hidden from view in the sylvian fissure, is proposed by a number of brain researchers.

Chapter 5

1. See, for example, special issues of the journal *Neural Networks,* 1997, vol. 11, no. 7, and 1994, vol. 8, no. 5/6. There is also relevant material on neural modeling of consciousness in Landau and Taylor (1997).

2. An important universal approximation theorem for neural networks states that any function can be approximated as closely as desired by a suitably chosen neural network with at most one hidden layer. This was proved by Hornik, Stinchcombe, and White (1989) after work of Hecht-Nielsen (1987).

3. An automaton approach was developed independently in Taylor (1991) in terms of more specialized systems called relational automata.

Chapter 6

1. Thus the $q'r'x't''$ firings in the past give meanings to input that caused qrxt firings insofar as the set of all related firings $q'' r'' x'' t''$ to $q' r' x' t'$ (with enough similarity between the sets) overlap with the qrxt firings brought about, say, by

Adrienne in the past. This could happen if one or more of $q'' = q$, $r'' = r$, $x'' = x$ or $t'' = t$. Then the qrxt firing would acquire the meaning possessed by whichever latter set of firings it agreed with.

2. Recent PET studies indicate the activation of frontal regions in semantic tasks, so there may be more than a single semantic module to consider.

3. There is considerable evidence for such early activation of all possible interpretations of a word, as observed by various experiments on word processing.

Chapter 7

1. This difficulty can be avoided by the existence of strong excitatory connections onto inhibitory neurons. Since about 10 to 15 percent of cortical neurons are inhibitory, such a possibility is feasible. However, "the excitatory gain of cortex appears to be controlled by a relatively weak inhibition" (Berman, Douglas, and Martin, 1992). This assessment of response is not universally accepted, and further clarification is required.

2. The resulting spatial structure of activity on NRT is difficult to predict analytically, since it arises from the saturating response of neurons (Taylor and Alavi 1993). The existence of such a wave pattern can be shown to occur by suitable mathematical techniques (Murray 1989).

3. In terms of figure 7.4, input I2 onto thalamic cell 2, supposed to be larger than I1 and I3 onto neighboring cells, causes stronger activation of the NRT cell N2 than its neighbors on NRT; this disinhibits both its NRT neighbors N1 and N3. If their activity is reduced, they have less disinhibitory action on their relay cells T1 and T3. These cells then allow less input onto NRT at N1 and N3. Overall, the activity of N1 and N3 will decrease, that of N2 increase; similarly the outputs of T1 and T3 decrease while that of T2 increases. Finally input I2 wins the competition. The cortical activity C2 will be maximum and that of C1 and C3 minimal. This is observed in the results of a simulation shown in figure 7.5, in which a set of five localized inputs is seen to be in lateral competition on NRT, with only three inputs succeeding to survive the competition to gain access to cortex.

Chapter 8

1. A PET study by Bottini et al. (1995) supports extended activation in a cortical site achieving consciousness. Cold water applied to the ear of someone who had lost the sensation of touch on the opposite side brought back the sensation during the stimulation (and for some minutes afterward) while the patient was imaged by PET. Brain activation was seen in his insula cortex (and some other regions). The ear stimulation would correspond to extravestibular input to various brain regions. These would become more sensitive to other inputs, such as touch. The set of regions where touch awareness emerges is not apparent from this study.

2. Bunching of activity on the clumping model of NRT allows a detailed mathematical description of the fastest growing mode of activity (Taylor 1996a).

Chapter 9

1. This also was shown by less controversial methods, for example, by studies of lexical priming (MacDonald et al. 1994).

2. A simple formula results for the reaction time RT(n, N) to the nth item of a list of length N (Hastings and Taylor 1994) is the universal forgetting formula:

RT $(n, N) = a \ln(b + ce^{d(n - N)})$,

where a, b, c, and d are universal constants, independent of n and N.

Chapter 10

1. Controversy still surrounds the areas activated in such tasks. See Crosson et al. (1996), Spitzer et al. (1996), and Moore et al. (1996).

Chapter 14

1. Considerable discussion also appears in Dennett and Kinsbourne (1992) and valuable additional material in that article. See also Velmans (1991) and Poeppel (1997).

2. Such shielding need not occur for intracortical interactions, where layers 5/6 or 2/3 can feed back to the same level, feed forward to layer 1, or even go laterally to all layers (Felleman and van Essen 1991).

3. Such activity in layer 5/6 cells connected to the thalamus may also be involved in explaining the V4 measurements of Leopold and Logothetis (1996).

4. This allows feedback modulation to earlier layers in the light of results of later processing, or for specially modulated top-down control, as in imagery.

5. Aspects of temporality in consciousness are perceptively analyzed by Poeppel (1997).

Chapter 15

1. The explanation of dreams may not be as simple as in the model of Hobson and McCarley; several further models have been suggested, such as by Ladd (1892).

2. An exception to this lack of reasoning ability and control in dreams is "lucid" dreams. In these it is possible to remember freely the circumstances of waking life, to think clearly, and to act deliberately on reflection, with the dream world appearing vividly real (LaBerge 1990). Lucid dreams are normally rare, with only about 20 percent of the population reporting having one more than once a month.

References

Adrian ED (1952). What happens when we think. In *The Physical Basis of Mind*, ed P Laslett. Oxford: Blackwell.

Alavi F and Taylor JG (1995). A basis for long range inhibition across cortex. In *Lateral Interactions in the Cortex: Structure and Function*, eds J Sirosh, R Miikkulainen, and Y Choe. Hypertext Book.

Aleksander I (1994a). The consciousness of a neural state machine. In *Proceedings of the international conference on artificial neural networks*, eds M Marinaro and P Morasso. Berlin: Springer-Verlag: pp 212–217.

Aleksander I (1994b). The ghost in the machine. *Times Higher Education Suppl* Nov 18, p 17.

Aleksander I (1995). Artificial consciousness: An update. In *Proc International Workshop on Artificial Neural Networks*, Berlin: Springer-Verlag.

Aleksander I (1996). *Impossible Minds*. London: Imperial College Press.

Alexander GE, DeLong R, and Strick PL (1986). Parallel organisation of functionally segregated circuits linking basal ganglia and cortex. *Annu Rev Neurosci 9*, 357–381.

Amari S-I (1977). Dynamics of pattern formation in lateral-inhibition type neural fields. *Bio Cybernet 72*, 77–87.

Andreason NC, O'Leary, DS, Arnalt S, Cizadlo T, Thistio R, Rezai K, Watkins GL, Boles, Ponto LL, and Achwa RD, (1995). Short-term and long-term verbal memory: A positron emission tomography study. *Proc. Natl. Acad. Sci (USA) 92*, 5111–5115.

Antrobus J (1986). Cortical and cognitive activation, perceptual thresholds, and sleep mentation. *J Mind Behav 7*, 193–210.

Arbib MA and Dominey PF (1994). Modeling the role of basal ganglia in timing and sequencing of saccadic eye movements. In *Models of Information Processing in the Basal Ganglia*, eds JC Houk, JL Davis, and DG Beiser. Cambridge: MIT Press: 149–162.

Armstrong DM (1968). *A Materialist Theory of Mind*. London: Routledge & Kegan Paul.

Atkinson RC and Shiffrin RM (1971). The control of short-term memory. *Sci Am* 225, 82–91.

Baars BJ (1988). *A Cognitive Theory of Consciousness.* Cambridge: Cambridge University Press.

Baars B (1994a). Consciousness creates access to working memory. Presented at the world congress on neural networks, San Diego, CA, June 9.

Baars B (1994b). A global workspace theory of conscious experience. In *Consciousness in Philosophy and Cognitive Science,* eds A Revonsuo and M Kamppinen. Hillsdale, NJ: Lawrence Erlbaum: 149–172.

Baars B and Newman JB (1993). A neural attentional model for access to consciousness: A global workspace perspective. *Concepts Neurosci* 4, 255–290.

Baars B and Newman JB (1994). A neurobiological interpretation of global workspace theory. In *Consciousness in Philosophy and Cognitive Neuroscience,* eds A Revonsuoa and M Kamppinen. Hillsdale, NJ: Lawrence Erlbaum: 211–226.

Baddeley A (1986). *Working Memory.* Oxford: Oxford University Press.

Baddeley A (1992). Is working memory working? *Q J Exp Psychol* 44, 1–31.

Baddeley A (1993). Working memory and conscious awareness. In Theories of memory. MA conway and PE Morris, eds. Hillsdale, NJ: Lawrence Erlbaum: 11–28.

Baddeley A and Hitch G (1974). Working memory. In *The Psychology of Learning and Motivation,* ed GA Bower. New York: Academic Press.

Baddeley A and Warrington E (1970). Amnesia and the distinction between long and short term memory. *J Verbal Learning Verbal Behav* 15, 575–589.

Bapi R, Bugmann G, Levine D, and Taylor JG (1998). Neural models of frontal function. Submitted to Behavioral Brain Sciences.

Barbas H and Pandya DN (1991). Patterns of connections of the prefrontal cortex in the rhesus monkey associated with cortical architecture. In *Frontal Function and Dysfunction,* eds HS Levin, HM Eisenberg, and AL Benton. Oxford: Oxford University Press.

Barlow H (1972). Single units and sensation: A neuron doctrine for perceptual psychology? *Perception* 1, 371–394.

Barsalou L (1987). The instability of graded structure: Implications for the nature of concepts. In *Concepts and Conceptual Development,* ed U Neisser. Cambridge: Cambridge University Press: 101–140.

Ben-Yishai R, Bar-Or RL, and Simpoubinsky H (1995). Theory of orientation turning in visual cortex. *Proc Natl Acad Sci (USA)* 92, 3844–3848.

Berggren KF and Huberman BA (1978). Peierls state far from equilibrium. *Physiol Rev B* 18, 3369–3375.

Berman NJ, Douglas RJ, and Martin KA (1992). GABA-mediated inhibition in the neural networks of visual cortex. *Prog Brain Res* 90, 443–476.

Binder JR, Bellgowan PS, Frost JA, Hammeke TA, Springer KA, Rao SM, Prieto T, O'Reilly W, and Cox RW (1996). Functional MRI demonstrates left medial temporal lobe activation during verbal episodic memory encoding. *Human Brain Mapping* 3(3), S530.

Bloom FE, Lazerson A, and Hofstadter L. (1985). *Brain, Mind and Behavior.* New York: WH Freeman.

Bottini G, Paulesu E, Sterzi R, Warburton E, Wise RJS,Vallar G, Frackowiak RSJ, and Frith CD (1995). Modulation of conscious experience by peripheral sensory stimuli. *Nature* 376, 778–781.

Bressler SL (1994). Dynamic self-organization in the brain as observed by transient cortical coherence. In *Origins: Brain and Self Organization,* ed K Pribram. Hillsdale, NJ: Lawrence Erlbaum: pp 536–545.

Brodzinsky DM, Gormly AV, and Ambron SR (1986). *Lifespan Human Development.* New York: Holt, Rinehart & Winston.

Brooks R and Stein C (1993). Putting cognition in COG. Unpublished research grant proposal, Massachusetts Institute of Technology, Cambridge.

Burani C, Vallar G, and Bottini G (1991). Articulatory coding and phonological judgements on written words and pictures: The role of the phonological output buffer. *Eur J Cogn Psychol* 3, 379–398.

Carmichael ST and Price JL (1994). Architectonic subdivision of the orbital and medial prefrontal cortex in the macaque monkey. *J Comp Neurol* 346, 366–402.

Carr TH (1992). Automaticity and cognitive anatomy: Is word recognition "automatic"? *Am J Psychol* 105, 201–237.

Chalmers D (1996a). Facing up to problem of consiousness invited talk. In *Toward a Science of Consciousness,* eds S Hameroff, A Kaszniak, and A Scott, eds. Cambridge: MIT Press; pp 5–28.

Chalmers D (1996b). *The Conscious Mind.* Oxford: Oxford University Press.

Cheesman J and Merikle PM (1985). Word recognition and consciousness. *Reading Res Adv Theory Pract* 5, 311–352.

Chevalier G and Deniau JM (1990). Disinhibition as a basic process in the expression of striatal functions. *Trends Neurosci* 13, 277–280.

Churchland PM and Churchland PS (1997). *Replies from the Churchlands.* In *The Churchlands and Their Critics,* ed R McCauley. Oxford: Blackwell: Ltd. pp 217–310.

Churchland PS (1986). *Neurophilosophy.* Cambridge: MIT Press.

Cohen D (1968). Magnetoencephalography: Evidence of magnetic fields produced by alpha rhythm currents. *Science* 161, 784–786.

Cohen DS, and Murray J (1981). A generalised diffusion model for growth and dispersal in a population. *Math Biol* 12, 237–249.

Cohen JD, Perlstein WM, Braver TS, Nystrom LE, Noll DC, Jonides J, and Smith EE (1997). Temporal dynamics of brain activation during a working memory task. *Nature* 386, 604–608.

Cohen JD and Servan-Schreiber D (1992). Content, cortex and dopamine: A connectionist approach to behavior and biology in schizophrenia *Psychol Rev* 99, 45–77.

Cohen NJ and Eichenbaum H (1993). *Memory, Amnesia, and the Hippocampal system.* Cambridge: MIT Press.

Courtney SM, Ungerleider LG, Kell K, and Haxby JV (1997). Transient and sustained activity in a distributed system for human working memory. *Nature* 386, 608–611.

Crick FHC (1989). Neural Edelmanism. *Trends Neurosci* 12, 240–248.

Crick FHC (1994). *The Astonishing Hypothesis.* London: Simon & Schuster.

Crick FHC (1996). Visual perception: Rivalry and consciousness. *Nature* 379, 485–486.

Crick FHC, and Koch C (1990). Toward a neurobiological theory of consciousness. *Semin Neurosci* 2, 237–249.

Crick FHC and Koch C (1995). Are we aware of neural activity in primary visual cortex? *Nature* 375, 121–123.

Crosby EC, Humphrey T, and Lauer EW (1962). Correlative anatomy of the nervous system. New York: MacMillan.

Crosson B, Rao SM, Woodley SJ, Rosen AC, Hammeke TA, Bobholz JA, Cunningham JM, Fuller SA, Binder JR, and Cox RW (1996). Mapping of semantic versus phonological versus orthographic verbal working memory in normal adults with fMRI. *Human Brain Mapping* 3(3), S538.

Damasio A (1989a). Time-locked multiregional retroactivation: A systems level proposition for the neural substrate of recall and recognition. *Cognition* 33, 25–62.

Damasio A (1989b). The brain binds entities and events by multiregional activaton form convergence zones. *Neural Computation* 1, 1231–32.

Davies M and Humphreys GW, eds (1993). *Consciousness.* Oxford: Blackwell.

de Garis H (1994). The CAM brain project. Presented at the int conf on neural information processing, Seoul, South Korea, ed. M-W Kim and S-Y Lee vol. 3, pp 1629–1634.

Delgado JMR (1969). *Physical control of the mind: Toward a Psychocivilized Society.* New York: Harper & Row.

Dennett D (1987). Consciousness. In *The Oxford Companion to the Mind*, ed RL Gregory. Oxford: Oxford University Press: pp 160–164.

Dennett D (1988). Quining qualia. In *Consciousness in Contemporary Science*, eds AJ Marcel and E Bisiach. Oxford: Oxford University Press: 42–77.

Dennett D (1991). *Consciousness Explained.* New York: Little, Brown.

Deschenes M, Madariaga-Domich A, and Steriade M (1989). Dendrodritic synapses in the cat reticularis thalami nucleus: A structural basis for thalamic spindle synchronization. *Brain Res* 334, 165–168.

Desimone R (1995). Invited talk, presented at the world congress on neural networks, Washington, DC, July 17–21.

Di Pace E, Longoni AM, and Zoccolotti P (1991). Semantic processing of unattended parafoveal words. *Acta Psychol* 77, 21–34.

Dixon NF (1981). *Preconscious Processing.* Chichester: Wiley.

Douglas RJ and Martin KAC (1991). A functional microcircuit for cat visual cortex. *J Physiol (London)* 440, 735–769.

Duclos SE, Laird JD, Schneider E, Sexter M, Stern L, and van Lighten O (1989). Emotion-specific effects of facial expressions and postures of emotional experience. *J Pers and Soc Psychol* 57, 100–108.

Duncan J, Martens Sand Ward R (1997). Restricted attentional capacity written but not between sensory modalities, *Nature* 387, 808–810.

Duncan J, Ward R, and Shapiro K (1994). Direct movement of attentional dwell time in human vision. *Nature* 369, 313–315.

Dupont P, Orban GA, Vogels R, Bomans G, Nuyts J, Schrepos C, DeRos M, and Motelmans L (1993). Different perceptual tasks performed with the same visual stimulus attribute activate different regions of the human brain. *Proc Natl Acad Sci (USA).* 90, 10927–10931.

Eckhorn R, Bauer R, Jordan W, Brosch M, Kruse W, Munke M, and Reibock HJ (1988). Coherent oscillations: A mechanism of feature linking in the visual cortex? *Biol Cybernet* 60, 121–130.

Edelman, GJ (1989). *The Remembered Present.* New York: Basic Books.

Edelman GJ (1992). *Bright Air, Brilliant Fire,* London: Allen & Unwin.

Engel AK, Konig P, Gray CM, and Singer W (1989). Oscillatory responses in cat visual cortex exhibit inter-columnar synchronization which reflects global stimulus properties. *Nature* 338, 334–337.

Ermentrout GB and Cowan JD (1978). A mathematical theory of visual hallucination patterns. *Biol Cybernet* 34, 644–647.

Farah M, Visual agnosia. Cambridge, MA: MIT Press.

Farah M, Hammond KM, Levine DN, and Calvanio R (1988). Visual and spatila mental imagery: Dissociable systems of representations. *Cogn Psychol* 20, 439–462.

Feijoo J (1975). Ut conscientia noscatue. *Cahir Sophol* 13, 14–20.

Feijoo J (1981). Le fetus Pierre et le loup. In E Herbinet and MC Busnel, eds *L'aube des Sens.* Paris: Stock.

Felleman DJ and van Essen DC (1991). Distributed hierarchical processing in the primate cerebral cortex. *Cerebral Cortex* 1, 1–47.

Fivush R (1987). Scripts and categories: Interrelationship in development. In *Concepts and Conceptual Development: Ecological and Intellectual Factors in Categories,* ed U Neisser. Cambridge: Cambridge University Press: 234–254.

Flanagan OJ (1984). *The Science of Mind.* Cambridge: MIT Press.

Fodor J (1975). *The Language of Thought.* Sussex: Harvester Press.

Freeman W (1995). *Societies of Brains.* Hillsdale, NJ: Lawrence Erlbaum.

Freeman W, Taylor JG, eds. (1997). Neural network models of consciousness. *Neural Networks* 11(7).

Freud S (1953–74). *The Standard Edition of the Complete Psychological Works of Sigmund Freud,* 24 vols, transl J Strachey. London: Hogarth Press and Institute of Psycho-Analysis.

Fries P, Roelfsma PR, Engel AK, Konig P, and Singer W (1996). Synchronised gamma frequency oscillations correlate with perception during binocular rivalry in awake squinting cats. *Soc Neurosci Abstr* 22, 282.

Frijda NH and Moffat D (1993). A model of emotions and emotion communication. In *Proc RO-MAN 93: 2nd IEEE International Workshop on Robot and Human Communication.* 29–34.

Frith CD, Friston K, Liddle PF, and Frakowiack (1991). Willed action and the pre-frontal cortex in man: A study with PET. *Proc R Soc Lond B* 244, 214–246.

Fuentes LJ, Carmona E, Agis IF, and Catena A (1994). The role of the anterior attention system in the semantic processing of both foveal and parafoveal words. *J Cogn Neurosci* 6, 17–25.

Fuster JM (1993). Frontal lobes. *Curr Opin Neurobiol* 3, 160–165.

Fuster J (1989). The *Prefrontal Cortex: Anatomy, Physiology and Neuropsychology of the Frontal Lobe,* 2nd ed. New York: Raven Press.

Fries P, Roelfsema PR, Engel AK, Konig P, and Singer W (1997). Synchronisation of oscillatory responses in visual cortex correlates with perception in interocular rivalry *Proc Natl Acad Sci (USA)* 94, 12699–12704.

Gallup GG (1979). Self-awareness in primates. *Am Sci* 67, 417–421.

Geisler WS (1989). Sequential ideal-observer analysis of visual discrimination. *Psychol Rev* 96, 267–314.

Georgopolous AP (1994). New concepts in generation of movement. *Neuron* 13, 257–268.

Georgopolous AP, Caminiti R, Kalaska JF, and Massey JT (1983). Spatial coding of movement: A hypothesis concerning the coding of movement direction by motor cortical populations. *Exp Brain Res* 7 (suppl), 307–336.

Godel K (1986). Collected works in 3 vols. ed. S Feferman. Oxford: University Press.

Graham MS (1989). *Visual Pattern Analysis.* Oxford: Oxford University Press.

Graham NS (1989). *Visual Pattern Analysis*. Oxford: Oxford University Press.

Grasby PM, Frith CD, Friston KJ, Simpson JR, Fletcher P, Frackowiak RSJ, and Dolan RJ (1994). A graded task approach to the functional mapping of brain areas implicated in auditory-verbal memory. *Brain* 117, 1271–1282.

Gray CM and Singer W (1987). Stimulus-specific neuronal oscillations in the cat visual cortex: a cortical functional unit? *Soc Neurosci Abstr* 13, 404: 3.

Gray CM and Singer W (1989). Stimulus-specific neuronal oscillations in orientation columns of cat visual cortex. *Proc Natl Acad Sci (USA)* 86, 1698–1702.

Gray JA (1995). The Contents of Consciousness: A Neurophysiolgical Conjecture. *Behav Brain Sci* 18, 659–722.

Greenwald AG (1992). New look 3: Unconscious cognition reclaimed. *Am Psychologist* 47, 766–799.

Grossberg S (1976). Adaptive pattern classification and universal recoding. I Parallel development and coding of neural feature detectors. *Biol Cybernet* 23, 121–134.

Grossberg S and Taylor JG (1994). Models of Neurodynamics and behaviour. *Neural Networks* 7 (6/7), 863–1190.

Hadeler K (1974). On the theory of lateral inhibition. *Kybernetik* 14, 161–165.

Hamalainen M, Hari R, Ilmoniemi R, Knuutilla J, and Lounasma O (1993). Magnetoencephalography—Theory, instrumentation and applications to noninvasive studies of the working human brain. *Rev Mod Physiol* 65, 414–497.

Hameroff S, Kaszniak A, and Scott A (1996). *Toward a Science of Consciousness*. Cambridge: MIT Press.

Hastings S and Taylor JG (1994). Modeling the articulatory loop. In *Proc International Conference on Artificial Neural Network 94*, eds Marinaro M and Morasso P. Berlin: Springer-Verlag: 1452–1455.

Hazlitt W (1946). *Selected Essays of William Hazlitt 1778–1839*. London: Nonesuch Press.

He S, Cavanagh P, and Intilligator J (1996). Attentional resolution and the locus of awareness. *Nature* 383, 334–337.

Hebb DO (1949). *The Organization of Behavior*. New York: Wiley.

Hecht-Nielsen R (1987). Kolmogorov's mapping neural network existence theorem. In *Proceedings on the Int Conf on Neural Networks, III*, 11–13. New York: IEEE Press.

Heimer L (1983). *The Human Brain and Spinal Cord*. Cambridge, MA: MIT Press.

Hepper PG and Shahidullah S (1994). The beginnings of mind—Evidence from the behaviour of the fetus. *J Reprod. Infant Psychol* 12, 143–154.

Herbert N (1993). *Elemental Mind.* New York: Penguin.

Hess WR (1957). *The Functional Organization of the Diencephalon.* New York: Grune & Stratton.

Hetherington EM and Parke RD (1993). *Childhood Psychology.* New York: McGraw-Hill.

Hikosaka O (1989). Role of basal ganglia in initiation of voluntary movements. In *Dynamical Interactions in Neural Networks: Models and Data,* eds MA Arbib and S-I Amari. Berlin: Springer-Verlag, pp 153–168.

Hilgard ER (1977). *Divided Consciousness.* New York: Wiley.

Hobson JA and McCarley RW (1977). The brain as a dream state generator: An activation-synthesis hypothesis of the dream process. *Am J Psychiatry* 134, 1335–1348.

Hodges W (1998). Turing's philosophical error. In *Concepts for Neural Networks,* eds. LL Landau and JG Taylor. London: Springer: 147–170.

Holender D (1986). Semantic activation without conscious identification in dichotic listening, parafoveal vision and visual masking: A survey and appraisal. *Behav Brain Sci* 9, 1–66.

Hopfield JJ (1982). Neural networks and physical systems with emergent collective computational abilities. *Proc Natl Acad Sci (USA)* 79, 2554–2558.

Hornik K, Stinchcombe M and White H (1989). Multilayer feedforward nets are universal approximators. *Neural Networks* 2, 359–366.

Houk JC, Adams JL, and Barto AG (1994). A model of how the basal ganglia generate and use signals that predict reinforcement. In *Models of Information Processing in the Basal Ganglia,* eds JC Houk, JL Davis, and DG Beiser. Cambridge: MIT Press: 249–270.

Houk JC and Wise SP (1993). Outline for a theory of motor behaviour: Involving cooperative actions of the cerebellum, basal ganglia and cerebral cortex. In *From Neural Networks to Artificial Intelligence,* eds P Rudomin, MA Arbid, and F Cervantes. Berlin: Springer-Verlag: 452–470.

Hume, D (1896). *A Treatise on Human Nature.* Oxford: Clarendon Press.

Humphrey N and Dennett DC (1989). Speaking for ourselves. *Raritan* 9, 68–98.

Iguchi I and Langenburg DN (1980). Diffusive quasiparticle instability toward multigap states in a tunnel injected nonequilibrium superconductor. *Phys Rev Lett* 44, 486–489.

Ioannides AA (1995). Estimates of 3D brain activity ms by ms from biomagnetic signals: Method (MFT), results and their significance. In *Quantitative and Topological EEG and MEG Analysis,* eds E Eiselt, U Zweiner, and H Witte. Jena: Universitatsverlag Druckhau-Maayer GmbH: pp 59–68.

Izard CE (1993). Four systems for emotion activation: Cognitive and noncognitive processes. *Psychol Rev* 100, 68–90.

Jackson SR, Marrocco R, and Posner MI (1994). Networks of anatomical areas controlling visuospatial attention. *Neural Networks* 7, 925–944.

Jacoby LL and Whitehouse K (1989). An illusion of memory: False recognition influenced by unconscious perception. *J Exp Psychol Gen* 118, 126–135.

James W (1950). *The Principles of Psychology.* New York: Dover.

Jeannerod M (1995). Mental imagery in the motor content. *Neuropsychologia* 33 (11), 1419–1432.

Johnson M (1987). *The Body in the Mind: The Bodily Basis of Meaning, Images and Reasons.* Chicago: Chicago University Press.

Kandel E and Schwartz JH (1985). *Principles of Neural Science,* 2nd ed. Englewood Cliffs, NJ: Prentice Hall.

Kawato M, Tayakawa H, and Inui T (1993). A forward-inverse optics model of reciprocal connections between visual cortical areas. *Network* 4, 415–422.

Kelley CM and Jacoby LL (1993). The construction of subjective experience: Memory attribution. In *Consciousness.* eds M Davies and G E Humphries. London: Blackwell: 74–89.

Koch C (1996). Re: 40-Hz TH-cortical activity and consciousness. Presented at a seminar on the contribution to thalamocortical foundations of conscious experience. http://www.phil.vt.edu/ASSC/newman.

Kohonen T (1982). Self-organised formation of topologically correct feature maps. *Biol Cybernet* 43, 56–69.

Kolb FC and Braun J (1995). Blindsight in normal observers. *Nature* 377, 336–338.

Krause BJ, Horwitz B, Taylor JG, Schmidt D, Mottaghy F, Halsband U, Herzog H, Tellmann L, and Mueller-Gaertner H-W (1997). Network analysis in episodic associative memory. Submitted to *Brain.*

La Berge D (1990). A network simulation of thalamocortical operations in selective attention *J Cogn Neurosci* 2, 358–373.

LaBerge D, Carter M, and Brown V (1992). A network simulation of thalamic circuit operations in selective attention. *Neural Comp* 4, 318–333.

Ladd G (1892). Contributions to the psychology of visual dreams. *Mind* 1, 229–304.

Lakoff G (1987). *Women, Fire and Dangerous Things: What Categories Recalibrate the Mind.* Chicago: Chicago University Press.

Landau LL and Taylor JG (1997). *Concepts for Neural Networks.* London: Springer-Verlag.

Lazarus RS (1991). Cognition and motivitation in emotion. *Am Psychol* 46, 352–367.

LeDoux JE (1992). Emotion and the amygdala. In *The Amygdala: Neurobiological Aspects of Emotion, Memory and Mental Dysfunction,* ed JP Aggleton, New York: Wiley: 339–351.

Leopold and Logothetis NK (1996). Activity changes in early visual cortex reflect monkeys' perception during binocular rivalry. *Nature* 379, 549–553.

Leslie AM (1987). Pretense and representation: The origins of theory of mind. *Psychol Rev* 94, 412–426.

Levelt WJM, Schriefos H, Vovbereg D, Meyer AS, Pechman T, and Havinga J (1991). The time course of lexical access in speech production: A study of picture naming. *Psych Rev* 98, 122–142.

Levine J (1983). Materialism and qualia: The explanatory gap. *Pacific Phil Q* 64, 354–361.

Levitan IB and Kazmarck LK (1997). *The Neuron,* 2nd ed. Oxford: Oxford University Press.

Libet B (1966). Brain stimulation in conscious and unconscious experience. *Perspect Biol Med* 9, 77–86.

Libet B (1982). Brain stimulation in the study of neuronal functions for conscious sensory experience. *Hum Neurobiol* 1, 235–242.

Libet B (1987). Consciousness: Conscious, subjective experience. In *Encyclopedia of Neuroscience* I, ed G Adelman. Boston: Birkhauser.

Libet B (1993). The neural time factor in "conscious" and "unconscious" events. In *Experimental and Theroretical Studies of consciousness,* ed T Nagel. London: CIBA Foundation Symposium.

Libet B, Alberts WW, Wright EW Jr, Delattre DL, Levin G, and Feinstein B (1964). Production of threshold levels of conscious sensation by electrical stimulation of human somato-sensory cortex. *J Neurophysiol* 27, 546–578.

Littlewood R (1997). The plight of the living dead. *Times Higher Educational Supplement,* p. 17.

Llinás R and Ribary U (1993). *Proc Nat Acad Sci (USA)* 90, 2078–2081.

Logothetis NK and Schall JD (1989). *Science* 245, 761–763. Neuronal Correlates of Subjective Visual Perception.

Logothetis NK and Sheinberg DL (1996). Visual object recognition. *Ann Rev Neurosci.* 19, 577–621.

Lu Z-L, Williamson SL, and Kaufman L (1992). Human auditory primary and association cortex have differing lifetimes for activation traces. *Brain Res* 572, 236–241.

Lucas JR (1961). Minds, machines and godel. *Philosophy* 36, 120–124. Series of neuronal population vectors. *Neural Comput* 6, 19–28.

Lycan WG, ed, (1990). *Mind and Cognition, a Reader.* Oxford: Blackwell.

MacDonald MC, Pearlmutter NJ, and Seidenberg MS (1994). Lexical nature of syntactic ambiguity resolution. *Psychol Bull* 101, 676–703.

Maddock RJ and Buonocore MH (1996). Functional MRI evidence for activation of retrosplenial cingulate and precuneate by autobiographical memory processes. *Human Brain Mapping* 3(3), S547.

Malsburg CH von der and Schneider W (1986). A neural cocktail party processor. *Biol Cybernet* 54, 29–40.

Mandler G (1975). Consciousness: Respectable, useful and probably necessary. In *Information Processing and Cognition: The Loyola Symposium*, ed R Solso. Hillsdale, NJ: Lawrence Erlbaum.

Marcel AJ (1980). Consciousness and preconscious recognition of polysemous words. In *Attention and Performance VIII*, ed RS Nickerson. Hillsdale, NJ: Lawrence Erlbaum: 435–467.

Marcel AJ (1993). Slippage in the unity of consciousness. In *Ciba Foundation Symposium* 174, *Experimental and Theoretical Studies in Consciousness*. Chichester: Wiley.

Mark V (1996). Conflicting communication behaviour in a split brain patient's support for dual consciousness. In *Toward a Science of Consciousness*, eds S Hameroff, A Kasznick and A Scott. Cambridge: MIT Press: 189–196.

Mark VH and Erwin FR (1970). *Violence and the Brain*. New York: Harper and Row.

Marshall JC and Halligan P (1988). Blindsight and insight in visuospatial neglect. *Nature* 336, 766–767.

Masulli F and Riani M (1989). Ambiguity and structural information in the perception of reversible figures. *Perception Psychophysics* 45, 501–513.

McCauley RN (1996). *The Churchlands and Their Critics*. Oxford: Blackwell.

McClelland JL, Rumelhart DE, and the PDP Research Group (1986). *Parallel Distributed Processing*. Cambridge: MIT Press.

McCulloch WS and Pitts W (1943). A logical calculus of the ideas immanent in nervous activity. *Bull of Math Biol* 5, 115–133.

McFarland D (1993). *Animal Behaviour*. London: Longmann.

McIntosh AR, Grady CL, Haxby JV, Ungerleider LG, and Horwitz B (1996). Changes in limbic and prefrontal functional interactions in a working memory task for faces. *Cerebral Cortex* 6, 571–684.

McNaughton BL and Wilson MA (1994). Reactivation of hippocampal ensemble memories during sleep. *Science* 265, 676–678.

Mead C and Mahowald M (1988). A Silicon model of early visual processing. *Neural Networks* 1, 91–97.

Melzack R and Wall PDP (1988). *The Challenge of Pain*. London: Penguin.

Mesulam MM (1981). A cortical network for directed attention and unilateral neglect. *Ann Neurol* 10, 309–325.

Mesulam MM (1985). Patterns in behavioural neuroanatomy. In *Principles of Behavior Neurology*, ed MM Mesulam Philadelphia: FA Davis: 1–70.

Metzinger T (1995). The problem of consciousness. In *Conscious Experience*, ed T Metzinger. Paderborn: Schoeningh: pp 3–40.

Monchi O and Taylor JG (1995). A model of the prefrontal loop that includes the basal ganglia in solving recency tasks. In *World Congress on Neural Networks*, INNS Press and Lawrence Erlbaum, Mahwah, NJ. III vol 3. 48–51.

Moore CJ, Price CJ, Friston KJ, and Frakowiak RSJ (1996). Phonological retrieval and semantic processing during naming tasks. *Human Brain Mapping* 3(3), S449.

Morton J (1991). Cognitive pathologies of memory: A headed records analysis. In *Memories, Thoughts and Emotions: Essays in Honor of George Mandler*. Hillsdale, NJ: Lawrence Erlbaum: 199–209.

Munn NL and Carmichael L (1974). *The Growth of Human Behavior*. Boston: Houghton Mifflin.

Murray JD (1989). *Mathematical Biology*. Berlin: Springer-Verlag.

Näätänen R (1992). *Attention and Brain Function*. Hillsdale, NJ: Lawrence Erlbaum.

Näätänen R, Ilmoniemi RJ, and Alho K (1994). Magnetoencephalography in studies of human cognitive brain function. *Trends Neurosci* 17, 389–395.

Nagel T (1974). What is it like to be a bat? *Philosophical Rev* 83, 435–450.

Nelson K (1993). Explaining the emergence of autobiographic memory in early childhood. In *Theories of Memory*, eds AF Collins, SE Gathercole, MA Conway and PE Morris. Hillsdale NJ: Lawrence Erlbaum.

Nicoll AA and Blakemore C (1996). Patterns of local connectivity in the neocorten *Neural Computation* 5, 665–680.

Norman DA and Shallice T (1980). Attention to action. Reprinted in *Consciousness and Self Regulation*, vol 4, eds PJ Davidson, GE Schwartz, and D Shapiro. New York: Plenum Press.

Ogmen H and Prakash RV (1994). A neural model for the initial stages of the sensorimotor level in development. In *COMPMED '94 Biotechnology Proceedings*.

Ohara PT and Lieberman AR (1985). The thalamic reticular nucleus of the adult rat: Experimental anatomical studies. *Neurocytology* 14, 365–411.

Papez JW (1937). A proposed mechanism of emotion. *Arch Neurol Psychiatry* 79, 217–224.

Pardo JV, Fox PT, and Raichle ME (1991). Localization of a human system for sustained attention by positron emission tomography. *Nature* 349, 61–64.

Pardo JV, Pardo PJ, Janer KW, and Raichle ME (1990). The anterior cingulate cortex mediates processing selection in the Stroop attentional conflict paradigm. *Proc Natl Acad Sci USA* 87, 256–259.

Paulesu E, Frith CD, and Frackowiak RSJ (1993). The neural correlates of the verbal component of working memory. *Nature* 362, 342–345.

Penrose R (1989). *The Emperor's New Mind.* Oxford: Oxford University Press.

Penrose R (1994). *Shadows of the Mind.* New York: Oxford University Press.

Perennin MT and Jeannerod M (1975). Residual vision in cortically blind hemifields. *Neuropsychologica* 13, 1–7.

Peterson SE, Fox PT, Posner MI, Mintun M, and Raichle ME (1991). Positron emission tomographic studies of the processing of single words. *J Cogn Neurosci* 1, 152–170.

Petrides M (1994). Frontal lobes and working memory: Evidence from investigations of the effects of cortical excisions in nonhuman primates. In *Handbook of Neuropsychology,* eds F Boller and J Grafman, Amsterdam: Elsevier: 59–82.

Piaget J (1945). *La Formation du Symbole chez L'Enfant.* Neuchatel: Delachaux & Niestle.

Picton TW (1980). The use of human event-related potentials in psychology. In *Techniques in Psychophysiology,* I Martin and PH Venables eds. New York: Wiley: 357–395.

Plaut DC and Shallice T (1993). Deep dyslexia: A case study of connectionist neuropsychology. *Cogn Neuropsychol* 10, 377–500.

Poeppel E (1997). A hierarchical model of temporal perception. *Trends Cogn Sci* 1(2), 56–61.

Poeppel E, Held R and, Frost D (1973). Residual visual function after brain wounds involving the central visual pathways in man. *Nature* 243, 295–296.

Pollack J (1989). *How to Build a Person: A Prolegomenon.* Cambridge: MIT Press.

Posner MI (1993). Seeing the mind. *Science* 262, 673–674.

Posner MI and Petersen S (1990). The attentional system of human beings. *Annu Rev Neurosci* 13, 25–42.

Posner MI, Peterson SE, Fox PT, and Raichle ME (1988). Localization of cognitive operations in the human brain. *Science* 240, 1627–1631.

Posner MI and Raichle ME (1994). *Images of Mind.* New York: Freeman.

Prigatano GP and Schachter DL (1993). Introduction. In *Awareness of Deficit after Brain Injury,* eds GP Prigatano and DL Schachter. Oxford: Oxford University Press: 3–16.

Putnam H (1995). Book review of *Shadows of the Mind. Bull Am Math Soc* 32, 370–373.

Pylyshyn ZW (1984). *Computation and Cognition.* Cambridge: MIT Press.

Redmond DE Jr (1985). Neurochemical basis for anxiety and anxiety disorders: Evidence form drugs which decrease human fear of anxiety. In *Anxiety and the Anxiety Disorders,* eds AH Tuma and JD Maser. Hillsdale, NJ: Lawrence Erlbaum: 533–555.

Reeke GN and Edelman GM (1995). A darwinist view of the prospect for conscious artifacts. In *Consciousness,* ed G Tratteur. Naples: Bibliopolis: 106–130.

Reiss M and Taylor JG (1992). Does the hippocampus store temporal patterns? *Neural Network World* 2, 365–393.

Riani M and Masulli F (1990). Modeling perceptual alternation by using ANNs. In *Second Italian Workshop on Parallel Architectures and Neural Networks,* ed ER Caianiello, Singapore: World Scientific.

Richards B (1989). *Images of Freud.* London: JM Dent & Sons.

Roediger H and McDermott (1995). Creating false memories; remembering words not presented in lists. *J Exp Psychol* 21, 803–814.

Roelfsema PR, Engel AK, Koing P, and Singer W (1997). Visuomotor integration is associated with zero time-lag synchronisation among cortical areas. *Nature* 385, 157–161.

Rolls E (1989). Functions of neuronal networks in the hippocampus and neocortex in memory. In *Neural Models of Plasticity,* eds JH Byrne and WO Berry. New York: Academic Press: 240–265.

Rovee-Collier C, Greco-Vigorito C, and Hayne H (1993). The time window hypothesis: Implications for categorization and memory modification. *Infant Behav Dev* 16, 149–176.

Ruhnau E (1995). Time-Gestalt and the observer. In *Conscious Experience,* ed T Metzinger. Paderborn: Schoeningh: 165–184.

Russell B (1921). *The Analysis of Mind.* London: Allen Unwin.

Sacks O (1996). *An Anthropologist on Mars.* Cambridge: Cambridge University Press.

Salmon E, Van der Linden M, Collette F, Delfiore G, Maquet P, Delguedre C, Luxen A, and Franck G (1996). Regional brain activity during working memory tasks. *Brain* 119, 1617–1625.

Salzman CD and Newsome WT (1994). Neural mechanisms for forming a perceptual decision. *Science* 264, 231–236.

Schank R and Abelson R (1977). *Scripts, Plans, Goals, and Understanding.* Hillsdale, NJ: Lawrence Erlbaum.

Scheibel AB (1980). Anatomical and physiological substrates of arousal: A view from the bridge. In *The Reticular Formation Revisited,* eds JA Hobson and BA Brazier. New York: Raven Press: 55–66.

Scheibel M and Scheibel AB (1966). The organisation of the nucleus reticularis thalami. *Brain Res* 1, 43–62.

Scheibel M and Scheibel AB (1972). Specialized organizational patterns within the nucleus reticularis thalami of the cat. *Exp Neuro* 34, 316–322.

Searle J (1983). *Intentionality: An Essay in the Philosophy of Mind.* Cambridge: Cambridge University Press.

Searle J (1991). *The Rediscovery of Mind. Cambridge: MIT Press.*

Searle J (1994). The problem of consciousness. In *Consciousness in Philosophy and Cognitive Neuroscience,* eds A Revonsuo and M Kampinnen. Hillsdale NJ: Erlbaum: 93–114.

Seyfarth RM and Cheney DL (1992). Meaning and mind in monkeys. *Sci Am* 267, 78–84.

Shallice T (1988). *From Neuropsychology to Mental Structure.* Cambridge: Cambridge University Press.

Shallice T and Warrington E (1970). Independent functioning of the verbal memory store: A neuropsychological study. *Q J Exp Psychol* 22, 261–273.

Sheinberg DL and Logothetis NK (1997). The role of temporal cortical areas in perceptual organization. *Proc Natl Acad Sci USA* 94, 3408–3413.

Singer W and Gray CM (1995). Visual feature integration and the temporal correlation hypothesis. *Annu Rev Neurosci* 18, 555–586.

Skinner JE and Yingling CD (1977). Central gating mechanisms that regulate event-related potentials and behaviour. In *Progress in clinical neurophysiology: Attention, Voluntary Contraction and Event-Related Potentials,* ed JE Desnedt. Basel: S Karger: 30–69.

Smith EE and Jonides J (1995). Working memory in humans: Neuropsychological evidence. In *The Cognitive Nerurosciences,* ed M Gazzaniga. Cambridge: MIT Press: 1009–1020.

Smithys JR (1970). *Brain Mechanisms and Behaviour.* Oxford: Blackwells Ltd.

Somers DC, Nelson SB, and SWM (1995). An emergent model of orientation selectivity in cat visual cortical simple cells. *J Neurosci* 15, 5448–5465.

Spitzer M, Bellemann ME, Kammer T, Gueckel F, Kischka U, Maier S, Schwartz A, and Brix G (1996). Functional MR imaging of semantic information processing and learning-related effects using psychometrically controlled stimulation paradigms. *Cogn Brain Res* 4, 149–161.

Steriade M, Jones EG, and Llinas RR (1990). *Thalamic Oscillations and Signalling.* London: Wiley.

Stevens JC (1968). Psychophysics. *Int Encyclopedia Soc Sci* 13, 120–126.

Streri A (1993). *Seeing, Reaching, Touching.* Cambridge: MIT Press.

Stubenberg L von (1992). What is it like to be Oscar? *Synthese* 90, 1–26.

Stuss DT (1993). Disturbances of self-awareness after frontal system damage. In *Awareness of Deficit after Brain Injury,* eds GP Prigatano and DL Schachter. Oxford: Oxford University Press: 63–83.

Stuss DF and Benson DW (1986). *The Frontal Lobes.* New York: Raven Press.

Tanji J and Shima K (1994). Role for supplementary motor area cells in planning several movements ahead. *Nature* 371, 413–415.

Tarassenko L (1994). Letter. *Times Higher Educational Supplement.*

Taylor JG (1973). A model of thinking neural networks. Presented at a seminar, Institution for Cybernetics, University of Tubingen, Tubingen, Germany.

Taylor, JG (1990). A Silicon model of the retina, *Neural Networks* 3, 171–178.

Taylor JG (1991). Can neural networks ever be made to think? *Neural Network World* 1, 4–11.

Taylor JG (1992a). Toward a neural network model of mind. *Neural Network World* 2, 797–812.

Taylor JG (1992b). From single neuron to cognition. In *Artificial Neural Networks* 2, eds I Aleksander and JG Taylor. Amsterdam: North-Holland: 11–16.

Taylor JG (1993a). A global gating model of attention and consciousness. In *Neurodynamics and Psychology*, eds. M Oaksford, and G Brown. New York: Academic Press: 157–180.

Taylor JG (1993b). Neuronal network models of the mind. *Verh Dtsch Zool Geselschaft* 86(2), 159–163.

Taylor JG (1993c). *When the Clock Struck Zero.* London: Macmillan.

Taylor JG (1994). Goals drives and consciousness. *Neural Networks* 7, 1181–1190.

Taylor JG (1995a). Modeling the mind by PSYCHE. Proceedings of the International Conference on Artificial Neural Networks, eds F Fogelman-Souilie and P Gallinari. Paris: EC2: 543–548.

Taylor JG (1995b). Toward the ultimate intelligent machine. Presented at the world congress on neural networks, Washington, DC, July 17–21.

Taylor JG (1996a). A competition for consciousness? *Neurocomputing* 11, 271–296.

Taylor JG (1996b). Breakthrough to awareness. *Biol Cybernet* 75, 59–72.

Taylor JG (1997). Mathematical problems of global brain modeling. Balzer Press In *Mathematics of Neural Networks,* eds SW Ellacott, JC Mason, and IJ Anderson. Boston: Kluwer Academic: 47–58.

Taylor JG (1998). Neural Bubble Dynamics in Two Dimensions I: Foundations to appear in Biological Cybernetics.

Taylor JG and Alavi F (1993). A global competitive network for attention. *Neural Network World* 5, 477–502.

Taylor JG and Alavi F (1995). A global competitive neural network. *Biol Cybernet* 72, 233–248.

Taylor JG, Horwitz B, Shah J, Mueller-Gaertner H-W, and Krause BJ (1998). Functional assignments and brain traffic in the paired-associate encoding and retrieval task. Submitted for publication.

Taylor JG, Jaencke L, Shah NJ, Noesselt T, Schmitz N, Himmelbach M, and Mueller-Gaertner H-W (1998). A three-stage model of awareness: Formulation and initial experimental support. *Neuro Report* 9, 1787–1792.

Taylor N and Taylor JG (1998). Abstract, submitted to the society for neruosciences meetings, 98.

Tootell RBH, Reppas JB, Dale AM, Look RB, Sereno MI, Malach R, Brady TJ, and Rosen BR (1995). Visual motion aftereffect in human cortical area MT revealed by functional magnetic resonance imaging. *Nature* 375, 139–141.

Tranel D and Damasio A (1988). Knowledge without awareness: An autonomic index of facial recognition by prosopagnosics. *Science* 228, 1453–1454.

Treisman A (1988). Features and objects: The fourteenth Bartlett memorial lecture. *Q J Exp Psychol* 40A, 201–237.

Treisman A and Gelade G (1980). A feature-integration theory of attention. *Cog Psychol* 12, 97–136.

Tulving E (1972). Episodic and semantic memory. in *Organization of Memory*, eds E Tulving and W Donaldson. New York: Academic Press.

Tulving E, Kapur S, Markowitsch HJ, Craik FIM, Habib R, and Houle S (1994a). Neuroanatomical correlates of retrieval in episodic memory: Auditory sentence recognition. *Proc Natl Acad Sci USA* 91, 2012–2015.

Tulving E, Kapur S, Craik FIM, Moscovitch M, and Houle S (1994b). Hemispheric encoding/retrieval asymmetry in episodic memory: Positron emission tomography findings. *Proc Natl Acad Sci USA* 91, 2016–2020.

Ungerleider LG and Mishkin M (1982). Two cortical visual systems. In *The Analysis of Visual Behavior,* eds DJ Ingle, RJW Mansfield, and MS Goodale. Cambridge, MA: MIT Press.

Velmans M (1992). Is human information processing conscious? *Behav Brain Sci* 14, 651–726.

Wang G, Tanaka K, and Tanifuji M (1996). Optical imaging of functional organization in the monkey inferotemporal cortex. *Science* 272, 1665–1668.

Warner R and Szubka T, eds (1994). *The Mind-Body Problem.* London: Blackwell.

Warrington E and Shallice T (1979). Semantic access dyslexia. *Brain* 102, 43–63.

Weiskrantz L (1986). *Blindsight: A Case Study and Implications.* Oxford: Clarendon Press.

Weiskrantz L, Barbow JL, and Salvie A (1995). Parameters affecting conscious versus unconscious visual discrimination with damage to the visual cortex (VI). *Proc Natl Acad Sci (USA)* 92, 6122–6126.

Weiskrantz L, Warrington E, Saunders M, and Marshall J (1974). Visual capacity in the hemianopic field following a restricted occipital ablation. *Brain* 97, 709–28.

Whitworth D (1997). Crash victim wins 950,000GBD for helpless flirtatiousness. *London Times,* 5.

Whybrow PC, Akiskal HS, and McKinney WT (1984). *Mood Disorders: Toward a New Psychobiology.* New York: Plenum Press.

Witherspoon D and Allan LG (1985). The effect of a prior presentation on temporal judgements in a perceptual identification task. *Memory and Cognition* 13, 101–111.

Young AW (1994). Conscious and nonconscious recognition of familiar faces. In *Attention and Performance*, XV, eds C Umilta and M Moscovitch. Cambridge: MIT Press: 153–178.

Zeki S (1993). *Visions of the Brain*. Cambridge: Cambridge University Press.

Zomeren AH van and Brouwer WH (1994). *Clinical Neuropsychology of Attention*. Oxford: Oxford University Press.

Index